DESPERATE GLORY

DESPERATE GLORY

At War in Helmand with Britain's 16 Air Assault Brigade

Sam Kiley

BLOOMSBURY

LONDON · BERLIN · NEW YORK

First published in Great Britain 2009

Bloomsbury Publishing Plc
36 Soho Square
London WID 3QY

www.bloomsbury.com

Bloomsbury Publishing, London, New York and Berlin
A CIP catalogue record for this book is available from the British Library

ISBN 978 0 7475 9996 8

10 9 8 7 6 5 4 3 2

Typeset by Hewer Text UK Ltd, Edinburgh
Printed in Great Britain by Clays Ltd, St Ives plc

For Melissa

Contents

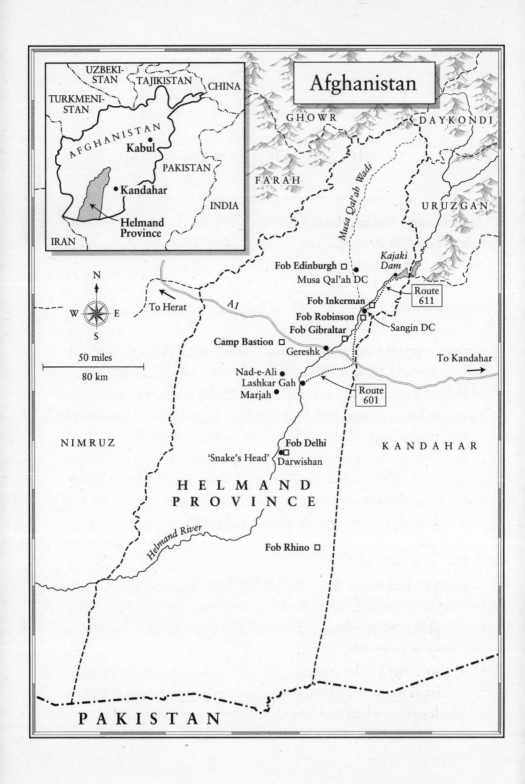

Afghanistan

UZBEKI-STAN
TAJIKISTAN
CHINA
TURKMENI-STAN
AFGHANISTAN
Kabul
PAKISTAN
Kandahar
INDIA
IRAN
Helmand Province

GHOWR
DAYKONDI
FARAH
URUZGAN

N
W   E
S

To Herat
A1

50 miles
80 km

Musa Qal'ah Wadi
Kajaki Dam

Fob Edinburgh □
Musa Qal'ah DC
Fob Inkerman
Fob Robinson □
Fob Gibraltar □
Sangin DC
Route 611

Camp Bastion □
Gereshk
Nad-e-Ali
Lashkar Gah
Marjah
Route 601

To Kandahar

NIMRUZ
KANDAHAR

'Snake's Head'
Fob Delhi □
Darwishan

HELMAND
PROVINCE

Helmand River

Fob Rhino □

PAKISTAN

INTRODUCTION

Afghanistan's Helmand valley has been uprooted and flipped on its side. Musa Qal'ah is now just off the A36 in Wiltshire. I'm sipping tea with a grey-haired warrior. His eyes are filling with tears. I can hear traffic outside. A young soldier humps enormous green boxes into the corner of the room – 'Alright here, sir?' – 'Thanks mate.'

We're sitting on hard, institutional chairs of metal piping and wood. I know that my ancient Land Rover is leaving an embarrassing stain of leaking radiator juice on the tarmac of the car park, next to the guard house. It's important that I fit in. I'm a civilian – but I need to look and sound efficient – I need to get along with these men.

Soon the people I am with will be trying very hard to kill other people and to stay alive themselves. I will be going with them. We're going into the Helmand valley together and I'm wondering how many of us will come out. What the old warrior is saying is scaring me.

This is a man who's come up through the ranks from private to captain. Before his first tour of Helmand in 2006 he'd fought in Northern Ireland, Iraq, Kosovo and Sierra Leone. His father was a soldier, as were two of his brothers; lately his son has joined the army. Warrior work has been his life; soldiering is in his DNA. He's also a hero – he picked up a Military Cross for bravery in Afghanistan in 2006. I imagine he's from the tough estates of Belfast or Londonderry where hard men drink hard and show no fear.

'Now, going back, I'm scared. I've got more trepidation than I have felt in my twenty-six years in the army; more than any time in my career,' says Captain Doug Beattie. I try to hide the discomfort of an acid bomb that's just gone off in my stomach.

'Why?'

'Because I know what's waiting for us out there. Young men are going to grow up very, very fast. They'll come back – those that make it – completely changed. I did.

'I killed close up. I killed at medium range, and I killed at long range. I now ask myself all the time – did I have to do it, could I have not killed some of them? Was there a way I could have not killed? I don't know – but you don't sleep very well when you've driven a bayonet through someone's throat. The guilt never goes away, it never does.'

'How many did you kill?' I sort of whisper, half hoping he won't hear. The memories my question drags up are obviously unwelcome. His eyes redden, water appears around the rims.

Captain Beattie is trim, and looks about fifty, though it turns out he's only forty-three. He has an easy authority among the forty men he will lead in Helmand. They call him 'Sir' and he calls them 'Mate'. Soon they will land in Kandahar to start life in the relentlessly grey-brown, dust-choking moonscape of southern Afghanistan. There's a quietness among these men. There's none of the usual 'slagging' which accompanies every moment of a British soldier's waking day. To civilian ears the non-stop vicious banter is a mixture of bullying and breathtaking vulgarity. Soldiers love it. They say this relentless verbal battering keeps them going. Today, though, it is quiet. Words seem to be fed out in treasured drips, none wasted.

Beattie's men are going to be fighting alongside and training Afghan Army *kandaks* – battalions of about 300 local men. They're going to be at the very front line of the military and political effort to rescue a fractious NATO alliance from stagnation, or even long-term defeat, in Afghanistan's south. Think-tanks, retired generals, and Lord Roberts, the former head of NATO, have been warning that the military campaign in Afghanistan 'risks failure'. Some experts claim that the Afghan government controls only 30 per cent of the country; 10 per cent is held by the Taleban, and the rest is 'tribal' – which generally means up for grabs, but mostly Taleban. The campaign these men have been training for is the Big One, if not the last throw of the British dice in Helmand, it's certainly Britain's biggest military gamble in decades. Defeat in Helmand could, most likely *would*, cause neighbouring Kandahar province to fall and the pro-Western Kabul government to collapse from within. Defeat cannot be contemplated.

British regiments are like tribes: they have their own plumage, language, customs and culture. Beattie's unit, the Royal Irish Regiment, was formed with the amalgamation of the Ulster Defence Regiment and the Royal Irish Rangers in 1992. It calls its private soldiers Rangers and recruits on both sides of Ireland's border. It's practically a family business. The father of the commanding officer, Lieutenant Colonel Ed Freely, commanded a battalion of the regiment. Major Hugh Benson is the regimental quartermaster. He tells me he'll be in Helmand with two sons and a nephew.

The Royal Irish Regiment, based in Shropshire, forms a Celtic fringe for 16 Air Assault Brigade with the 5th Battalion the Royal Regiment of Scotland, based in Canterbury in Kent. The two infantry regiments are specially trained for air assault by helicopter and with the 2nd and 3rd Battalions of the Parachute Regiment as well as logisticians, signallers, Pathfinders, a medical regiment, artillery and airborne engineers, form Britain's biggest brigade of over 8,000 men and women. Trained for rapid deployment, 16 Air Assault Brigade has had the lion's share of operations over the last decade in Sierra Leone, Kosovo, Iraq and Afghanistan. With its headquarters in Colchester it doesn't fall under the command of other army divisions but answers to the Joint Helicopter Command and the Commander in Chief of Britain's Land Forces, directly.

This is 16 Air Assault Brigade's final exercise on Salisbury plain:

the climax of a year's training for the brigade's return to Helmand. Today 'Musa Qal'ah' is actually Knook Camp – a collection of prefabricated huts and warehouses next to the tea-shop typical Wiltshire village of Upton Lovell on the River Wylye. Musa Qal'ah itself is legendary in British military lore as a latter-day Rorke's Drift. In the summer of 2006, 16 Air Assault's Pathfinder Platoon fought off waves of Taleban attacks on their mud-brick fortress for fifty-two days. Relieved by Danish commandos and men from the Royal Irish Regiment, the town was then held for another fifty-six days. Perhaps sensing that overrunning a British position would be a massive boost to Taleban prestige, and a devastating blow to their enemies, the fundamentalist fighters hurled themselves into the battle for the British compound in waves that crashed in death at the walls. Defending themselves, the Royal Irish fired a quarter of all the bullets fired by British troops in the whole of Afghanistan in 2006. Seven men died fighting for Musa Qal'ah back then, and many more have died since.

'My wife hates it that I'm going back. I feel like I'm abandoning my wife at a very vulnerable time for her. We've been married for twenty years. People set celebrities on pedestals but they never know what an army wife goes through,' says Beattie.

In 2006 Beattie ended his tour in Garmsir, in the south of the Helmand valley. He'd been sent out to Afghanistan expecting to find himself in an office job, looking after the welfare of young soldiers or some other comfy gig. Due to a gap in personnel he was sent, with twelve other men, to run a training team for Afghan police in a desert town on the Taleban's opium smuggling routes to Pakistan and Iran.

During his first four months in Afghanistan, Beattie was the target of four suicide-bombing attacks. On the last a young man managed to get through two different groups of Afghan police who were supposed to be guarding the local 'cop shop' in Garmsir, where Beattie was advising the commander quietly over a glass of *chai*. There was a crack and a flash.

Beattie was flung onto his back; his face was burning and he could not breathe through a fog of black acidic smoke. There was silence, and then groaning and screaming. When he stood up the police station was a butcher's shop of body parts. Someone was lying in two pieces and smoking entrails curled across the dirt. Beattie bent to collect a hand, perfectly severed.

'They were the worst sights I have ever seen in my life. There's not a lot you can do when you're picking up the broken limbs and body parts of ten people. I saw the hand, I think, of the bomber. And it was an awful thing to think this had just been a person who once lived, who loved and laughed just like any other human being, and now was just a mess on the floor.'

I'm gripped by an unexpected loneliness. Benson, Beattie, their sons, nephews, comrades, they're part of a fighting clan. They seem born into it. Ranger Phil Gillespie, who is only nineteen, and is returning to fight another round in the Helmand valley, admits he's 'only going back because if I'm not there who will my mates have on either side of them?' Sergeant P. J. Brangan, twenty-seven, who, with Gillespie, fought at Musa Qal'ah in 2006, says: 'When you're seeing the tracer hitting the walls right beside you and you get hundreds of near misses, and you can turn and laugh. You know, it's the best drug I ever heard or read about.' Whether they are fearful, or are mad keen to hurl themselves into the enemy with their bayonets fixed, these soldiers at least are going to be with their military families.

But I am a civvy – an outsider – and worry that is how I will always be seen while I'm at war with the brigade.

I buy a new set of body armour ahead of my scheduled deployment at the beginning of May 2008. I also try to get fit, but the runs around the fields by my home leave me a sweaty gasping mess of middle-aged flubber, and with the horrific realisation that I might need to purchase a sports bra.

As the date of my departure with 16 Air Assault Brigade approaches,

I begin, for the first time, to fear that I will not come back alive from this, the biggest challenge of my life. I have seen a lot of wars: I've covered conflicts on three continents for seventeen years and survived more as a result of good fortune than skill. Dozens of my friends and colleagues have been killed on assignment. I try to hide these feelings from my family. My wife and children maintain their resolute enthusiasm for a project which has taken me two years to put together. But I am now beginning to think it is an absurd risk. Four days before my flight I collapse with a raging fever, a throat infection and crashing headaches. (I now suspect my illness might have been a psychosomatic attempt by my subconscious to kill off my attempt to write this book, before it killed me.)

I am not a war or adrenalin junky. I have spent most of my life trying to communicate how stupid and ugly war really is. But there is no more addictive drug than the thrill of being where history is happening. There is no more important historic event than when your own countrymen are at war. I needed to go to Helmand. And if I was going to do a proper job, and do justice to whatever was going on over there, I had to do a full tour of duty with a brigade. It became a compulsion. There was another compulsion, too – I just didn't want to miss this one.

When I returned in October 2008 from Operation Herrick Eight, after five months of war – frequently on the front line – I felt, as I confessed to my wife, more relaxed than I had been for more than a decade. I had been the 'Helmand Hitchhiker' catching rides on busy Chinooks all over the province – from Garmsir to Kajaki and Lashkar Gah to Now Zad. I had been on air assaults, logistic convoys, and infantry patrols, with almost every unit in the brigade. I had a great deal of luck too.

I was in a fuel truck which passed over two bombs which blew up vehicles behind us. I got off a Land Rover shortly before it also drove over an Improvised Explosive Device, which blasted a back wheel through the seat that had been fashioned for me by Sergeant Terry Wait of the Royal Logistic Corps. Terry was thrown clear by the blast which injured only his arm.

But I need not have feared loneliness. The men and women of 16 Air Assault, in units as tribal as the SCOTS and as cultish as the Paras, treated me with the greatest courtesy, kindness and with extraordinary openness.

I was not 'embedded' in the contemporary meaning of the word. I did not have an escort and I was given access to every level of every unit serving in the brigade. No attempt of any kind was made to limit what I could see, where I went, or who I could talk to.

Though I have travelled widely throughout Afghanistan over the years, canvassing the views of local people, this was not one of the occasions on which I had much access to Afghan civilians. This is a book about British soldiers at war, not a polemic, nor a report card on the latest bloody tour.

I am conscious that I have not done justice to the many thousands of soldiers, sailors and airmen who served on the tour, in this book. Soldiers tend not to talk about what they did when they get home. They might share a few war stories with comrades who were with them at the time, but they will rarely open up to civilians. They fear that they will be accused of bragging, or lying; above all they fear that they will not be understood. I hope that this book might help to explain to those who were not in Helmand, or at war in general, what it was like for those who were.

This book is the product of my own observations and interviews on the ground, and back in the United Kingdom, as well as the personal diaries, letters, videos and photographs of hundreds of personnel and other documents. Any errors between these pages are entirely my responsibility and I would welcome the opportunity to correct them in future editions.

Between 9 April and 15 October 2008, thirty-three service personnel died on Operation Herrick Eight.[1]

This book is dedicated to their memory.

Senior Aircraftman Graham Livingstone, Royal Air Force Regiment, aged 23 from Glasgow

Senior Aircraftman Gary Thompson, Royal Auxiliary Air Force Regiment, aged 51 from Nottingham

Trooper Robert Pearson, Queens Royal Lancers Regiment, aged 22 from Grimsby

Trooper Ratu Sakeasi Babakobau, Household Cavalry Regiment, aged 29 from Fiji

Trooper James Thompson, 21 Special Air Service Regiment, aged 27 from Whitley Bay

Marine Dale Gostick, Armoured Support Company, Royal Marines, aged 22 from Oxford

Private Nathan Cuthbertson, 2nd Battalion The Parachute Regiment, aged 19 from Sunderland

Private Daniel Gamble, 2nd Battalion The Parachute Regiment, aged 22 from Uckfield

Private Charles Murray, 2nd Battalion The Parachute Regiment, aged 19 from Carlisle

1 Source: www.mod.uk/DefenceInternet/FactSheets/OperationsFactsheets/
OperationsInAfghanistanBritishFatalities.htm

Lance Corporal James Bateman, 2nd Battalion The Parachute Regiment, aged 29 from Staines

Private Jeff Doherty, 2nd Battalion The Parachute Regiment, aged 20 from Southam

Corporal Sarah Bryant, Intelligence Corps, aged 26 from Liverpool

Corporal Sean Reeve, Royal Corps of Signals, attached to 21 SAS, aged 28 from Brighton

Lance Corporal Richard Larkin, 21 Special Air Service Regiment, aged 39 from Cookley

Trooper Paul Stout, 21 Special Air Service Regiment, aged 31

Warrant Officer Class 2 Michael Williams, 2nd Battalion The Parachute Regiment, aged 40 from Cardiff

Private Joe Whittaker, 4th Battalion The Parachute Regiment attached to 2 Para, aged 20 from Stratford-upon-Avon

Warrant Officer Class 2 Dan Shirley, 13 Air Assault Support Regiment, Royal Logistic Corps, aged 32 from Leicester

Lance Corporal James Johnson, 5th Battalion The Royal Regiment of Scotland, aged 31 from Strathclyde

Corporal Jason Barnes, Royal Electrical and Mechanical Engineers, attached to 2 Para, aged 25 from Exeter

Lance Corporal Rowe, Royal Army Veterinary Corps, aged 24 from Newcastle

Sergeant Jonathan Mathews, 4th Battalion The Royal Regiment of Scotland, aged 35 from Edinburgh

Private Peter Cowton, 2nd Battalion The Parachute Regiment, aged 25 from Basingstoke

Signaller Wayne Bland, 16 Signal Regiment, Royal Corps of Signals, aged 21 from Leeds

Corporal Barry Dempsey, 2nd Battalion The Royal Regiment of Scotland, aged 29 from Ayrshire

Ranger Justin Cupples, 1st Battalion The Royal Irish Regiment, aged 29 from Co. Cavan, Ireland

Warrant Officer Class 2 Gary O'Donnell GM and Bar, 11 Explosive Ordnance Disposal Regiment, Royal Logistic Corps, aged 40 from Edinburgh

Private Jason Rawstron, 2nd Battalion The Parachute Regiment, aged 23 from Clayton-Le-Moors

Lance Corporal Nicky Mason, 2nd Battalion The Parachute Regiment, aged 26 from Aveley

Trooper James Munday, Household Cavalry Regiment, aged 21 from Birmingham

Staff Sergeant Henrik Christiansen, Danish Battle Group

Warrant Officer 2nd Class Ivan Brok, Estonian Army

Corporal Jesper Pederson, Danish Battle Group.

Departure

A man usually at ease with going away, he lay beside his sleeping wife and allowed a few tender tears to roll through the cracks at the corner of his closed eyes. Beyond the pre-medieval yard-thick walls of his home on the Welsh borders, not far from Hereford, the unseasonable April warmth of the earth was swelling flower bulbs. The crocuses were already over, even on the cold windswept hill where the brigadier had made his home. He could almost hear the ground crackling with life and the promise of a shimmering summer. His children were similarly blooming into their own, emerging as sporting stars of their schools. He would miss the rest of spring, their months of cricket and horses. The leaves would be falling from the trees by the time he returned home.

He crept from his bed aching with sadness. There was barely a blue hint of dawn off to the east as he fumbled with his luggage and dragged himself out of his home life. His driver waited outside with the interior light on. He closed the car door shut with a gentle thump and looked up at his home. Only a corridor shone. He sighed. His son and his girls; his wife and their daughter, were asleep, warm and safe.

Over the next weeks thousands of other men and women would

be kissing the eyes of the people they loved, coughing away the lumps in their throats, and secretly praying, praying very hard, that they would return from combat alive. Alive, and in one piece. Everyone in the army knew that the wards at Birmingham's Selly Oak Hospital had seen a steady, and increasing, flow of mangled men. They were missing arms, legs, both. Young adults were stumbling painfully like drunken toddlers at Headley Court in Surrey, learning how to walk again on false limbs. Modern body armour and modern medicine conspired to save the lives of those who had lost a half, or two thirds, of their bodies.

Mark Carleton-Smith had a better idea than most of what lay ahead. Every time he had commanded troops during his career it had been in some kind of a war or other. Originally an Irish Guardsman, he'd spent most of his life with the British Special Forces: as an SAS squadron commander in Bosnia, as the commanding officer of 22 SAS in Iraq and Afghanistan until only three years earlier. Now he was off again. Promoted to brigadier, he would be commanding thousands of men and women in a conflict that would leave minds and bodies shattered, and many dead. The thoughts jarred against the warming dawn as he headed south towards RAF Brize Norton. But there was no escaping reality. Britain's undeclared war in Helmand, which the government insisted on calling a 'peace support mission', was a major insurgency draining blood and treasure. The battlefield was complex, the background politics opaque; even the reasons for the war in the first place seemed to be constantly shifting.

Most soldiers like clarity. An easily understood mission statement, a clear set of orders and a simple plan. There was nothing in Helmand that was likely to produce anything like clarity. Carleton-Smith prepared his senior officers to embrace complexity and contradictions. A couple of months before 16 Air Assault Brigade was due to leave for Afghanistan he spoke to the entire brigade staff, the middle managers and senior officers who would be leading the troops into battle. Leaning against a podium on their final exercise, he said: 'We never make war as we ought – but how we can.'

His voice with its slightly metallic edge, his mouth moving in the exaggerated way trained singers use to enunciate every word, he told his audience: 'We'll be constrained by international, British and Afghan national political considerations not military imperatives. War is, and will always be, that way . . . At the core of our operation is the *perception* of what we are doing in the capitals around the world, in the Afghan theatre, and up and down the Helmand River. Not of *what* is happening but of what *appears* to be happening. We have to ask ourselves "What is important? The activity, or the assessment of the outcome?"'

He was telling the leaders of his brigade that they could win all the little battles they wanted. The question would be – so what? Would the Afghan population support what the British were doing in their country?

If the Afghans of Helmand did not believe the British were worth having around, and that the British would win – then the British would most certainly lose. For how long would the British public support the war? If the British public decided that the fight for Afghanistan wasn't worth the price – then domestic support for the war would evaporate; and the British would lose. He was telling his officers to ask themselves every time they planned an operation, or fired a shot, 'What will the consequences be?' Failure to do so, he told them, would mean that young British lives could be squandered.

'There's no moral justification for sending young men to die unless you have a good idea of what they're trying to achieve. It's that simple,' he added.

Carleton-Smith flew to Afghanistan on a vast Boeing C17 military transport jet. It resembles a great grey flying shark. Compared to the ancient TriStar planes which shuttle back and forth carrying troops to Afghanistan, the C17 is a luxury airliner. He could throw a sleeping bag down in the back, among the Sea King helicopters and

aviation parts, and get a few hours' kip. Only a decade or so old, the
C17, leased from America, felt less like it was held together by mere
hope: the fifty-year-old TriStars had been bought secondhand from
a failed US airline and broke down frequently.

With its tail to a sinking sun, after nine hours the C17 was over
the playing fields of the 'Great Game' – one that Britain had been
part of for almost 200 years.

Since the early nineteenth century, Britain and its empire and the
United States had struggled with Russia for influence over central Asia.
The British spy and explorer Arthur Conolly is believed to have coined
the term 'Great Game' when in 1829 he wrote to a friend of the 'beauty'
of the rivalry between Russia and Britain to 'civilise Asian races'. In fact
the game, from the British perspective, was all about trying to make
sure that the Russian empire's steady southward creep would not allow
the Tsar to use Afghanistan as a bridgehead into India.

The real-life adventures of men like Conolly, his attempt to rescue
fellow British spy Charles Stoddart, their execution in Bukhara, Sir
Francis Younghusband's expeditions into Kashmir and Tibet, and
dozens of other Victorian and Edwardian heroes, became the inspiration for great fictional characters of espionage and intrigue. Rudyard
Kipling's *Kim* and *The Man Who Would be King*, John Buchan's
Richard Hannay and Sandy Arbuthnot, Ian Fleming's James Bond,
and even Robert Ludlum's Jason Bourne, owe their very existence
to the dashing multi-lingual players of the Great Game. Travel
through Afghanistan has remained a rite of passage for some of
Britain's bravest and best writers. Eric Newby's *A Short Walk in the
Hindu Kush*, Jason Elliott's *An Unexpected Light* and Rory Stewart's
The Places In Between are already classics of twentieth- and twenty-
first-century travel literature. Lurking in the subconscious of some
of the latter-day adventurers who find their way to Afghanistan
is, perhaps, the sense that they might become part of a League of
Intrepid Gentlemen and join a brotherhood of dash with a pedigree
stretching back twenty decades. Or die in the attempt.

Carleton-Smith had read history and politics at Durham and knew very well that the Great Game frequently degenerated into war. Britain had already fought three major campaigns in Afghanistan. The first began with victory in 1839 and ended in defeat in 1842 with the massacre of around 14,000 troops and civilians on the retreat through the Gandamak Pass east of Kabul. Britain invaded again in 1878 to prevent Russia from establishing a diplomatic foothold. This time the Second Afghan War ended with a British victory, of sorts, and the installation of a friendly emir, Abdur Rahman Khan, who agreed to hand control of his country's foreign policy over to the British. The British Raj then set about trying to draw Afghanistan's administrative frontier between Russia, India and Afghanistan. Today it remains a vague and notional border, drawn on a map, but not on the ground, and named after the British diplomat, Sir Mortimer Durand, who drew it in 1893. It cuts through the largely ethnic Pashto tribal areas, which lie in both Pakistan and Afghanistan. Today it remains the scene of bloody civil war in Pakistan and the source of recruits for Afghanistan's Taleban and al Qaeda.

Abdur Rahman Khan's grandson, Amanullah Khan, found the strictures of British influence in Kabul overbearing. In 1919 he launched a brief campaign for full independence. Although the British fought the Afghans to a stalemate, using aerial bombardment for the first time in Afghanistan, independence was agreed by 1921. But Afghanistan remained a buffer between British India – and later the interests of the West in modern Pakistan – and Russia.

A pink twilight patina is spreading over the snow-capped peaks of Kazakhstan and Turkmenistan as Carleton-Smith's C17 swoops slowly into Afghanistan airspace from the northwest. He knows the landscape very well. Half an hour out from Kandahar he looks down at a thin necklace of lights running north to south, the Afghan villages and compounds strung out along the Helmand River.

One of his last jobs as a commanding officer in Afghanistan in

2005 had been to drive along the green ribbon of the Helmand River valley on a secret reconnaissance mission, ahead of the possible deployment of British troops there. He had encountered no direct hostility but had been staggered by the scale of opium production. Fields that had once been sown with wheat were being turned over to poppy by armies of temporary labourers. They in turn would watch the small group of soldiers trundle by, wave, smile openly, then return to their ploughs. Four years after the Taleban had been driven from power, poppy production in the Helmand region had trebled in twelve months.

In Lashkar Gah, the provincial capital, Carleton-Smith had met with a small contingent of US Special Forces soldiers of a Provincial Reconstruction Team which was trying to extend the rule of Kabul's central government. They told him they had watched dozens of pickup trucks, so overloaded with greasy opium resin leaking out of plastic sacks that they almost dragged along the ground, shudder by to markets in Iran and Pakistan every day.

Helmand's governor, Sher Mohammed Akunzada – a member of the Alizai, the dominant Helmandi tribe – had been appointed by President Karzai and now commanded a police force drawn from local militia. He managed to keep the peace because, through his tribal connections, he knew many of those involved in the drug trade. The Taleban, meanwhile, was creaming off millions every year in protection rackets and 'tax' from the opium growers to fund its campaign. This was a typical Afghan balance of power – an accommodation had been reached between terrorists determined to destroy the government, the government's own representative, and drug lords, which allowed them all to coexist and the latter (ie the drug trade) to make lots of money.

When Carleton-Smith returned to Britain he told his masters that he'd found a region rich in opium, relatively peaceful, and apparently quite happy with the idea that it was beyond the control of the government in Kabul. Helmand was happily lawless. He told the British Ministry of Defence that 'there is no insurgency in Helmand now. But we can give you one [if we send in British forces].'

A year later, 16 Air Assault Brigade delivered on Carleton-Smith's prediction. British troops entered Helmand in the early summer. Within weeks they were facing full-blown insurgency. The reasons for sending 4,700 British soldiers into Helmand were not properly debated in Parliament before 26 February 2006, when the Secretary of State for Defence, John Reid, issued a statement to the House announcing the first deployment of the brigade. If the army wanted clarity, they were not going to get it from him. He stated that the aims of the mission were:

To 'deny terrorists an ungoverned space in which they can foment and export terror. 11 September taught us that terrorism thrives where there is no stability, no effective government, no security'.

To 'help the people of Afghanistan build a democratic state with strong security forces and an economy that will support a civil society'.

That 'Afghanistan must be restored as a secure and stable state'.

To 'support international efforts to counter the narcotics trade which poisons the economy in Afghanistan and poisons so many young people in this country. 90 per cent of the heroin which hits our streets originates in Afghanistan.'

That 'the Helmand Provincial Reconstruction Team will work with UK officials from the Foreign and Commonwealth Office and Department for International Development to deliver a tailored package of political, developmental and military assistance. Specifically, its mission will be to help train the Afghan security forces, to facilitate reconstruction, and to provide security, thereby supporting the extension of the Afghan Government's authority across the province.'

He went on to say: 'I want to make a few things clear. The size and structure of the Task Force has been guided by a careful assessment of the likely tasks and threats it will face. What matters is that we put the right forces in to do the job and do it safely and do it well.'

Within five months it was clear that John Reid's assessment of the numbers of troops needed was woefully wrong. Paratroopers, Gurkhas, Danish commandos, the Royal Irish Regiment, dog handlers, logisticians, helicopter pilots, military police and Royal Engineers were all fighting, day-in-day-out, on a six-month tour of duty codenamed Operation Herrick Four.

The predictable and predicted explosion of violence came as a surprise to the British government. Rather than employ the 'asymmetric' hit-and-run tactics, combined with suicide attacks and bombings that had been seen in Iraq, the Taleban had taken the fight to the British. They had fought more than 300 battles in those six months. The areas around British bases, which the Taleban attacked again and again, had been flattened. Tens of thousands of civilians had fled the main towns; hundreds of schools had been closed. Britain had, indeed, delivered an insurgency.

Carleton-Smith was flying in as the new commander of 16 Air Assault Brigade on Operation Herrick Eight. Three other brigades had taken up the fight in Helmand on three tours since 2006. Troop numbers had steadily climbed to around 8,300. They were spread in Forward Operating Bases (Fobs) from the far south to the edge of the Uruzgan Mountains at the Kajaki Dam in the north. Over the previous two years eighty-nine British soldiers and airmen had been killed in Helmand. The fighting had been so intense that it had been compared to D-Day and the Korean War. And it had begun to be judged in terms of body counts and by the sheer volume of bullets, rockets, artillery shells and grenades that British forces had fired at the enemy.

As Carleton-Smith looks down on Helmand from his C17 he knows these statistics are meaningless. You can create walls of lead and explosives and 'hose down' suspected enemy positions with machine-gun fire all day. But what will it achieve aside from a fairly juvenile thrill? The more bullets you fire and bombs you drop, the greater the chances are that someone innocent will get killed. The moral high ground is the most important tactical asset. If you want to win a counterinsurgency campaign you have to drain the sea that the insurgents swim in. Killing the people you are supposed to protect is the best way of adding recruits to your enemy's cause.

Sitting on the flight deck of the C17 shark as it dives towards the ground, Carleton-Smith follows the Standard Operating Procedure for landing at Kandahar airfield. Body armour on. Helmet on. This isn't likely to save anyone's life if the plane is shot down, but the airfield has been rocketed fairly regularly. He knows the scene. A two- or three-man team of Taleban creep out into the desert down a wadi and wait. After dark, they crawl out of their hiding places and lay one or two Chinese-made 107mm rockets at an angle against the rocks. Peering along the green tubing of the 1.5-metre-long missiles they line them up against pre-set markers, usually cairns built between the aiming point and the target. Then one of the team attaches a heavy-duty radio battery to the rocket fuse and a simple electronic alarm clock, sets the time for the missile to be launched, and then scuttles back into the desert.

Hitting back at the Taleban rocketeers is most often a waste of time: shelling a patch of scorched earth does nothing to raise morale for the NATO troops. At Kandahar airfield rockets have been exploding at the base regularly enough for there to be a rule that everyone has to be within a ten-second dash of their helmet and body armour.

Carleton-Smith isn't too worried about the rockets, but it would be embarrassing to end his tour of Helmand before he even gets there. So he pulls on the body armour without complaint. He notes the time as he comes in to land: 1742 hours Zulu (army time). That means 18.42 at home, and confusingly 2212 hours local time: only Afghanistan could be three and a *half* hours different from London.

The moment he feels the warm dry air catch his face as he leaves the plane, he feels that he's never left. It has been twenty-three months since he flew out of Kandahar, and exactly three since his last reconnaissance ahead of the tour. The place doesn't get any more pleasant. The former Kandahar International Airport has been turned into an unloved military town, housing more than 13,000 troops who live in rows of white container housing like giant Tupperware boxes. There is no relief from the grey-brown monochrome of the whole place. Cars crawl along gravel roads throwing up lazy plumes of powdery dust that settle on top of grey concrete box-like bunkers, scattered around as shelters against rockets. When the breeze is in the north the stench from the lakes of shit in the sewerage plants catches in the throat.

Captured from the Taleban in 2001, the airfield is the hub of all NATO and American operations in southern Afghanistan. Though 15 kilometres outside Kandahar city and a day's drive from the capital, Kabul, it seems more like a lunar space station. Its centre-piece is a raised boardwalk where soldiers can buy a pizza, a cup of coffee, a local rug, or get their uniforms fixed and altered by a tailor. Encircling a dusty football pitch and roller-blade hockey rink, its boards creak all day to the desultory wanderings of tired men and women, wondering why they bothered to take the promenade at all.

Carleton-Smith cannot wait to get out. He has a couple of days' briefings in Kandahar and Kabul before taking over command in Lashkar Gah on 9 April 2008. When he finally takes off for his new brigade headquarters the helicopter carrying him almost falls from the sky. The synchronisation mechanism, which keeps the main rotors from ripping into the flying blades on the tail, breaks down and his pilot is forced to make a shuddering return to Kandahar airfield. The aircraft would have torn itself to pieces in seconds if the two sets of swirling rotors had connected. When he finally arrives at Lashkar Gah District Centre he finds himself in a camp that more closely resembles a prison (it is known as 'Lashkatraz' to its inmates).

Its high, reinforced walls block any view in or out. There is accommodation for about 500 troops in tents and around 150 civilians in a blockhouse. But at least someone has thought of planting a garden to relieve the relentless tan and grey.

He feels a surge of energy. His aide-de-camp, Julian Roberts, a blond Irish Guards captain of extraordinary charm, whose father is a serving major general, is waiting for him in Kandahar. He smoothes the way with his huge smile. The rest of the headquarters team await him in a low, windowless, white building in a corner of the camp. His key players, it is noted, have the same pedigree as the brigadier. And they all seem to have physical abnormalities. Whether these mutations are a result of being a member of the Special Forces, or what is needed to get through the six months' hell of Special Forces selection, no one quite dares ask.

Carleton-Smith stands no more than a wiry five foot nine. His calf muscles bulge like knotty marrows below his knees. Wellington boots gather in a rubber concertina just above his ankles. His Chief of Staff, Major X, originally a Gurkha officer, has spent most of his career in Special Forces. Most recently he has been the officer commanding A Squadron SAS, and has followed his boss to 16 Air Assault Brigade. X is no exception to the SAS bulge-in-the-wrong-places phenomenon. Tall, slim, with brown hair, he has a narrow face and a slightly pointed nose which emphasises his beaky intelligence. He is quick to smile and prides himself on creating a culture of fun to offset the intensity of the work at headquarters. His upper body is in proportion to the rest of him, and athletic. But he has bison's thighs.

Head of the planning desk, a younger major and former SAS troop commander, Major Y is tall and slim too. A man with the easy charm that Eton and birth into the aristocracy can breed, he doesn't seem to have any obvious physical anomaly, apart, as Major X observed, from a perfect bottom. Lieutenant Colonel David Wilson, commanding officer of 23 Engineer Regiment (Air Assault), who is believed to have a Special Forces background, is very proud of his 'low slung ears', which means that he can grow his sideburns further down his face than anyone else and still conform to military dress regulations.

'All the blokes who appear in newspaper photographs with blacked-out faces have expensive haircuts,' a jealous junior officer observes, in a whisper.

The British in Helmand now have a small number of Apache attack helicopters, a battery of 105mm guns from the 7th Parachute Regiment Royal Horse Artillery, and a half battery of a Guided Multiple Rocket Launch System. Carleton-Smith has armoured infantry, Harrier, F16, F18, and even B51 bombers on call. There are drones and high-altitude spy planes, and the Royal Marines have left their Viking armoured troop carriers behind. No one fears that a significant British base can be overrun.

Little serious fighting is expected over the next few weeks because all of Helmand's energies are focussed on the poppy crop. The fields on the outskirts of Lashkar Gah, south into the Red Desert, and all the way north into the mountains at Kajaki, are roaring with colour. Carleton-Smith knows that fighting will be low in intensity until the scratched cheeks of billions of poppy heads have wept their last tears of opium resin. The Taleban will watch, they will wait, but they will not attack. Not yet. War at this time would be bad for business. Intelligence reports say that the Taleban have agreed with the poppy farmers and drug barons not to fight with the British until after the wheat has been reaped, which closely follows the poppy harvest. Fighting before the crops are in would be economic suicide – for all Afghans in Helmand.

Over the previous two years Helmand had gone through a staggering drugs boom. There was a 62 per cent increase in the amount of land under poppy in 2005–06. A year later this had gone up by another 53 per cent. The acreage in Afghanistan being used to grow opium is more than all of the land used for coca cultivation in the

whole of the South American continent. Afghanistan produces 93
per cent of the world's opium. Helmand's drugs industry generates
half of Afghanistan's $4 billion total drug revenues. Poppy, British
intelligence analysts say, is worth $100 million a year to the Taleban
in taxes taken in Helmand and is a major source of their funding for
the war. But it is also, overwhelmingly, the only source of income
for the farmers in Helmand. Wheat prices have been driven down
by the free distribution of surplus grain as food aid from Europe and
America so little has been planted this season and Helmandi farmers
will be unable to benefit from the global spike in cereal prices.

Fighting up and down the Helmand valley means that farmers
cannot get perishable crops to market in Kandahar. The British do
not interfere with the poppy harvest and are left to patrol mostly
unmolested through the vast plantations of gorgeous flowers.

Carleton-Smith goes straight into a session with the civilian boss
of the Provincial Reconstruction Team (PRT), Michael Ryder. A tall
super-fit fell-runner and veteran of the Foreign and Commonwealth
Office, he has held senior posts in security policy. Now he is in
charge of the British reconstruction and development effort in
Helmand and has £30 million to spend over three years. Based in the
Lashkar Gah District Centre, a short walk from the military headquarters, the PRT is supposed to help the Afghan administration
spread its influence into Helmand – and undermine the insurgency
with successful development projects.

Ryder, gangly, bearded, and donnish, is working for a Whitehall
department which does not appear to relish the challenges that a
real war brings. On the eve of Carleton-Smith's arrival, Ryder – the
senior British civilian official in Helmand – has sent an 'e-gram',
a short electronic message, to the Foreign Office headquarters in
King Charles Street, Westminster, expressing deep reservations
about NATO plans to send an entire US Marine Expeditionary
Unit (MEU) into Garmsir in southern Helmand. Carleton-Smith
knows that the Foreign Office is worried that his brigade's plans

will be pulled out of shape by having to supply troops to reinforce territory taken by US Marines once the MEU has left. But he is convinced that the plan to send the Marines into Garmsir offers the best chances of success in the province in 2008.

The 2,200-man 24 MEU consists of a small army in its own right. Designed to be a self-sufficient fast-moving sea- and air-borne force, every MEU generates awe, and envy, among British officers and men. A MEU travels with its own armoured vehicles, artillery and field hospital. It has at least four CH46 double-rotor, medium-lift helicopters, which can carry at least fourteen men in full combat gear. A MEU has its own AH-1W Super Cobra attack helicopters. These are a special favourite. They have been around since Vietnam. They carry a pilot and a gunner in a tiny cockpit which hangs beneath two rotor blades, which make an unmistakable slow *wack-wack-wack-wack* noise. The Cobra looks like a gigantic hornet. You can see when it is preparing to kill. A three-barrelled proboscis pops down from beneath its chin. This means that the 20mm Gatling gun is engaged. The weapon's aiming mechanism is hard-wired into the pilot's helmet so all the pilot has to do is look at something and the gun swings onto the target. Its three barrels can fire up to 1,500 rounds, the size of a fat carrot, in a minute. It makes a formidable farting sound when it fires. Slung in the armpits of its stubby wings the Cobra also carries Hellfire computer-guided 'fire and forget' missiles.

'They don't fuck about, these Yanks. They really don't fuck about,' one senior British officer observes as he watches the arrival of 24 MEU at Kandahar airfield. The Marines also have their own Harrier jump jets on call. In short, they have almost the same amount of fire-power as the whole British brigade, which has four times as many men.

Hardened by several tours in Iraq and Afghanistan, the Marines have been eagerly anticipated in Helmand. The British are keen to keep them for the whole of their scheduled six-month tour – even

if the Americans are, technically, the 'theatre reserve' for the overall
NATO commander, American General Dan K. McNeill. As far as
the British officers in charge of Helmand are concerned, there is
every advantage of having the huge extra help the MEU can bring –
and no reason not to welcome them in.

But the might, and style, of the MEU has spooked the Foreign
Office as much as it has won the admiration of the British Army:
it isn't a ground-holding organisation. The Foreign Office assumes
that US Marine Leviathan is a giant ground-grinder. That it will tear
through enemy-held territory leaving nothing but smoking ruins in
its wake. There is a danger that the US Marines might actually be
too successful.

The Marines have a mission in two parts. Their main aim is to
re-establish Forward Operating Base Rhino, deep in the Red Desert,
not far from the border with Pakistan, and try to stop the seem-
ingly endless supply of men and ammunition pouring in from
Afghanistan's eastern neighbour.

To get to Fob Rhino the Marines will need to pass through
Garmsir district, about 40 kilometres south of Lashkar Gah. The
area is known as the Snake's Head because of the way the Helmand
River bulges at this point into a network of irrigation canals, and
then tails off south into the desert. Low lying and chopped into a
grid by irrigation channels built by the Americans in the 1950s, it has
been the scene of vicious fighting for over two years. In late 2007
two members of the Mercian Regiment were killed, and seven other
wounded, in one firefight. Six other British soldiers have died there
in a battle over an area known as 'Three Walls'. But the fighting over
the potentially rich area has reached stalemate. The British, with a
company of around 140, have been able to do little more than hold
the ground they stand on.

They are based at Fob Delhi, which is about the size of three
tennis courts, set up in what had been an administrative building
for American contractors working on the canals fifty years ago.

The Helmand River runs slowly past the western walls. Within them is a gravel area just large enough to land a helicopter. Two other interlinked compounds house men in medieval conditions of extreme heat in summer, and extreme cold in winter. The Fobs in Helmand are part fashioned from local mud-walled buildings which are surrounded by thick and towering earth barricades. About 500 metres north, a dozen or so soldiers from the base do two- or three-week stints manning a mini-fort known as J-Tac Hill. This artificial kopje is believed to have been built by the British during the Second Afghan War, 120 years before. Another small number of troops are perched on a similar mount southwest of Fob Delhi called Hamburger Hill.

The fighting with the Taleban has degenerated into First World War trench warfare. On one side the heavily outnumbered British manage to defend themselves with superior weapons and training. On the other, often no more than 200 metres away, the Taleban have built trench systems which connect hundreds of underground bunkers to firing positions, hidden anti-aircraft machine guns, and rocket launching sites.

The first that fighters coming in from Taleban camps in Pakistan see of the British is at the Snake's Head. South of Fob Delhi the area is entirely depopulated for about 8 kilometres. Farmers have abandoned their compounds for safety elsewhere, leaving behind a maze of broken buildings and earth chewed up by bombs. Fob Delhi stands on the eastern edge of Darwishan village, which once boasted a bazaar with over 150 shop fronts. These are now silent and empty; their steel doors long ago torn aside by looters, windblown dust piles up in empty corners. A small detachment of Afghan police and secret agents occasionally run the gauntlet, from their lonely compound in the middle of the village, to meetings with the British in a base which is attacked every day.

British officers hope that if the MEU can be persuaded to launch their campaign in the Snake's Head, their firepower will sweep the Taleban south, pushing the front line away from the gates of Fob Delhi. This, they believe, would allow local farmers to return to their land. It would also damage the enemy's ability to reinforce their operations further north into the Helmand valley. The MEU commander agrees. But Ryder and many of his colleagues in London say that neither the Afghan security forces, nor the British Army, have the resources to hold such a large area. There is a danger of 'mission creep' – that military success will require additional investment in men and materiel at a time when the focus of the Foreign Office is to find a way for Britain to extract itself from the sands of Helmand, not dig itself in deeper.

Carleton-Smith disagrees. What, after all, is the point of fighting in Helmand? To take territory away from the Taleban. That is precisely what the MEU is planning to do. The British know that after two years of heavy fighting they need every bit of help they can get. Helmand isn't improving, if anything it is going backwards. But the problem remains: how will British and Afghan troops hold and control the Snake's Head after the Marines pull out?

The Kabul-appointed administrators that the British are trying to support can hardly move anywhere within the province – and then only under heavy guard. Carleton-Smith himself has to be escorted in an armoured Land Cruiser just to get to the governor's office five minutes away from his Lashkar Gah base. There are only two ways to get to any of the other bases around the province: by helicopter, and there are very few of them, or as part of a road convoy, in what is called a Combat Logistics Patrol, and these are guaranteed to get attacked.

'The theme is freedom of movement – without it, there is no ability to link the government to the people and there is even less effective governance. This stops development and produces a vacuum which is exploited by the Taleban. They are not strong but they are better placed geographically than local ministers,' Carleton-Smith tells Major X as they cross from the cookhouse to headquarters.

'No bloody kidding,' he mutters to himself. Earlier that day he'd learned that the citizens of Gereshk, the economic hub of the province, had seen their first government minister in twenty-eight years – 'with a life expectancy of forty-three, that's a once in a life-time event!'

Meanwhile, because government is limited to small enclaves in Lashkar Gah, Gereshk, Sangin and Musa Qal'ah, the rule of law is based not on any central government legal system but on the ancient cultural codes of *pashtunwali*. Carleton-Smith has been told that 99 per cent of disputes, and criminal cases, are settled by elders sitting in court and deciding matters in the way they always have. Criminal prosecutors in Lashkar Gah are handling just five cases a week, mostly of petty theft. The prison is jammed with children, women, old men – above all the poor. None have been subjected to a judicial process of any kind; they are just too poor to bribe their way out. Beyond the urban concentrations, Taleban structures mirror *pashtunwali*, with added reinforcement from the Koran. The Taleban sets up courts and land dispute committees very quickly in areas where they are dominant, and just as quickly bring a brutally enforced rule of law where there has been almost none.

The American MEU offers the British the chance to take territory away from the Taleban, to repopulate it, and to extend the central government's rule into new areas. This is precisely what the brigad-ier and his whole brigade think is the reason they are fighting in Afghanistan. Their mission is to 'close down the ungoverned space'. Doing so, the British government has said, will make the British homeland safer by removing any chance that Afghanistan could again be used as a safe haven for al Qaeda.

But six days after he finds out that Ryder is arguing against the MEU's plans, the Foreign Office South Asia desk sends word that it wants both the brigadier, Carleton-Smith, and Ryder, the top British civilian in Helmand, to compile and send the Foreign Office an e-gram analysing how UK and US plans would fit together in the Snake's Head. It would then be used in talks with Washington and Kabul to argue against sending the MEU into Helmand at all. Carleton-Smith refuses to endorse this view and hears nothing more about the 'e-gram'.

The command structure of the British mission in Helmand is chaotic. Carleton-Smith must serve the interests of the British government and is in constant contact with his military masters in the Permanent Joint Headquarters in Norwood, Middlesex, and the Foreign Office. But his 16 Air Assault Brigade also falls under NATO's mission in Afghanistan, the International Security Assistance Force (ISAF) and the ISAF commander, American general, Dan McNeill.

When General McNeill and his entourage arrive for a conference in Lashkar Gah they look as if they have wandered into the Bost Hotel conference rooms from a planet that is one and a half times the scale of our own. Compared to the small and delicately boned Pashto, and the wiry British officers, they seem to be entirely of the wrong dimensions. McNeill reveals a buzz-cut squarish head as he pulls his helmet off and tucks it under his arm. Close to the end of his two-year stint in the country, he knows it intimately. His subordinates and rivals know not to underestimate the man because of his bullish shape and size. He's been an officer in the US Special Forces in Vietnam; he's served in Iraq too. He's sixty-two, but looks ten years younger.

He sinks into one of the sofas that lines the walls of the hotel's meeting room. One end of it is decorated with a puzzling mural: Afghan armoured personnel carriers pick their way through what looks like a Swiss Alpine landscape. Another American, Major General Robert Cone, plants himself on the same sofa and Carleton-Smith thanks his ancestors for the genes which allow him to squeeze in next to the two giants. The room is quickly lined with local dignitaries in gold, black or white turbans. At one end of the meeting room sits the bare-headed governor of Helmand, Alhaj Gulab Mangal,

senior Afghan army commanders in their Soviet-era wide-brimmed
flat caps, and other top officials. They are gathered for a Super *Shura*
– a top-level meeting. A smartly dressed man with a close-cropped
beard stands in the centre of the room, opens both of his palms to the
heavens, throws back his head, and bursts into song. Carleton-Smith
smiles to himself. Naim has a subtle and cadenced voice, for a secret
policeman. Naim, the provincial head of the National Directorate of
Security (NDS), knows that extremist Taleban supporters would be
outraged at hearing the Koran sung. The Taleban banned all music
when they were in power. He also knows how much Afghans pride
themselves on their musical heritage, which is now only dimly recalled
after thirty years of war. So he sings.

Sitting directly opposite him, Carleton-Smith recognises Sher
Mohammed Akunzada. He notes how well the black-haired grandee
hides any animosity he surely feels towards the British. In December
2005, he was sacked by President Hamid Karzai, at the insistence
of the British, after 9 tonnes of raw opium, which he said he had
himself confiscated from drug dealers and was just storing, had been
found in his compound. But Akunzada is a powerful figure: his
younger brother is the deputy governor of Helmand, and several
of the local police chiefs are part of his network. Now a senator in
Kabul, he remains a presidential confidant. Carleton-Smith smiles
a greeting at him, nods in respect, and wonders how far Akunzada's
tendrils reach into the region.

Mangal explains that in the twelve districts of Helmand only
eight actually have local governors. The rest are entirely in the
control of the Taleban. The government and British forces have
tenuous control only over Musa Qal'ah, Sangin and Kajaki – and
only in small areas. Travel is dangerous for ordinary Afghans, and
this is holding up development. And there is one major priority –
Darwishan in Garmsir district.

'The Snake's Head!' thinks Carleton-Smith.

As if speaking to a script deliberately written to frustrate the

British Foreign Office, Helmand's governor is telling NATO's top general that taking the Snake's Head from the Taleban is his top priority.

'The government has a tiny footprint in Darwishan, no more really than a checkpoint – and it is a vital district. It is a gateway to Helmand and a safe haven for the enemy. It is extremely important that we extend government control over the district . . . without control of the south, and the border with Pakistan, we will never establish enduring stability in Helmand. If necessary we must deploy additional forces there,' Mangal declares.

McNeill nods. Carleton-Smith sneaks a quick look at Michael Ryder, who remains entirely inscrutable. But the message is unmistakable – send in the Marines.

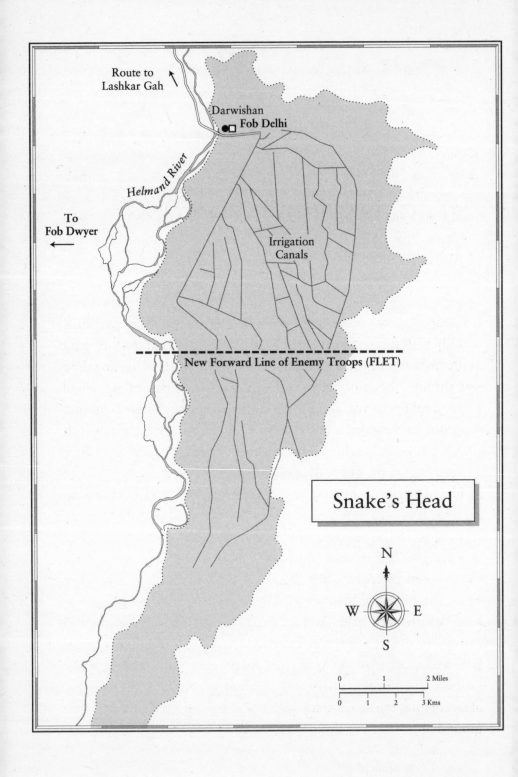

Route to
Lashkar Gah

Darwishan
Fob Delhi

Helmand River

To
Fob Dwyer

Irrigation
Canals

New Forward Line of Enemy Troops (FLET)

Snake's Head

N
W   E
S

0   1   2 Miles

0   1   2   3 Kms

2

CATASTROPHIC SUCCESS

An empty green metal machine-gun ammunition box is filling steadily with cigarettes and ash. Mastiff, the camp cat, is staring up at the front legs of a hairy yellow camel spider which are feeling their way through the joint between the mud wall and the ceiling. Small plastic beakers of tea, thick with sugar, are being handed around. Someone has revealed a previously hidden packet of biscuits, which the visitors politely refuse. The camp looks wobbly through the heat which bends light, like it does over the kettle.

The officer in command of Fob Delhi has deep shadows around his eyes. It is hard to tell what colour his hair is: like everything else it is coated in the tan dust of Helmand. Bubbles of baked air bloat and burst in flurries and eddies, briefly whisking talcum dust into the noses of the party with Brigadier Mark Carleton-Smith. They sit on three rows of benches made from black plastic tubes, six feet long, which once held Javelin missiles. Explosions, somewhere in the middle distance, manage to force themselves through the stifling haze with a lazy *whump*. As the sun rushes to its zenith it pours white heat over the top of the plywood partition, on the left of the briefing area, cooking the camel-back water bags and rucksacks lying on the ground.

'What we have here,' says Major Neil Den-McKay, 'is catastrophic success.'

He beams, delighted with the phrase. Until four weeks ago 'A' Company of the 5th Battalion of the Royal Regiment of Scotland (the Argyll and Sutherland Highlanders), lead by Den-McKay, had been holding the line alone at Fob Delhi. Then 2,200 US Marines from 24 MEU, backed up with Harrier jump jets, Cobra attack helicopters, Bradley fighting vehicles, Humvees and other machines of war, roared into town. 'A' Company had watched the movement with envy and delight.

This was war porn at its best. Jets screamed low overhead, heralding the move of the MEU to Fob Dwyer, a sun-baked fort two hours west of Fob Delhi, out in the desert. The Cobras came through the sunrise and behind them, grinding up the sandy roads; then came the tall and mighty American armoured personnel carriers, the Cougars, some pushing wheeled ploughs designed to set mines off ahead of the speeding column.

'They're not worried about being blown to fuck? They're just driving along and crossing their fingers they won't get blown up,' Corporal Lachlan 'Lachie' MacNeil said, as he watched the Marines barrel along the roads. Years of experience in Northern Ireland had taught the British Army to painstakingly search any 'vulnerable points' (VPs), like bridges, culverts and junctions, for hidden Improvised Explosive Devices (IEDs) by using metal detectors. The Americans didn't bother; they roared through like cavalry. Two US Marines died on the way to Fob Delhi when their Humvee jeep charged along the road from Kandahar and hit a bomb hidden under the tarmac. The Americans seemed to shrug and accept these sudden deaths.

In Kabul, General McNeill had lost patience with the British Foreign Office's equivocation over Garmsir's future. And on 28 April he'd sent the Marines in. He told them they were to sweep past the eastern edge of the Snake's Head, break any resistance they found, and then head about 50 kilometres further into the desert to re-establish Fob Rhino. While the Foreign Office dithered and worried about the consequences of capturing a large tract of land from the Taleban, McNeill sent a personal message to Colonel Peter Petronzio, commander of 24 MEU. He wanted the US Marines to 'stir it up in Garmsir – stick around – and get some defeating done'. He was getting fed up with the under-resourced British.

Carleton-Smith had been tipped off about McNeill's message to the MEU commander. He had agreed with it, but decided that he would let American diplomats explain what was going on and put some steel into their British colleagues – 'lest they wilt again'.

The Argylls, who had taken over from the Gurkhas after a winter tour, had been in Fob Delhi for only twenty days when McNeill's orders came through. In that time they'd killed eleven Taleban. The Fob had been hit with five 107mm Katyusha rockets. They'd been stuck in a back-and-forth shooting match with the Taleban over a 200-metre no-man's-land, every day. The fighting was intense. But the status quo was stifling. No one admitted it, but the idea that they would be stuck in Fob Delhi for six months, providing targets for the Taleban and having no material effect on the war in Helmand, was chafing under the company's skin. They knew that with just 140 men there was little, or no, chance of interrupting the jet stream of hundreds of guerrillas who came through from Pakistan in the south.

The British had only enough troops to hold the front line with the Taleban. But behind the Taleban trenches the British knew that insurgents were using the Snake's Head as a Taleban gathering point. It was also the Taleban's training base, and where they were blooded for the first time. Newly arrived from Pakistan, young guerrillas would have a quick crack at Fob Delhi, then move on north up the Helmand valley to fight in Sangin or Musa Qal'ah. The Jocks hated being thought of as a warm-up for the main events in the north of the province. But they knew that they were. Fob Delhi, sitting in an

ultra-violent prison moonscape of smashed mud walls and charred
fields scorched grey by high explosives, was just a tiny breakwater in
the Taleban sea.

The MEU plan, Operation Azada Wosa ('Stay Free' in Pashto)
would give the British a focus for doing what they most wanted to
do – offensive operations. Den-McKay grabbed at the chance to be
part of what was going to be an operation to seize and hold ground
– rather than fight and then withdraw, which had been the pattern
in most areas for two years.

'A' Company had led the breakout from the Fob to prepare the
ground for what the army calls the 'forward passage of lines' – when the
MEU would pass through the British-held area into enemy territory.

Den-McKay is hyperactive. Constantly smiling, his favourite
words are 'robust' and 'balanced', and he sees to it that 'A' Company
are always both. Popular and approachable, he loves being far away
from his battle group headquarters in Lashkar Gah, with no colonel
to look over his shoulder.

He leans forward as he speaks, and finds it hard to use the middle-
class, frequently euphemistic, language favoured by some of his
fellow officers. He doesn't speak of 'neutralising' the Taleban – he
speaks of killing them. He also has a habit of thinking out loud. So
when he is in the field, anyone around him, and everyone on his
radio network, knows what he is thinking, and why.

One morning, Lachie says, nodding towards his company
commander Den-McKay, 'That, Mister, is the best fucking officer
and the best fucking soldier I've seen in my fuckin' life,' and then
stalks off.

Standing in the briefing area at Fob Delhi at the end of a month
of fighting which has been led by the Americans, Den-McKay tells
Carleton-Smith: 'Sir, the enemy has been smashed, to be honest.
All we see now is covert groups trying to get to cached weapons and
bodies. What matters now is what we do with this success. It is, I say
again, a catastrophic success!'

The capture of the Snake's Head began with 'A' Company heading east and then south down a road called 'Route Cowboys' that runs alongside a 10-metre wide canal with concrete sides that drops steeply into the water. The company moved at night in Mastiff armoured trucks and Land Rovers. The whine of the engines broadcast their move to the Taleban. Lachie, a Glaswegian who'd joined the army aged sixteen and illiterate, and who was now writing a blog on his war, imagined the Afghan fighters lying face down in their foxholes, watching the trucks head towards checkpoint Balaklava, which marks the junction for the dog-leg turn south. As the trucks lurched and took the turn, everyone's breathing changed. The trucks swung south. Like teenagers caught gossiping in church, the whispered banter faded quickly to nothing. A lot of men clenched their jaws hard – no one wanted to bite off his own tongue if the Mastiff leapt into the air after hitting a bomb in the road. There was a certainty of battle.

The moon was down. Feral crops sucked what little light shone from the stars out of the air. Fields appeared as straight-edged black holes in the dark. The compounds on the right, to the west, were jagged and looked white in the night vision goggles used by the top gunners. Steel telegraph poles, shorn in half by gunfire, rested their heads on the ground. Irrigation ditches cut the landscape up like a chessboard and gave the Taleban a ready-made trench system.

Den-McKay stared into these shapes as they flickered by in the eyepiece of his goggles. In the last few weeks he'd watched video downlinks from spy planes and drones which had followed Taleban fighters and their supply columns, as they scuttled along the 'rat runs' of ditch complexes – and then vanished. They'd become invisible to thermal-imaging cameras, as if they'd evaporated. It had been maddening. Worse still, when he had clearly seen men carrying ammunition to a known firing point of a heavy machine gun, which threatened helicopter landings at Fob Delhi, he had not been allowed to attack them. They had not posed a direct threat to the lives of his men so, under the British rules of engagement for what is not, officially, a war but a 'peace support mission', the Taleban could not be shot that night.

2 Platoon disgorged from the backs of the Mastiffs and began their patrol down either side of the road. The night was gently bluing towards dawn. Silence. The sand absorbed the sound of feet moving across it.

Lachie had fought during the siege of al Amarah in Iraq. But his section was full of very young men – teenagers – fresh out of training. He'd been in for a dozen years. The army, and reading, were now his life. He sat against a wall before the patrol began and took a long look at the hungry group of stringy boys he led.

'If something happens these lads will smash the fuck out of the enemy,' he thought to himself, and chuckled. Looking at Private Nick Whelan he could see the excitement. These teenagers wanted to go to war. 'Fucking good on them. Britain needs a few more like these, then we wouldn't be in the shit we are today. More of these and we'd still be ruling half the world, not on our knees and weak.'

He'd grown up in some of the toughest parts of Glasgow. It showed on his face. His sloping nose with its punched look; his skin worn, his mouth curved down; his hair cropped close. In Fob Delhi, if he wasn't working, he could be found tucked into the shade somewhere, reading. It had been an obsession of his for almost a decade – ever since he mastered letters. He can lose himself in anything – military history, Mills and Boon, it doesn't matter; his dirty knotty hands are always wrapped around a book.

But this morning, he took his men south, through compound after compound. They had found lost sandals, abandoned Taleban bivouacs, walls with 'murder holes' cut into them looking out over the road ready for an ambush.

On the other side of the river the steady thumping *dum-dum-dum-dum* from an insurgent 12.7 'Dushka' heavy machine gun formed a back beat to the firework swishes of Taleban rockets.

The fields were abandoned; the Afghan fort-like homes, with their compound walls 4 metres high and courtyard gardens, a shambles of overgrown prickly bluish weed and hip-high grass. Doors to homes and granaries, which were usually locked against the prying eyes of neighbours, slumped against their frames like old drunks.

The day had opened with an artillery barrage against an oblong collection of compounds marked 'Jesters' on the British maps. Artillery guns at Fob Dwyer fired their cone-shaped rounds, stuffed with high explosive, 'danger close' to Lachie and the rest of 2 Platoon. The howl and crash of the artillery makes bile rise in the throat for the first few rounds. When 'danger close' is called over the radio, you know it is indeed going to land dangerously close. If there's a minor glitch, a miscalculation of wind speed or humidity, you'll be torn to pieces.

Fountains of brown dust kicked up by the barrage spurted from the 'Jesters' compounds. Shards of metal shell-casing hummed through the air and fell to the ground. Rills of smoke rose from them as they cooled. But when Lachie and the rest of 2 Platoon got to Jesters, there was nothing much left to clear – just rubble and torn mud walls.

That night 2 Platoon settled down in a small abandoned compound. They'd just been told that the next stage of the move south had been postponed for twenty-four hours. It meant that they could get some sleep. Lachie and Colour Sergeant Davey Ure, commander of the Javelin missile platoon, climbed onto the roof to start sand-bagging it against mortar attack.

They saw movement in a compound marked 'Charlotte' on their maps. The air began to crackle with bullets. Rocket-propelled grenades screamed overhead and they both returned fire. Taleban mortars began raining in, about 20 metres short of the compound walls.

'Incoming! Incoming!' someone yelled.

'That's pretty fucking obvious,' someone else shouted as grey smoke shot up into the air from the impacts. Machine gunners rattled back in the general direction of the mortars and a helicopter was called in to attack the Taleban on the edge of Charlotte. In a few moments, and as dusk fell, it was as if a giant hand had been slapped down on the mud fortress and crushed it.

At dawn the next morning collared doves called back and forth across the compounds to each other. Other birds sang a disjointed and defiant chorus as the platoon set off to clear Charlotte. It was huge – more like a village within a compound. 'We're definitely going to get bumped this morning,' Lachie said as his section painstakingly picked its way between walls and ditches. There was no sign of the Taleban who had attacked them last night. The British followed each other in single file along a route cleared by the lead scout with a metal detector. Instructions were murmured; the grass crackled with heat.

'I can smell them. I can fucking smell the bastards. There's people in here for sure, I can smell their stink, their human stink,' whispered Lachie.

Den-MacKay had been clear with his orders – 'I want every inch of land either side of the canal made safe for the Marines when they push through, every fucking inch must be turned over. I don't want our allies being ambushed because we haven't done a proper job.'

Lachie's platoon commander, Lieutenant Olly Bevan, twenty-three, from Gloucestershire, is like a well-muscled schoolboy, with blond hair that sticks up almost vertically; he has even teeth, a wide smile and conventional good looks. Having pushed out to the east of Lachie's section, he was having to walk back to talk to the Glaswegian because his Bowman radio was, predictably, on the blink. Bevan felt the overgrown weeds which had taken over the abandoned compounds begin to close in. The spiky grass plant was chest-high in places, 'a great place for a stay-behind gunman to use as an ambush', he thought.

Channelled through doorways by battered mud walls, which

could be rigged with bombs, Bevan kept his voice as calm, measured and as quiet as he could. But there was an edge to it as he stepped through a narrow gap in a wall and found himself in a small courtyard. On his right a two-storey mud minaret-like building overlooked him – 'a perfect spot for a Taleban sniper'.

A path led away into a jumble of tumbling buildings to the side of the minaret. Straight ahead the courtyard opened into a dense orchard. Lachie was on the left, resting on his knee and looking intently into the orchard.

'Lachie,' whispered Bevan, his vocal chords stretched with tension . . . 'Lachie!'

Something made Bevan bring his rifle to his shoulder. He could hear voices. A flicker of white moved in the fruit trees. 'Can't see,' he thought.

'Who the fuck?' Bevan blurted out loud. No civilians here. Taleban.

'There's the enemy! Get out the way – fucking move!' he yelled at a private soldier who'd strayed into his sights.

Lachie and Bevan fired seven shots between them at four armed men who'd emerged from the trees 30 metres in front. Another twelve rounds followed.

Lachie saw a crimson flash as one of his rounds went through a fighter's right shoulder.

Bevan's victim had been hit in the chest and side. He doubled up but stayed on his feet, ducked into the trees, and made off down an alleyway to his left.

'Follow me. The rest of you watch the fucking rear,' Lachie roared and took off after the Taleban group like a dog after rabbits.

'Two zero – two zero Alpha – contact wait out.' Bevan quickly sent a message telling Den-McKay that he was in a fight and then ran after Lachie.

Lachie rushed down the tight alleyway with his section. Bevan and five others ran parallel to him, and stopped. Ahead was an overgrown walled garden half the size of a tennis court. It was thick with abandoned vines and cut up by irrigation channels. The wounded Taleban fighter was trapped and hiding somewhere inside it. Bevan ordered his men to form an extended line across the compound and pick through it.

Nick Whelan, a good-natured soldier aged just nineteen, and with a reputation for his easy-going, smiling vanity, appeared alongside Lachie on the threshold of the garden.

'I-can-see-his-feet,' he whispered, bringing his rifle up to his shoulder. Nick fired.

'Stoppage!' he yelled, as his Minimi jammed.

Bevan and another soldier ran up and fired into the vines which partially hid the Taleban fighter.

Nick was silent as he contemplated what he'd done and kept his rifle trained on the body. Bevan walked up to the dead man. He looked about twenty-five and was very, very thin. Next to him lay his PKM machine gun. He'd been shot in the side and the chest and head. Bevan marvelled at how he'd managed to stay upright let alone run away after he'd been so mortally wounded. 'Tough. Nails,' he said to himself as he used the bayonet on the end of his rifle to lift the dead man's shirt to check for hidden weapons.

'Check that out. Fucking "Gucci" trainers,' said Whelan. Most local people wore *chapels* – leather or plastic sandals made of two pieces of leather crossed over the top of the foot leaving a V-shaped opening at the toe. These shoes were new and well-made Western-style trainers. 'Must be a new arrival from Pakistan.' There were no shops for dozens of miles in any direction.

He turned his back and rejoined the rest of the platoon, which was chasing the other two Taleban off to the east. Splashes of blood in the dust led the British troops into another series of compounds, and more jungles of overgrown gardens, irrigation ditches and walls, endless walls.

'Go firm [stop],' Bevan ordered. The whole platoon was buzzing.

He'd felt the surge of triumph, the adrenal elation that comes with combat and the added thrill of being in on a kill. His men had forgotten that they had been in the field for nearly forty-eight hours and were charging ahead like huntsmen. They risked running into a Taleban trap or counter attack.

Popcorn. The air was full of snap and crackle, like popcorn bursting in a saucepan. *Thump, thump, thump*. Machine gun. Taleban. 2 Platoon's own 'Jimpy' and Minimi gunners scrambled on top of a wall, spotted the smoke and returned fire. Someone else from the platoon was up on a roof setting up to fire a 66mm Light Anti-Structure Missile (LASM) – the ISAF equivalent of a rocket-propelled grenade. This hand-carried missile and disposable tube is a favourite with soldiers – it makes a big bang. Two were fired at the Taleban machine-gun nests, setting off cheers and whoops from the Jocks. Another platoon could see Taleban wounded being carried to a donkey and evacuated. They radioed 2 Platoon to tell them that fighters were running away from the battle. Bevan did not want the Taleban to regroup so he called for mortars to be dropped. The bombs made a crunching sound as they exploded among the fleeing insurgents.

By now 'A' Company had reached its objective, the point at which the Americans would take over the battle with the Taleban with their 2,200-man MEU. Lachie patrolled 100 metres into the fields on the east of the road to make sure that it was clear. He found snail trails of thickening blood which disappeared off into fields of patchy self-sown wheat. But no bodies, dead or alive.

2 Platoon's experience turned out to be typical of the next three weeks of fighting as the US Marines pushed down the far eastern edge of the Snake's Head and cleared it east to west. Artillery bombardment and bombing raids by jets preceded infantry attacks on Taleban positions. It became clear, as the fighting wore on, that the Taleban who stayed to fight were a screen – a rear guard with

orders to protect the withdrawal of the main force. Small groups of two or three men were able to survive for days.

The mystery of how they managed to defy attempts to kill them quickly emerged: the Snake's Head was riddled with a network of underground bunkers, connected by tunnels. Most of the bunkers had been built under the roots of the huge thick-limbed mulberry trees. Under the vaulted roof of roots eight men could survive anything but a direct hit by a 500lb bunker-busting ground-penetrating bomb. Hellfire missiles from helicopters and cannon rounds soaked into the earth like spilled water. It was a Third World Maginot Line – an almost impenetrable series of defences. Each bunker had an escape hole the size of a badger's sett, and carefully camouflaged murder holes for the gunmen inside. The mouths of the caves were less than a metre across and each one had a well-fitted hessian curtain across it.

'That's where the fuckers we've been watching have been going when they've vanished off our screens. They have been diving into the bunkers and pulling the curtains – the hessian absorbs the heat from their bodies, so we can't see them with any of our thermal-imaging gear. Clever bastards,' said Den-MacKay on a day in which engineers attached to his company blew up seventy-five separate bunkers.

The fighting had eased off, but the patrolling was intense. The Taleban had planted IEDs in the paths and bunker entrances. Nick Whelan walked carefully behind the man leading the patrol, through the maze of ditches south of Fob Delhi. The man in front had a metal detector.

Nick was on his backside. He couldn't hear anything and thick grey dust or smoke blinded him. He could just make out the guy in front as a heap on the ground.

Nick leapt to his feet and sprinted forward shouting 'Man Down! Man Down!'

Cartwheeling forward he landed on his face, as if running into a low brick wall. Blackness – then more thick dust. Nick, as soldiers always do when they've been blown up, checked his crotch. 'Thank fuck for that.' Then he felt spurting blood on his thighs.

Someone else was shouting 'Man Down! Man Down!' They meant Nick. He had triggered a second bomb, hidden by the Taleban to catch someone rushing to help an injured comrade.

A face appeared.

'Keep still.'

It took an hour to get the two wounded British soldiers back to the Fob's one-roomed field hospital where Captain James Lyon, a tall and unflappable doctor from 16 Medical Regiment, straightened the nasty broken femur of Whelan's friend and patched up the tears and holes in Whelan's lower body.

'Can't wait to gob off about this when I get to the pub,' said Nick.

Operation Azada Wosa had culminated in the capture of the ancient Jugroom Fort, which sits on a commanding bend in the Helmand River looking west into the desert. This was where a British Royal Marine, Lance Corporal Matthew Ford, had been killed a year earlier, apparently by friendly fire, during a failed assault on the Taleban. This time it took the US Marines just three hours to overrun the citadel, without a single ISAF death.

By the end of May, the Americans and 'A' Company of the Argylls had captured about 50 square kilometres of new territory for the government in Kabul. The front line lay about 1,000 metres south of Amir Aga, a village strung out across the Helmand River valley about 7 kilometres south of Fob Delhi. It had been under Taleban control for more than two years. The village has survived mostly intact. The Taleban, like any intelligent guerrilla movement, has avoided a self-destructive defensive fight.

Curious children emerge from their houses to stare at the Americans and beg for sweets. A handful of adult men wait quietly outside a small base which the US Marines have opened and are

using to canvass locals for 'quick impact projects', or Quips, which
the Americans can fund on behalf of the Afghan government to win
the support of local people.

Sayed Gul, a tall man with jet-black hair spilling out the sides of
his black turban and coal-coloured eyes which soften as he speaks,
gestures towards a group of children who are dancing around his
legs: 'I can teach these young people now. The Taleban destroyed our
school because it had been built by the government in 2003. They
said that we were teaching American ideology and that they didn't
want that in the schools because they were fighting the Americans.
There were a lot of very powerful Taleban people here. But most
of them have run away to Pakistan now. It was a terrible time here
when they were in charge, they killed and tortured people that they
said were spies for the government and for the Americans,' he says.
He is waiting to meet with American officers to ask for a grant to
restart his school.

'The Taleban believed they were the government here and I have
to admit I didn't think that we'd ever see the real government come
to help us. But I am happy. I want to see security, clinics and schools
back here. We don't want to be taken back in time like the Taleban
want, we want to be part of the world.'

The local head of the NDS, Mir Hamza, is beaming. He has not
been able to get to Amir Aga for years and has travelled down from
Darwishan in Garmsir district next to Fob Delhi with the American
vanguard. 'This is the beginning. In a few days you will see farmers
returning to their fields and rebuilding their homes. The foreign
fighters have all run away – many have gone north and many have
also gone to Pakistan. We will stay here and keep the Taleban out.'

But many officials in the British Foreign Office are dismayed.
This is an unwelcome victory. British forces could never have taken
the Snake's Head. They are already stretched, spread thin across
Helmand. The US Marines have shown up two embarrassing truths.
First, that if they want to prevail in Helmand, the British will need

more troops. And second, that there are not enough British – or Afghan – troops available to hold the ground that the Americans have taken. This, the Foreign Office fears, will be a political problem, on the domestic scene. How will ministers cope with the military necessity of more troops for a war in Afghanistan which they will not admit is a war, and for which public support is wavering?

During a video conference between Foreign Office officials in Afghanistan and London, Whitehall mandarins moan about the capture of Garmsir district and the inconvenient challenges it poses. It takes the intervention of the British ambassador to Kabul for the civil servants to comprehend that the capture of the Snake's Head is to be celebrated, not condemned. 'Rejoice! Rejoice!' Sir Sherard Cowper-Coles shouts at a startled room of officials in their London conference room. He observes that, since the British military and civilian mission to Helmand is to expand the reach of the Afghan government, it is churlish to complain when they have done just that.

The US Marines are still tasked to go on to occupy Fob Rhino. But Colonel Petronzio tells Mark Carleton-Smith that he is happy to remain in the Snake's Head for the rest of his tour, up to August or September. If he does, this will buy the British time to cobble together some Afghan government troops and maybe bring in more British troops from a reserve force based in Cyprus to hold the newly captured territory.

If the Marines do not stay, the British could face humiliation – they could be forced to withdraw back close to Fob Delhi. For the time being Carleton-Smith has no spare troops.

'I have not got any second echelon forces [reinforcements and reserves] to hold captured ground or manoeuvre around the Taleban. Most of what we have is fixed in Fobs. To generate men for battle-group operations means we have to cut down on manpower in the Fobs. This means that at the moment [outside the Snake's Head] we're just mowing the grass,' he tells his senior officers in Lashkar

Gah before heading to Garmsir. 'We are being asked to do counter-insurgency *lite*.'

It has taken American firepower and men to deliver the Snake's Head. Carleton-Smith has already sensed frustration in the American command of ISAF that the British are unable, or unwilling, to expand the territory under government control.

But the success of the Snake's Head operation means that he feels confident in declaring: 'The Taleban are not used to having two battles at the same time. We have definitely pre-empted their opening gambit and we're shaping the agenda. I've got the Taleban in my space and I'm in his head. His plan was to fix us in bases and restrict movement – pick us off on the main routes with land mines. He doesn't want to stand and fight at the moment, he wants to outlast us because he cannot outfight us.'

The Taleban, however, have other plans.

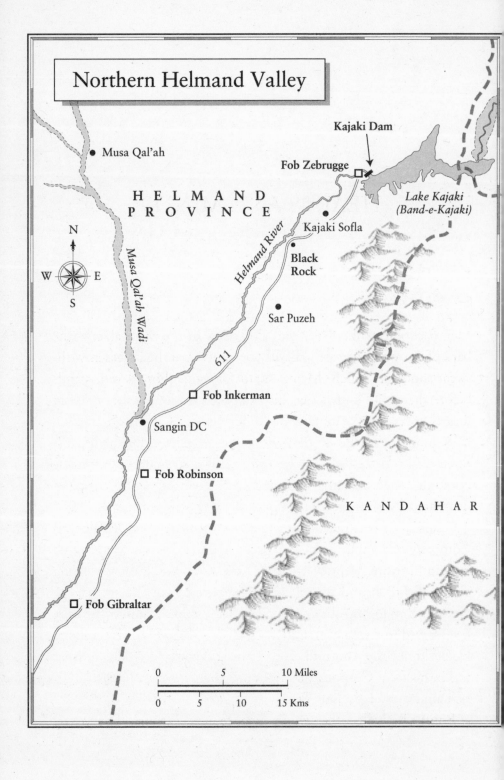

Northern Helmand Valley

Musa Qal'ah

H E L M A N D
P R O V I N C E

Kajaki Dam

Fob Zebrugge

Lake Kajaki
(Band-e-Kajaki)

Kajaki Sofla

Black
Rock

Sar Puzeh

Musa Qal'ah Wadi

Helmand River

611

Fob Inkerman

Sangin DC

Fob Robinson

K A N D A H A R

Fob Gibraltar

```
0            5         10 Miles

0     5     10     15 Kms
```

3

HEARTS AND MINDS

12 June, Fob Gibraltar

Men pack into rows of benches either side of the map table; at the
back of the room they are so tightly crammed that their greased-with-
sweat shoulders touch. Major Adam Dawson, thirty-seven, stands
before them. He knows that his troops are no longer interested in
'hearts and minds' campaigning. Four days ago at Fob Inkerman,
'B' Company of the 2nd Battalion, the Parachute Regiment, lost
three men – three well-known and much-liked men – in a suicide
bombing when a young man had emerged from a side alley and
detonated a vest packed with explosives and ball bearings.

Yesterday it was the turn of his own men, from 'C' (Bruneval)
Company of 2 Para. In the early minutes after dawn, a lean, shaven
man in his early twenties had approached a patrol. He was wearing
a blue dishdash and a skull cap. The patrol kept him at bay by
ordering him to stop about 30 metres short of them. Smiling broadly
he gestured to a yellow grain bag which was slung over his shoulder.
He beckoned the paratroopers to come and have closer look at what
was in his sack. Corporal Scotty Bourne held his men in check.

'Don't move lads. Stay firm.'

Bourne signalled the young man to lift his shirt. The young

man grinned, and staring into Scotty's eyes, he lifted the bag to his chest. There was a metallic click and a crack. The air whirred and hummed and the paratroopers dropped onto their faces – ball bearings skidded past their ears and kicked dust into their eyes.

They stood up and stared at where the young man had been – now there was nothing but scorched earth: 30 metres back the bomber's leg lay in the road. It was retrieved, strapped to the side of a day sack, taken for DNA sampling, then burned on the Fob Gib rubbish tip.

The only one way to defeat insurgents is to turn their host population against them. But the Taleban's skilled use of suicide bombers in rural areas totally destroys any British enthusiasm to 'engage with the local population'. Dawson knows he has to break this barrier down if he is going to get the farmers around Fob Gibraltar onside. British troops have arrived uninvited in the heart of the opium industry: can they be believed when they say they are in the country to help rebuild it? What kind of friendship can be built when the only contact they have involves a squaddie roaring '*Wadarega!*' (Stop!) in thick Geordie?

Two months of relentless patrolling, of chatting with farmers and handing out sweets, have been met with what the soldiers now see as betrayal. If local people can know, or suspect, a suicide bomber is among them and say nothing to the foreign troops picking their way across the country, then the locals, surely, are on the wrong side. So are the complaints about fighting with one hand tied behind their backs. Soldiers know from the intercepted radio communications of the Taleban that they are being watched, every step they take, by 'dickers' – unarmed men and children who mingle with the civilians and relay details of British movements to Taleban commanders. Young men in black clothing watch British troops lumbering through ditches and along canal tracks, and carefully note the way soldiers react to threats, what their 'Standing Operating Procedures' are.

Dickers have spent the last two months getting a live demonstration of paratroop infantry procedures. It is as if in the weeks before D-Day the Nazis have been invited to Salisbury Plain and given a ringside seat, while the British show them what equipment they have, how it works, its weaknesses and limitations, and how they will move across the ground. The paratroopers have to tolerate the blatant spying which dogs their every move. They can hear the dickers on the push-to-talk radio intercepts. They can see them chatting into mobile phones with extended high-powered antennas. They are even starting to recognise the faces of men who seem to be 'simple farmers' and who appear standing in a field holding a spade and watching them – wherever the troops go.

British rules of engagement in Helmand are intended to preserve some of the moral high ground. They are also meant to reinforce the obvious notion that if foreign soldiers kill profligate numbers of Afghan civilians they have no chance of winning a counter-insurgency war. In fact, civilian deaths in Afghanistan will only drive people into the Taleban camp. The Taleban want the British to hate and mistrust the Afghan people. They want British troops to kill Afghans so that the hatred will be mutual.

Soldiers are cooking. The sun's relentless energy bears down on the metal parts of their weapons which scald their hands. Anyone touching the armour plate of a vehicle risks a frying-pan burn, and soldiers wear tight leather gloves for protection. There is little relief at night, when the low-slung bunkers, built of rammed dirt, turn into roiling torments of thumping heat, like giant pizza ovens. Men rise from a night on the creaking army cots so wet with their own sweat they think they've pissed themselves. Most soldiers opt to sleep outside, where there is no protection from mortars or rockets, but at least the temperature drops far enough to allow a little sleep in the couple of hours before dawn. But still the thick, smothering pillow of hot air presses down into the face all night. During the day they wade through dust so fine it flows like liquid across the ground and dries into sharp pebbles inside their noses.

Everyone stinks. Sweat-starched cotton uniforms reek of ammonia. The standard-issue brown shiny nylon T-shirt, which is supposed to wick sweat away, works too well. It holds back so much of the body's effluent and other muck in the fabric that when you try to get it off, and it snags in your chin stubble, it makes you retch and gag.

It's early Wednesday evening, 11 June. Dawson gathers his officers and senior NCOs together for an 'orders group' and tells them he has planned to take two platoons and his own headquarters about 4 kilometres north of Fob Gibraltar to meet with local elders as part of the brigade's continuing policy of 'key leader engagement'. He has to remove the wedge that the Taleban's suicide bombers have driven between his men and Afghan villagers. This will be an opportunity to speak with community leaders, to explain to them that the British, and other foreign troops in Helmand, are there at the invitation of the Afghan government, not as invaders. He will listen carefully to their complaints and try to find out what, if anything, Britain can do for them.

The company has done dozens of patrols like this. In April and May they meandered through the vast plantations of flaming red, white and blue poppies. Soldiers marvelled at the slash of colour between the stark tan-coloured mountains to the east and the crumble-crust desert to the west. Corporal Matthew 'Des' Desmond loved to savour the contradictions laid out in front of him. As the shaven-headed cockney struggled along, his body armour chafing on his back where the straps of his radio pack dug in, he grinned wide and happy at the magnificent beauty of the landscape.

'Here we're surrounded by amazing flowers, which produce opium, which produce money for the Taleban to buy weapons to kill us. We're telling local people we're here to bring security, and we bring fear and fighting and might blow up their homes. It's a beautiful landscape, and we can't stand being here. It's fucking mad really,' he muttered out the corner of his mouth, with a barrow-boy grin.

This June evening, 'C' Company prepares to leave Fob Gib and move by night, silently, across country to an abandoned compound. 8 Platoon's commander, the lanky Lieutenant Sam Aiken, is on leave so Sergeant Chris Lloyd is in charge with Des, who has stepped up from corporal to platoon sergeant. 7 Platoon is led by Lieutenant Murray McMahon, who enlisted in the Paras from Cape Town, where he grew up. He dropped out of the University of Cape Town and joined 3 Para as a private. After serving two tours in Iraq he was selected for officer training and sent to Sandhurst.

McMahon issues wind-up radios to his men with orders to hand them out to local people. It is hoped this might win some friends and at least put the Afghans within reach of NATO propaganda.

They cross the Fob, down the short alleyway between the mud walls of 8 Platoon's improvised barracks and the small engineers' compound. Their shadows slide along ahead of them as they clip on their gear. They pass the memorial to the four men who were killed fighting around Gibraltar in the previous tour a few months ago. As they trot down a 30-metre earth ramp the shadows lengthen and blend into one as the two platoons prepare to leave. In the gathering moment before they step out the gate, into the Green Zone, the natter and banter fades away. Stooped by the weight of their gear, the young men ease themselves onto the ground and sit like toddlers in the dirt with their legs sticking out straight.

Corporals and sergeants stand above them, muttering in low tones; everyone is smoking. The Taleban has opened the fighting season. Outside the thick rocket-proof walls of the Fob, the poppies have been harvested of their resin, dried and scythed, leaving crew-cut fields of six-inch stalks as hard as bamboo. The wheat, too, has been cut and winnowed, the chaff left behind in piles four feet high.

All is brown. Only the mulberry trees lining the irrigation ditches defiantly hold their green.

Jeff Doherty and Pete O'Neill are sniggering together, plotting in a corner. It has been nine months since they first met, at the end of a ten-mile run.

Dried gob shone through the stubble on his chin. He had a hangover which mingled nausea with a raging hunger for greasy food. Jeff's lungs were sticking to his ribs. Bent double, he rested his hands on his knees to gasp in rasps of the freezing rain-wet air of an English October morning. He cocked his gaze right, drawn to the whiff of burning tobacco.

A paratrooper, with drooping thick dark eyebrows and a long face, which gravity gathered into his thick lips, clutched a packet of fags and sucked the smoke in hard. Warmth and naughtiness shone beneath those hangdog brows. The ten-miler was done, 'smashed'. Jeff now also needed to smoke to ease the pain in his chest and attack the churning in his stomach. He wanted a fag off this bloke who'd just joined 'C' Company.

'Mate, could I have one of those?' Jeff asked.

Pete O'Neill, at twenty-five one of the older 'Toms' – privates – thought: 'Christ, he's just like me when I joined up: cocky.' There was a spark of instant friendship. Over the next six months, 8 Platoon watched the new friends with growing fascination. Lugubrious Pete and sparkly Jeff began to merge into a double act. Pete was from Wolverhampton, where pollution stains from long-dead heavy industries blacken the glum Victorian architecture of the Midlands. Jeff joined the army from Southam, a Warwickshire market town where Elizabethan timber-framed buildings smugly nestle in rich green fields, between the Stowe and Itchen rivers. Southam boasts a healing spring, several polo teams, and a thirteenth-century church.

Jeff was a naughty child at school and left at sixteen. He was especially close to his father, Jeff senior, who owns a taxi and courier business and a pub and who'd fought for custody of his son in a bitter divorce. For four months the two Jeffs lived in a van. Even as a young paratrooper the son would lay his head on his father's lap to watch television. Jeff senior had been terrified when his son joined the army, and offered him £600 a week not to sign up. When he took Jeff to the station for the last time before he was sent to Afghanistan, Jeff senior recalls: 'I cried and cried and begged him not to go. I knew he wasn't coming back. I just knew it.'

Jeff inspired devoted friendship wherever he went. 'We were always together. He was my shadow and I was his,' Pete remembers.

'You two should get married,' someone said.

Same-sex partnerships, or gay marriages, had become an accepted part of British military life. A number of men, including officers, had remained in the forces after becoming women, in much publicised sex-change operations. So Jeff and Pete took the suggestion seriously. They came up with what they believed was a brilliant scam. They would claim to be a gay couple and go through a civil partnership. Then they would qualify for a 'pad', a proper house in 'married quarters', and each get a £900 'disturbance allowance' to help them with the move.

'We reckoned that we'd do it twice. Get married, move in, get our allowances, leave it a while, get divorced, move back into the [single accommodation] block, get another allowance for that, and then get married again and move back to the pad, with more allowances again.' There appeared to be a wondrous £2,700 'gay supplement' for two straight paratroopers, one of whom − Jeff − had a long-standing girl-friend called Chloe. All they had to do was to get it past Chris Lloyd, the platoon sergeant, and Lieutenant Sam Aiken, their 'boss'.

'Every time we'd go on leave or home at weekends we'd go to bridal shops and take pictures of ourselves and send them through to the bosses,' said Pete. They gave Chris Lloyd designs for wedding outfits in which their ceremonial paratrooper uniforms, known as 'blues', were cut in half and spliced with wedding dresses.

The apparent sincerity of the scam had caused such consternation that, in the plans for the newly built accommodation at the Paras' garrison in Colchester, Jeff and Pete were allocated neighbouring rooms to try to make sure that they wouldn't go through with it. The idea was that if they were put in rooms close to one another they might give up on the joke of their plans for 'marriage'.

'I kept telling them to fuck off and grow up, and they kept at it,' recalled Sam Aiken.

Pete was a veteran. He'd done four operational tours, one before to Afghanistan, two in Northern Ireland and one in Iraq. Given the publicity which had surrounded Helmand no one would have been expecting a tour by a Parachute battalion to be quiet. Pete was apprehensive. During the endless training in Belize, Kenya and the UK, as the date for deployment to Afghanistan approached, the jokes about who wasn't going to make it back started in 8 Platoon.

'If anyone got killed we planned to get tattoos on our backs with a totem pole and graves at the bottom with our dead mates' names on. Jeff would have mine, and I would have his – just in case. Stupid stuff like that,' remembers Pete.

They all go through their equipment checks one last time. Carrying body armour and ammunition is hard enough. Now they have an extra 2 litres of water each, rations for twenty-four hours, and extra ammunition because they are going to be out overnight, and extra radio batteries, each weighing over three pounds. Swaddled in ceramic, steel and Kevlar body armour, covered in backpacks with pouches hanging off every available surface, including their legs, today's modern warriors resemble a cross between a medieval knight and a pack mule. Jeff and the rest of the lads of 8 Platoon most resent having to carry the heavy equipment supposed to protect against radio-controlled bombs.

Their solution is simple. They get the oldest member of the platoon, thirty-three-year-old Brendan Wadsworth, a Territorial

Army soldier from 4 Para, who left his job as a welding instructor to come to Afghanistan, to carry it. 'Wadders' is different. He is teetotal for a start, a character trait as unlikely in a paratrooper as philately or flower arranging. He is also quiet, well read, and spends most of his time watching Japanese manga cartoons. His heavy wrinkled brow and intense stare unnerve some of his comrades, but there is no doubting his physical strength. So, Wadders gets to carry the heavy Electronic Counter Measures equipment which is designed to jam the Taleban's signals to radio controlled bombs. He cannot pass a member of 8 Platoon without the unison football cry of 'WAAADDDEERRRSSS'. He is the platoon's favourite oddball and he bears this treatment, which among paratroopers is what passes for affection, in silence.

Adam Dawson leads his company through the wooden gates of Fob Gibraltar at exactly 1933 hours. The sun has almost finished setting to his left, out in the desert. He heads north along the track which will take them through a village built on slightly raised ground. It appears on the army's satellite imagery maps in the exact shape of the hammer which crossed the sickle on the old Soviet flags and so its two parts are called the Hammer's Head and the Hammer's Handle.

The mountain range to the east of the Helmand valley glows orange and red. The route is cross-country, across the shin-spiking stubble which gouges thin strips of skin from their calves. Shadows from the mulberry trees shift in the thermal currents, which continue to thump heat into the air long after sunset, and take on human form. Dickers flicker in and out of view along the irrigation ditches.

Soon everyone is drenched in their own sweat; it runs down their backs and chafes between their thighs. The lucky ones are able to cool off by sitting in the fast-flowing water of the irrigation channels. The game is to piss in the water if you have a mate sitting downstream, and tell him what you'd done when you calculate your body-warm urine wrapping itself around him. There is a perennial fear that someone will contrive to crap in the water.

It is slow going through the chequerboard landscape of ditches and fields, avoiding natural paths and only crossing them after painstaking searches for mines and IEDs with metal detectors. But by the early hours of 12 June, 'C' Company make it to what is marked on their maps as the H4 (Hotel Four) operations box: a typical village of walled compounds separated from each other by alleys wide enough only for a donkey to pass. It includes a compound which intelligence sources know the Taleban have been using as a logistics base; cars and vans come and go frequently. But it is also near the home of an obviously wealthy man, Abdul Wahab. He lives in an immaculate, whitewashed compound with its own mosque and orchards – where almond and apricot trees are forming young fruit, figs are bulging and pomegranates ripening.

Abdul Wahab sits Dawson down for tea and talk at 0619 hours, according to the signals log books. A typical 'key leader', Abdul has businesses in Dubai and Iran, where he spent many years as a refugee and met his wife. He said he knows of Taleban in the area but not much about who they are, or what they do. He complains about intermittent electrical supplies from the Kajaki Dam and welcomes the British as his guests. Dawson responds warmly to his natural Afghan hospitality. But three other figures who gather in the background stare with unreserved contempt and hatred at the British troops.

It is unhinging to be stared at with genuine hatred. When men have murder in their hearts you can see it in their eyes. It is as intimate and unblinking as a lover's look into the soul. They want you to know that they want to get to know you. They want to hear the sound of your laugh, your cough, the angle of your smile. The stare is searching, black and with a twinkle of humour. It says 'I'm going to watch your last breath leave your body. I'm going to kill you, and I'm going to like it.' It comes with a warm smile. When you catch it, the blood floods out of your head and hands, you feel cold – and violated, raped.

At least three people at this mini *shura* give the British the 'stink eye'. They are photographed, some scowling, some grinning. By 0701 hours it is over and time to start moving back to Fob Gibraltar, well before the Taleban are expected to be out of bed. So far the insurgents have shown themselves to be deeply habitual. They seldom do anything much before ten in the morning. The peak period for suicide bombings is between ten and lunchtime.

If the Taleban are planning an attack, or to move men around during a battle, they often manage to broadcast their intentions over their walkie-talkie radios, which British troops can intercept. Sure enough, as the British leave Abdul Wahab's compound and head south, intercepts pick up the Taleban dickers telling their bosses that the British are on the move. It is the last Taleban signal that is heard that day.

Murray McMahon leads 7 Platoon south through compounds and then across yet more fields of stubble and ditch. Sergeant Lloyd and Des take 8 Platoon on a parallel route a few hundred metres east of McMahon, starting in a vineyard and working their way due south. There are very few farmers around for this time of day – Helmandis always take advantage of the relative cool of the early morning to get as much work done in the fields before the heat becomes unbearable. But the fields are far quieter than expected. Des puts this down to the company's new drills which keep all civilians at least 50 metres away. Interaction is no longer being encouraged.

Further south McMahon's scouts spot two men on motorbikes, and wearing black dishdash, race at high speed past them. One covers his face with his turban. This is suspicious but nothing much to worry about – it isn't, after all, combined with a spike in intercepted radio chatter from the Taleban. In fact the Taleban, who always seem to be in a state of rage and shout into their radios, are

quiet this morning. Des, meanwhile, has split his platoon into two
and is moving them south towards a river which has high banks,
known as 'bunlines' because the baked earth rises out of the ground
like muffin tops. Between the bunlines the stream is about 2.5
metres deep and wide. Jeff, who is the lead scout in 2 Section, and
Pete, who is in 3 Section, have somehow contrived to meet while the
platoon 'goes firm' (stops) and take a breather. While their leaders
figure out what to do next, they sit and joke.

'Give us a chockie bar, go on mate, I'm fucking starving. Starving,
c'mon you Jack bastard, give us something to eat,' Jeff implores.

Pete is unmoved: 'You're fuckin' jokin' aren't you? Your admin
stinks as bad as you do, man. Where are your rations? Did you bring
any? Have you scoffed the lot? I've only got one chocolate bar left
and you're not having it.'

Adam Ireland, leading 1 Section, 8 Platoon, is tall with blond
crew-cut hair and newly cultivated Edwardian side-whiskers. Always
charismatic, he'd revelled in being the chief barrack room wretch as
a younger soldier. Now he is evolving into a calm and natural leader
of men at war. A group of four children are standing by the edge of
the ditch and through his translator he asks where the best crossing
place is. They point to his right as he looks south across the stream.

Lance Corporal Jay Bateman, Adam's second in command, clambers up the high bunline while Jeff Doherty does the same further
down. The two sections are about 50 metres apart.

The air fizzes and crackles with bullets. There seems to be no
space between them as if they are being poured from a hose. Rounds
are smacking into the ground; the dust is leaping around their feet.
Des can hear the fizzing sound made by bullets which are within a
foot of his ears. He can feel the hot whip of them on his face. He
scours the landscape behind him and to his left, looking for the
Taleban firing points. Three weapons are being fired in coordinated
volleys to the rear and left from a group of small buildings. There is
the clatter of AK47 rifles, the ripping of PKM machine guns and a

steady relentless and measured *duff-duff-duff* of a 12.7 Dushka heavy machine gun, a weapon that fires a bullet the size of a man's thumb and travels with such kinetic force that it can tear your arm off or stop your heart without hitting you.

Someone is yelling 'Contact Left! Contact Left!' Someone else is shouting 'Man Down! Man Down!'

Pete's guts turn to jelly. Everyone is stunned. This is better than a textbook ambush, better than they have ever seen done on exercise, better than they have ever heard of. They are stuck in what is called the 'killing zone'. It is a place where everyone is supposed to die.

'Where the fuck are they? Where the fuck are they?' No one can see where the Taleban are firing from. The enemy have dug themselves into ditches and tree lines and have cut murder holes in the mud walls of compounds to shoot through. Red tracer rounds are punching through 1 Section like a sewing-machine needle – now from the front left and from straight ahead. There is no break in the Taleban fire. The high-pitched clatter of rifles gives way to seamless percussive volleys of up to six Rocket Propelled Grenades shot in unison from ditches.

Des, stuck at the rear of the platoon, is lucky. He is able to take cover in a bunline. He watches the bulbous green RPG warheads *sheesh* through the air – they look like pointed marrows with a stiff tail of piping. The rockets skateboard off the bank in front of him, sail over his head, and burst.

Adam Ireland, up at the front of 1 Section, watches in disbelief. RPGs cartwheel and skid across the ground towards him. The stubble in the fields is set alight by the exploding rockets, making it harder to see what to shoot at. Des feels no fear – he doesn't have enough thinking time for that. He immediately sends a 'contact report' back to company headquarters, and then calls fire onto positions which the Taleban are now giving away with the smoke from their own guns.

A paratrooper begins chucking his missiles into the short metal pipe of his 51mm mortar, and watches them rain down onto the Taleban firing points. With Des's help, he fires ten rounds before anyone else has the chance to change their rifle magazines. 'Not bad for a Stab [Stupid Territorial Army Bastard],' thinks Des.

8 Platoon are now trying desperately to win the firefight. They will be slaughtered if they cannot force the Taleban off their guns and into cover themselves. Des's bunline, a low mud wall either side of a shallow ditch, gives him a perfect spot to fire from, a kneeling position with good cover from the blizzard of bullets.

Then he gets a signal over his radio headset that someone is hurt up ahead. 'Doc, Doc,' he yells to Captain Akbar Lalani, who recently qualified as a doctor and is on patrol having joined the Paras fresh from training. 'Peel around me and get up to that tree on the edge of the river in the corner – they've had a casualty,' Des tells him.

Lalani, and the company sergeant major, Mark 'Skid' Ewan, step forward from behind a pile of poppy stalks where they have been taking cover. Before anyone moves they have to shove the Taleban heads down. Doing that means looking straight into the shower of incoming bullets and shooting more back. Skid quickly gets through his 30-round magazine. Lalani realises Skid will be vulnerable as soon as he stops firing to change the magazine and rushes into the open to cover the changeover. But the moment he moves, the sergeant major goes down. He's been shot in the ankle. Lalani runs out to drag the older soldier back out of sight. Tearing off his boot he finds that Ewan's injury is not life-threatening – but he cannot walk.

Des meanwhile grabs Andrew Palmer, a soft-spoken eighteen-year-old medic, and tells him to rush the 50 metres across to where he knows 2 Section's casualty is lying. Andrew sprints across the now-burning field. Everything around him is acutely defined. He can feel and see the bullets sowing their way towards him across the smoking stubble. As he looks right he can see the strike of Des's ammunition on the enemy positions. The air feels thick and cool and healthy as he pulls it into his lungs; and the eight pounds of equipment on his back is entirely weightless. He runs on tiptoe like a sprinter and vaults over the bank of the stream, throwing himself down next to the wounded man.

He's forgotten about Des, who watches from his own safe position, and then thinks: 'Fuck me, I've gotta run through the bullets without any cover.' It is a mad idea. Firing from the hip off to his right and running for his life will not stop the Taleban machine gunners from fixing him in their sights. 'This is fucking stupid,' Des thinks. He charges across the field, pulling his trigger in short bursts and screwing his face up like a kid afraid of the dark.

Leaping over the raised river bank he hears: 'I'm Hit! I'm Hiiiiit!' It is Brendan 'Big Gay Mo' Morris, a former stripper and semi-professional rugby player from south Wales with male-model looks. Mo is lying on his back. He's been knocked over by the force of a bullet which has hit him on the right of his lower jaw, slicing through the chinstrap of his helmet. 'I've been shot in the face! I've been hit in the face, hit in the face. There's blood!' he is screaming. His mates tell him to calm down: he's been grazed by a bullet, that is all. After a few seconds Des sees that he is 'back in the room' and up against the bank hammering away at the enemy again.

Jeff Doherty seems calm amid the screams and explosions. He is lying motionless on the bank, with a hole in his temple. Lalani sets off towards him, across the open field into the burning and ploughed-up ground. Paratroopers watch in awe as the doctor, who has minimal military training, ignores Taleban bullets, falls under the weight of his body armour and a huge medical pack, staggers up, runs some more, falls again, emerges from the ground and runs on – just to get to a man who is probably dead.

Watching the young doctor charge across that open field, Adam Ireland thinks: 'Mega – that's a proper officer: head up and charging, not scuttling about like a spider – head up and proud. Fuckin' mega.'

Lalani had called for covering fire before he made his dash – assuming there were at least fifteen paratroopers available to spray

the Taleban positions. In fact, he got the support of just three – one
of whom changed his magazine just as the doctor stumbled past to
the ditch to join Des and Andrew. Mo has already pushed forward
along the ditch and dragged Jeff down onto the side of the bank
before moving on another couple of metres to continue the fight.
He turns to look at Paul Lloyd, the section commander, and shakes
his head. Paul reports over the company net that Jeff is 'T4' – a low
priority casualty, which tells everyone he is dead. Andrew can do
nothing.

Des helps Lalani move Jeff so that he can double check – they
don't want to give up if there is the slightest sign of life. In moving
the once ebullient soldier Des causes him to exhale a huff of blood
into his face. For a moment Des thinks it is a breath.

'Jeff?'

Nothing. Des can taste blood. Lalani knows that Jeff was killed
the instant he was hit, but somehow cannot let go of the idea that a
miracle might happen and gives the dead man a morphine injection
'just in case'.

'He didn't feel a thing,' Lalani tells Des.

Cradling the dead man, as though he is a sleeping baby, they ease
his body off the bank and into the ditch. Taleban bullets continue
to smash into the ground by their heads sending spurts of dust and
dirt into their eyes. They are standing up to their chests in water. If
they stay in the stream, and can safely get to a rendezvous point 400
metres to the west where the ditch hits a track, they might make it
out. There is nothing for it. Jeff's body, still in his body armour and
helmet, is slowly pulled along by the two of them.

'We've got to keep his head out of the water,' Des says, mostly to
himself. 'We'll make sure you don't get hurt any more,' he tells Jeff.
He pulls weeds away from the blasted head. Blood leaks into the
water, giving it a ferrous shine.

Steve 'Geordie' Lewis and Frank 'the Yank' Ward, who was with
1 Section when the shooting started, dive into the stream for cover

and then wade east towards the Taleban to try to spot firing points. They push beyond Des and Jeff and, scrambling into the storm of bullets, they find themselves at the top of the river bank. Very quickly they see a two-man Taleban machine-gun team on top of a compound 170 metres away. Steve shoots one dead with his 7.62mm long-barrelled sniper rifle. Frank kills the other with a burst from his Minimi, a light machine gun with a bulge underneath where the bullets hang chain-linked in a plastic case.

The sniper pair, acting as the platoon's scouts and as its fire support, run back along the stream to cover Adam's section. While they run, there is another radio message. News of another T4. Lance Corporal Jay Bateman, the lead scout of 1 Section, has been killed in the same volley of fire which triggered the ambush.

Adam looks to his west and only one other paratrooper is visible to him when the first rounds come in. The Taleban's Dushka ploughs up the banks of the stream. He turns to make sure that his men are in cover and notes they are all lying on their belt buckles face down. Except Jay, who is sitting against a wall.

Jay is a legendary figure in the company. A paratrooper for eight years, he reminds his friends of an enthusiastic Labrador. Big, blond, and always smiling, he is perpetually enthusiastic and staggeringly strong. He is also incapable of malice, and can see none in others. He became an easy target of practical jokes soon after he joined. As a young Tom he had been told to get twenty Benson & Hedges cigarettes from the Naafi by a corporal who had said: 'If you can't get B & H get anything.' An hour later Jay returned with a pork pie. While at Fob Gibraltar he had taken the order very seriously to self-medicate with anti-malarial tablets, which were issued in strips with the days of the week marked off like contraceptive pills to ensure that no one missed a day. He had been found searching for one marked 'Tuesday' in the communal bowls of malaria pills left in the cook house. He had also been suckered into asking the store man for 'bubbles for my section's compasses' and had caused uproar when someone had told him that the enormous Nikon binoculars used in the Fob's observation towers needed tokens, like a spyglass on a seaside pier, and he'd gone looking for them. He could be tricked so easily, his mates knew, because he could never imagine wanting to make a fool of anyone else.

On patrol it is always Jay, as the section second in command, who will individually check that every other soldier is safe and happy before he takes cover himself. So Adam doesn't think twice when he notes that only Jay does not appear to have taken cover like the rest of the section. He is always forgetting about his own safety.

'Jay's been hit. He's been hit,' someone yells through the leaping dust.

He is sitting because that's the way his body buckled when a round hit him in the head. Adam crawls to him and presses his fingers into his neck to feel for a pulse. He checks his wrists too; his hands are limply cradling his rifle. Nothing. Jay, of all people, is dead. The radio net is jammed with frantic situation reports and orders being given. And before he can send out the message that Jay is gone, Adam hears from Paul Lloyd, his oldest friend in the regiment, that Jeff is dead too.

He is devastated. Jeff was one of his closest friends and Jay was his closest work mate. For a few seconds Adam is reeling. He feels sick and almost collapses onto his backside. For the first time in his army career he thinks 'right that's fucking it – I'm getting out – this isn't worth it', but flames from the burning field are gathering speed and racing towards Jay's body in an angry wave.

'Get Jay, get Jay,' he yells. 'He's not going to be left here to burn.'

Wadders and Kris Williams rush to their dead friend. *Sheesh!* Another RPG warhead crashes in between Adam and the two guys, skids along the ground, hits the bunline and explodes in the air about two metres above their heads with a crack. Shards of metal from the warhead whack into the ground. Rills of smoke rise from tiny holes where the razor-sharp shrapnel has cut into the hard dried earth.

Not far away Pete picks up the same message about Jeff's death. He is by now with the rest of his section, strung out east to west along the stream. None of them can see a safe angle to shoot at the Taleban because their own people from 1 and 2 Sections are in the way. But the moment Pete hears that Jeff is dead he feels a surge of rage. Terry Jones, a short and wiry Welshman from Cardiff, is next to him. Pete lets out a gurgling roar which rises from deep in his guts; he then charges up the river bank towards the enemy. Seeing a fellow paratrooper apparently preparing to assault, Terry goes with him.

Gaz Storey, his section commander, is quick witted and quick moving enough to get a hand on the back of Pete's webbing and drag him back into cover. He moves before the 'red mist' hits, the ultra-violent madness which can overcome troops in the heat of battle and lead to acts of breathtaking savagery, and bravery, but that could infect the rest of 'C' Company's men.

'Don't be fucking daft. We need you here. Get into cover and get on your fucking weapons,' Paul says as he drags the two men back by their webbing like toddlers on reins.

The air is now thick with smoke from the burning fields and cordite from the British guns which are keeping up a constant rate of fire into the Taleban positions to the east and north. The distant thump, thump, thump of Fob Gibraltar's mortars, sent in high arcs before crashing into the Taleban's tree lines, give some reassurance to the teams of soldiers now trying to evacuate their dead and wounded.

Skid Ewan is being helped across the field behind the main bulk of 8 Platoon. Des and Lalani are dragging Jeff along the stream, gasping with exhaustion. Jay's body is lying where he fell on the edge of the bank but the field next to him is now towering with flames. Adam is about 25 metres away and can see that his friend will be burned unless he's moved. Wadders and Kris are the other side of Jay and now the flames have cut them off from Adam.

'Wadders – bring Jay here before he's set on fire will you,' Adam yells.

Wadders says nothing. He just throws his left arm across his face, and uses the other to lever Jay onto his shoulder. Kris does the same. Adam is shooting back at the Taleban trying to force their heads down but the insurgents' bullets are still whipping past and smacking into the ground around them. Then the two men carrying Jay, the biggest man in his platoon, plunge into the burning field. The flames roar around their heads and wrap themselves around the staggering paratroopers who emerge next to Adam and put Jay down. Every stitch of their clothing is smoking and on the point of ignition.

'I couldn't leave him to burn in that fire. What do you want next?' Wadders says to his section commander.

Adam, Kris and Wadders strip Jay of his weapon and webbing and put him onto the folding stretcher he'd been carrying. They move fast. Adam wants to get him back to Chris Lloyd. The three of them set off at a jog, ignoring the snap of Taleban bullets which follow them. The stretcher is unbalanced and Jay falls off into the stubble. A fourth soldier joins the stretcher party for the final 50 metres.

'Right. That's done,' says Wadders. 'What do you want next?'

'Hit that point we just left again and then we'll extract down the river,' Adam shouts back. Wadders dumps his ECM, and the welding instructor and part-time soldier who had been the butt of 8 Platoon's jokes since he arrived takes off at a sprint back across the flaming fields to the rest of his section.

'Brilliant. Fucking brilliant. That's fucking, fucking brilliant. Wadders, you're still a fucking weirdo – but you're our weirdo now,' Adam shouts at Wadders's back as he races off.

Des and Lalani have had to stop floating Jeff's body down the stream between them because it has narrowed, leaving space for only one of them to drag it. So for the last 300 metres Des, alone, works like a pit pony to pull his dead friend's body to safety. As the acting platoon sergeant he knows he will need to appear calm and on top of his game when he gets to the meeting point. But while he has Jeff this close, tears are flowing. Jeff had been in his section for two years, since he'd come to the battalion. Des thought he was a 'diamond'. 'The sort of bloke who was like your little brother, always getting into scrapes and you'd have to get him out.' He talks to Jeff's body constantly. And he desperately, desperately, needs to drink. Surrounded by water he is almost dying of thirst but cannot suck on the pipe to the water bladder on his back because he still has Jeff's blood in his mouth. He thinks it would be disrespectful.

'Corporal Desmond. You're going to plough in. Give it a rest or let me take over. C'mon – I'll take over.'

Lalani, who is behind Des, can see that he is near to physical collapse. The doctor keeps telling Des to stop and take a breather. But he plunges on. 'I'll screw the nut for you,' Des says to his dead friend.

Most of the shooting has died down. Des can hear blood hammering inside his skull. He has hold of Jeff by the dead soldier's webbing and is towing him along under one arm. The sinews in his legs are burning and when he stumbles and almost submerges himself he makes a noise somewhere between a sob and a roar.

Jeff's trousers are being tugged off by the water. 'That's not going to happen, no way, that's not going to happen,' Des snarls, snatching them back up and plunging on. When he finally arrives at the rendezvous point, dragging his friend out of the stream gently is almost impossible. 'It's weird. Even though he was dead we wanted to show respect. To screw the nut for him and make sure he didn't get hurt or damaged. It's undignified, being dead. We didn't want to make it worse.'

As he approaches the end of the ditch where it meets a road junction he prepares in his head what he was going to say to the rest of the platoon. He takes deep breaths. He doesn't want the men to hear the tears in his voice. But the moment he begins to speak, his voice cracks. He stops and breathes in and out, hard.

Jay is already lying on the ground. But Des and Chris Lloyd can see no wounds on him and so tell the men to back away, because they are going to get his helmet off and check his head for wounds. That is when they find the tiny entry on the back of his head, and the swelling in his jaw, where the bullet which killed him is trapped.

Someone sees a wheelbarrow full of stalks and other rubbish and asks one of the platoon's interpreters to empty it into the stream. He misunderstands and throws the whole thing into the water. 'No you fucking prick, we just wanted you to get the stuff out of it. We want to put Jay in the wheelbarrow to get him back,' Adam yells.

The red-faced Afghan dives in head-first and drags the barrow back out. Jay is settled into it. Mauled and smoking from their ordeal, 8 Platoon know that there is a Chinook helicopter in-bound to collect Skid, Jeff and Jay. An Apache attack helicopter is overhead to provide security and a landing site has been found in a field. 8 Platoon have been locked in combat for twenty-eight minutes. The first ten have been the most intense. Now it is relatively quiet. Quentin 'Q' Daniels, the Joint Tactical Air Controller, who has been on almost every patrol of the tour, knows the ground intimately and declares the landing site for the helicopter safe. But the pilot of the Chinook will not land; he says the site isn't safe – even though there is no shooting now and the Apache, which has been hanging about overhead for ten minutes, says there is little danger.

'Fucking, fucking, RAF cunts. Cunts,' Adam rages as he looks at the rest of his mates in the platoon. Des is shattered, physically exhausted. Everyone is carrying some piece of a dead man's kit. It has taken three men to move Skid Ewan who has been carried about 200 metres by them linking hands as a cradle. They are still 3 kilometres from the Fob and now, it seems, they are being left to manhandle bodies and wounded all the way back. The Chinook is suddenly called away to evacuate soldiers injured in fighting which is going on simultaneously further north, in Musa Qal'ah. Jeff is laid on a stretcher, and Pete picks up one of the corners. Jay is in the wheelbarrow and Skid is given a three-man lift.

This is a classic Parachute Regiment moment. Feeling abandoned by the Air Force, burned and bloodied with the enemy at their backs, this is what the Paras do best – they 'reg it out'. They love to tell each other that 'Paras don't die – they go to hell and re-group'. They have re-grouped.

Murray McMahon's 7 Platoon have been unable to be of much use in supporting 8 Platoon in the first stages of the fight. They were patrolling 500 metres west and south and had stopped in a cluster of buildings when the ambush was triggered. After coming under inaccurate fire from RPGs, PKM machine guns and AK47s, McMahon orders two sections forward, to a track running north–south to flush out the enemy. Someone has spotted a dicker about 100 metres south down the track. He has a walkie-talkie and is crouching down by a wall and gesturing to the Taleban out of sight, warning them about 7 Platoon's movements. Armed or not, he is a threat and is shot. He flops to the ground as if the air has been let out of him. Adam Dawson is pleased. The dicker has been caught red-handed with his radio in the middle of a battle.

But as he moves back up the road he notices a tractor with three men sitting on it. They are relaxed and are watching his every move. One smiles at him – it is Abdul Wahab, the wealthy host of that morning's *shura*. Now, two hours after they had been drinking tea together and forty minutes into a vicious fight, here is Wahab treating war like a spectator sport. Unless, of course, he was somehow involved. There is nothing Dawson can do. He stares back at the grinning 'farmer' as hard as he can. He feels in his bones that Wahab knew about the ambush, perhaps even set it up. British rules of engagement mean he just has to walk on, while McMahon has his men clear through compounds to the east of the north–south track. Troops burst in through the compound gates; they can smell cordite from Taleban weapons; they can see the murder holes cut into walls used by Taleban gunmen. But they only find old women and children. 'We're fighting fucking ghosts,' McMahon mutters.

By 0835 hours, 7 Platoon's most southerly section is about 400 metres away from 8 Platoon and can see a man skulking 200 metres away behind them, to their northwest. He is watching them closely. The company have already been caught in a brilliantly executed L-shaped ambush which was a kilometre long. The Taleban know that the British will have to return to their base and are now channelling them along the main track, while their dickers report every British move on the flanks. Three warning shots are fired at the man who is dressed entirely in black, with a black turban. Each time the bullets snaps into the ground next to him he simply takes cover and finds a better observation point. The fourth shot is used to kill him.

After another fifteen minutes 8 Platoon begin moving south and 7 Platoon help with moving Skid. Pete is still carrying Jeff, and talking to him. Jeff's arms keep flopping off the stretcher and getting caught in Pete's legs. Each time they do, Pete apologises: 'Oh, sorry, sorry, mate. Didn't mean to hurt you Jeff – honest.' The track is easier going. But it still takes three people to push Jay's wheelbarrow, one on each of the handles and one in front to keep his feet from getting stuck under the wheel. He has been tied into it, with a stretcher on top and a T-shirt covering his face. Someone found another wheelbarrow and put Jeff in that, again held in with a stretcher and with a *shemag* over his face. Within a few minutes a third wheelbarrow is found for the injured Skid. He is pushed the entire way by a translator who refuses help, or rest. When help is offered he elbows it away. No one, however, can remember his name.

Steve Lewis and Frank Ward take up the lead and head south down the track towards the Hammer's Head. They know of a compound where an estate car can be found, and the keys demanded from its owner.

'Give us your car and we'll give it back later,' barks Lewis. Ginger-haired and built like a prize-fighter, he is a terrifying sight. His orange moustache curls down either side of his mouth. In repose he has a disconcerting, intense stare. Now, with two friends dead, he is in a cold rage. His face is blackened. He has killed that day and looks like he might do so again if crossed. The car is a white Toyota Corolla estate. Skid takes a front seat.

Kris, a paratrooper from 9 Platoon who's been attached to Adam Ireland's section for the patrol, helps him carry Jeff to the back of the car. As he bends to lift Jeff by the head Adam can see that the rifle he'd slung across his back is slipping around and forward.

'Don't you fucking dare let that weapon hit him on the head,' Adam snarls. His section can see him shaking. Someone comes to Kris and gently leads him away telling him they can see that Adam is close to snapping. Kris walks about 50 metres off into a field by himself, sits down, and weeps.

7 Platoon guard the rear while most of the rest of the men are pushed out to the left and right flanks. The heat is growing more intense. Insubstantial creatures, small tornados which Africans call Dust Devils, are leaping out of the middle of fields and spinning an erratic dance among the soldiers. They are now 2.5 kilometres from home. Water supplies are getting low or the last few drips have already been sucked from their camel-backs. Dawson now faces leading his exhausted men down a predictable route which, after what has just happened, he fears will lead into another ambush – but this time a massacre.

The car is not long enough for the two bodies. So Adam climbs in with them. He's seen dead friends before in Iraq. Then he'd had to clear up a comrade who'd been decapitated and another who'd been blown up. Jeff and Jay still look like Jeff and Jay, he thinks.

Then he takes hold of his dead mates and the car lurches away. Pete runs alongside the vehicle like a bodyguard on a presidential cavalcade. The whole platoon sees what is happening and starts running too.

Adam holds Jay and Jeff's hands. With everything outside the car no longer his problem, he can now focus on his friends. 'Why did you die Jeff? Why? Why you? Jay I'm so sorry mate, I dunno what happened . . .' Adam is choking with tears. How could he undo this? Make it not the way it was? At the southern edge of the Hammer's Handle village, the Taleban have dug a wide ditch right across the road with only a small bridge of earth left for pedestrians and their little Chinese 125cc motorbikes.

The Quick Reaction Force from Fob Gibraltar, which has been sent to meet 8 and 7 Platoon with their Land Rovers, fear an ambush when they are stopped by the ditch, and have quickly pulled out, dismounted, and secured the flanks against a Taleban attack. They load one body across the front of a quad bike, the other into a Land Rover with Skid, and race them away. 'C' Company now have about a kilometre to walk back. But the high drama is over. Adrenalin and rage subside, leaving empty grief and bodies so hollowed out by exertion that they are floppy. Some men are shaking and dizzy with bad cases of 'sugar-debt' – hypoglycaemia; their bodies have burned every bit of food and fat in their systems and are trying to shut down. No one can swallow any more. Their already pasty mouth mucus has dried solid. Murray thinks his tongue feels like a strip of biltong – dried meat – from back home in South Africa.

Still the local Afghans stare. Warning shots are fired at two men who refuse to go indoors. As they pass a shop selling Pakistani biscuits and tinned food, a group of middle-aged men give Dawson the 'stink eye'.

Jeff and Jay, now wrapped away in body bags, are put on stretchers and kept in the *shura* bay, a walled off area near the entrance to the

Fob. It is now 1005 hours. A helicopter comes to pick them up, with Skid, thirty-five minutes later.

The whole company stands in silence and at attention while the Chinook churns up an obliterating cloud of dust and throws tiny pebbles in their faces as it takes their friends away.

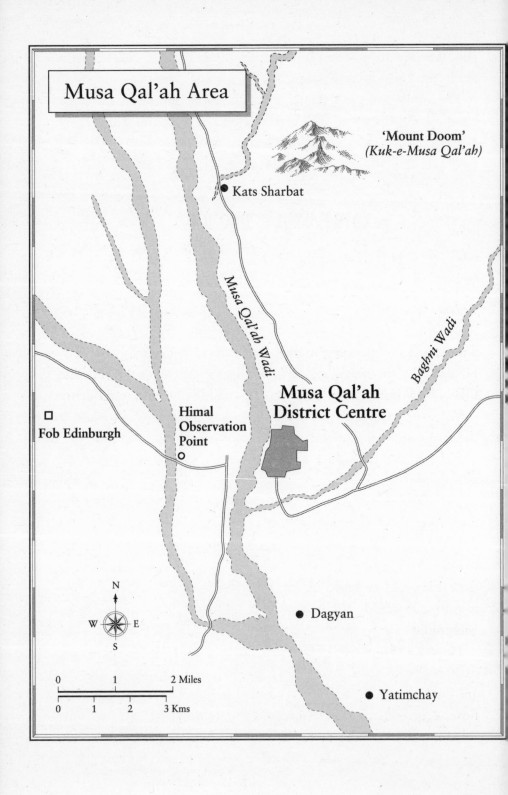

Musa Qal'ah Area

'Mount Doom'
(Kuk-e-Musa Qal'ah)

● Kats Sharbat

Musa Qal'ah Wadi

Baghni Wadi

**Musa Qal'ah
District Centre**

Himal
Observation
Point
○

□
Fob Edinburgh

● Dagyan

● Yatimchay

N
W E
S

| 0 | 1 | 2 Miles |
| 0 | 1 | 2 | 3 Kms |

4

ONE-WAY TICKET

12 June, Musa Qal'ah

Something is bothering him. He is on a train; that much is obvious. He can hear the *tickety-tick tickety-tick* as it goes over the sleepers. Like a half-drunk commuter who has nodded off and is suddenly jerked awake, David Richmond's vision is blurred. He can make out the rhythmic flashes of light and shadow made by telegraph poles as the train rushes through the country. But: 'Why am I on a train? Where am I going?'

He isn't terribly worried. But it would be nice to know. In the meantime there is something else. His nose. Christ, his nose is itching. It feels like a cockroach has crawled into a nostril. He goes to scratch it but his left arm will not work. It itches. It fucking itches. He tries to move his left arm, but nothing happens; it will not do as it is told. 'Hah! I've got another arm, I'll use that,' thinks Richmond.

He reaches up to his face. His right arm feels heavy; it has little points of pain. As it comes into view he can see that tubes are growing out of it. Never mind, his finger is coming for his nose. A huge black face looms into the picture and snarls at him: 'Nononono,' says the face. Richmond's hand is taken away. He feels he shouldn't say anything – shouldn't be a bother. Maybe he can't. Either way, he doesn't. He just screws up his face and tries to get rid of the itch by wriggling his nose. Someone thinks he is asking for water, and puts a salty-tasting liquid on his lips. It doesn't help. Now he is thirsty and that itch, that itch makes him want to scream. Another hand, not his, appears and scratches his nose for him. Aaaah, better.

Richmond fixes his eyes on the porthole window of the train and forces himself to focus on what is beyond. If he shoulders his way through the pillowy feeling in his head and looks out of that round window, he can see the telegraph poles flashing and hear the *tickety-tick*. He focuses harder. Blades. Helicopter blades. They are going *wok-wok-wok* through the air. He is near the back, which is open; he knows that because he can smell ice-cream vans. That's what helicopters smell like, old ice-cream vans with coolers run on paraffin – helicopters run on paraffin. I'm in a helicopter. My leg hurts. I feel sick. We're coming into the station. The train is landing. That took ages, that journey, ages. Hospital. A friendly face. 'Anything we can do for you, we will.'

'Can you take this tourniquet off? It's killing me. Not sure what is more painful, getting shot or this strangling of my leg,' says Richmond as the ketamine painkiller he's been given on the heli-copter (on top of two or three big doses of morphine) begins to wear off. And as it wears off, what has happened pours back into his head.

Fob Gibraltar is almost silent. Paratroopers mooch about, speaking quietly over cups of tea, huddled in small groups. They are mourning. Pete O'Neill and Adam Ireland begin to pack Jeff's cot up, folding his possessions into a cardboard box ready to be sent back to his family. There is a group doing the same for Jay; and there's some fond sniggering as they recall their favourite 'Batemanisms'. It is almost lunchtime. They have been back in the Fob for three hours and there is a merciful quiet.

At exactly the same time as they wander into the cookhouse to try to gag down some slushy pasta in a reddish brown sauce, the Taleban are raking more British troops with machine-gun fire 50 kilometres north in Musa Qal'ah.

David Richmond is hopping about on one leg, screwing his head into his neck, hunching his shoulders up and thinking: 'Fuck me, that's close, that's too, too close.'

This isn't supposed to be happening. Richmond is the commanding officer (CO) of 5 SCOTS (the Argylls). But COs don't get into this much trouble. Taleban bullets are passing his ears so close they sound like supersonic bumble bees. He can feel the change in air pressure as they suck past him.

Something kicks him in the thigh. He loses control of his leg which is suddenly useless.

'Christ, my leg's broken,' he thinks, and falls flat on his back. He looks up at the fierce blue sky. He doesn't want to look back where he'd been standing and talking to Nick Calder, the officer commanding 'D' Company, and the rest of his head-quarters group. He would see a pile of bodies. Pinned down by the pain which now shoots up his leg, and by the weight of his own armour, he feels like an upended tortoise. He dares himself to look. Richmond arches his neck painfully and looks over his eyebrows.

Everyone is fine. 'How did that happen? How did I get hit? How did the bullets miss everyone else and hit me when I was standing behind them? That's weird,' he thinks. He can see Calder shooting back at the Taleban.

'Nick,' he says. 'I seem to have broken my leg.'

'No, sir, you've been shot. That's why it's broken.' Calder chuckles. The exchange reminds him of some stiff-upper-lip dialogue he'd heard in a movie about the Battle of Waterloo.

Richmond has been hit by a heavy and long burst of Taleban machine-gun fire as he stood up, after he'd given his orders to Nick.

The bullet has smashed through the back of his right thigh, shattering his femur.

He's been shot on day two of a major drive against the Taleban. It had begun the previous evening. 'D' Company had headed off into the desert northeast of Musa Qal'ah District Centre. Leaving the Helmand River at their backs they had squeezed into the heavily armoured Mastiff trucks and all but vanished into the vastness. Richmond and the bulk of his headquarters staff, including the artillery battery commander, Major Andy Thomson, joined the company.

Mount Doom, a breast-shaped massif that rises 1,000 metres from the valley floor, is allegedly so sacred to locals that neither side ever patrols its summit. It lours over Musa Qal'ah to the north. The British are going to hook east around the mountain and attack suspected Taleban locations at Qaryeh-e Kats Sadar, a village which quickly becomes just 'Kats' to the Jocks. The Afghan National Army, with its mentors (known as an Operational Mentor and Liaison Team – or 'Omelette') from the Royal Irish Regiment, will patrol due north up the edge of the Musa Qal'ah wadi on the west of Mount Doom. 'B' Company of 4 SCOTS armoured infantry, in ageing Warrior fighting vehicles, will drive up the western bank. The aim is to use these two groups to lure the Taleban south – and then the Jocks and Mastiffs will smash them from behind.

Musa Qal'ah town has been in the control of the British and Afghan government for only six months. It had been retaken from the Taleban using a combination of money, guile, and guns. The British supplied the money and the guile. By offering him cash and playing on inter-clan rivalries with other Taleban leaders, they turned a local Taleban warlord, Mullah Salaam, over to the government's side. The guns came from the British Army and the Afghan National Army (ANA), who stormed the town in December 2007.

The recapture of Musa Qal'ah was seen as essential to redress the humiliation of having been forced out in 2006, at the end of 16

Air Assault Brigade's last tour of Afghanistan. British Pathfinders, Royal Irish, Danes, and a grab-bag of any available troops, had been heavily outnumbered and besieged for months, fighting from a tiny 'platoon house' in the middle of the town. They had been almost entirely cut off and risked being overrun many times. Eight British soldiers died defending the District Centre. They had run low on water, ammunition and food. They left the town after months of intense fighting had flattened much of its centre in a deal brokered between local elders and the Taleban in October 2006. By February 2007 the Taleban were back in full control. They accused the elders who had brought peace to the town of collaboration, and hanged them from trees along the wadi.

After they retook Musa Qal'ah the British wisely avoided returning to the previous platoon house. It was almost in the middle of Musa Qal'ah, surrounded by buildings which the Taleban could use as cover in their attacks. It was almost undefendable. The new District Centre (DC) is on the south-western edge of the town in a derelict three-storey blockhouse of a building, which, locals say, was once a hotel. Now it is a windowless concrete skeleton with a charred interior. Spaghetti coils of wiring hang between makeshift partitions and curl down the walls into military laptops. On the roof, sentries stand behind heavy machine guns in sand-bagged observation towers – sangars – looking west over the grey shale of the Musa Qal'ah wadi's dry bed. Next door the Afghan National Army and the National Directorate of Security, the secret police, cook delicious meals of okra, stewed onion and goat kebabs. About 75 metres south of the main building, 'D' Company of the Argylls camp in tents. Diagonally across open ground, covered in crushed rock, a platoon of Americans from 2nd Battalion the 7th Marine Regiment have set up camp. They have been sent, officially, to help train the Afghan police. But finding that job is already being done by members of the British Territorial Army's 21 SAS Regiment in Musa Qal'ah, the Americans have offered themselves to David Richmond.

The fortressed District Centre spreads west and up a steep hill to a building known as the White House, which accommodates Mullah Salaam, the new district governor, his *shura* rooms, and the local police. The Musa Qal'ah wadi runs almost directly north to south and meets the Helmand River 35 kilometres south at Sangin. The green and richly irrigated strip of land either side of it generates tens of millions of dollars in opium, the first crop of the year, every year. On top of that the farmers produce thousands of tonnes of wheat, and then maize which grows twelve feet tall and turns the landscape into a gridiron jungle of heavily irrigated fields in the autumn.

No one in Musa Qal'ah can remember a time of peace, much less of proper government, since 1979. The countryside is quilted with what are quaintly known as 'legacy minefields' – great swathes of territory planted with hidden explosives by the Soviets, or the muja-hideen fighting them, between 1979 and 1989. One of the biggest legacy threats is around Mount Doom – its lower slopes are not even grazed by goats.

Musa Qal'ah is central to the British effort to prove to ordinary Afghans that NATO is worth backing. It has totemic status as a political and commercial centre for Helmand, and as a transit point for guerrilla groups operating in the east around Kajaki, south to Sangin, west to Now Zad, and north into Uruzgan. The British message is that they are in for the long haul, and that they will win.

Civilians are returning to the town. The ANA has set up an outer ring of patrol bases to act as a first line of defence. But there is a steady flow of intelligence which says that the Taleban are building up their forces about 3 kilometres north and south of the settle-ment. British and Afghan patrols know that if they walk more than a couple of kilometres from the District Centre itself, they will get into a fight.

A confluence of information from local agents and NATO's other sources indicates that Mullah Sheikh, the leading Taleban commander to the north of Musa Qal'ah, is using a compound in

Kats as a base. There are signs that other top leaders are with him, plus a medical centre and a factory for making roadside bombs. There are up to a hundred fighters, possibly massing for an attack on Musa Qal'ah itself.

Richmond and Mark Carleton-Smith are determined that the Taleban should not be able to choose the time and place of every fight. There is a horror of being 'fixed', stuck in heavily fortified compounds unable to influence events beyond rifle range, while the Taleban move freely. This is what has happened to British forces across Helmand for much of the last two years.

'We're going into their back gardens, we're going to rattle their cage and make them fearful that they'll be hit anytime, anywhere,' Richmond tells his men.

Mastiffs, named – like all the army's latest vehicles – after breeds of dog, look like very angry container trucks crossed with a massive wild boar. Their long snouts snarl with cross-laced bar armour which wraps itself back to the body and over thick haunches of tan-coloured steel. It can run on only two of its three axles and four of its six tyres. Underneath, its body is V-shaped, like a chicken's breastbone, to deflect blast from mines. A gunner sits on top in a rotating turret armed with a heavy .50 calibre machine gun or a 40mm grenade launcher, which spits explosive lumps of metal from a thin black proboscis. Clambering into them through the back doors is always a relief. Inside the belly of this metal dinosaur, you feel safe. A driver and his mate are separated up at the front and have to crawl back down through its thorax into where six men can sit on padded seats, and suck on water cooled in bottles shoved into the air conditioning unit. A broken air conditioning unit turns the truck into a bread oven on wheels. It has no windows. Passengers groaning in the heat can see out via a TV monitor mounted in the back right-hand corner. The disorientating images make you feel seasick in minutes.

As Richmond's eight Mastiffs bump out across the desert to swing onto the northern shoulders of Mount Doom, which soldiers like to call 'The Dark Side of Doom', Second Lieutenant James Adamson, commander of 'D' Company's 10 Platoon, is dismayed to find that the air conditioning in his truck is not working. He is crammed in with eight other men. He wonders briefly whether he'd have been better off with the enormously tall colour sergeant, who'd just introduced himself as 'Strawman'. Strawman, he assumes, is at least enjoying the fresh air, riding in a borrowed open-topped American armoured vehicle – like a metal cattle truck – called an Armadillo.

He likes what he's seen of John 'Strawman' Brennan. The rangy soldier uses Irish idiom and speaks with a Mancunian accent. The commander of a platoon mentoring Afghan government troops, he's turned up to help 'D' Company with an eight-man section of Afghan soldiers. With him, Adamson is delighted to discover, is an intriguing Afghan sergeant called Razza. An ethnic Uzbek from the north of the country, Razza gleefully explains that he was once a member of the Taleban himself. Strawman, an imposing figure with a broad chest and the long powerful arms of a boxer, scowls from beneath a head of thick light brown curls.

'He's a fucking top soldier – the best – top bloke,' he growls quietly while nodding towards Razza.

Towering a foot taller than most Afghan soldiers, his phenomenal strength and endurance have won them over. He, meanwhile, is amazed by how ferociously brave the government troops are, how they seem to have a sixth sense for danger, and how it is almost impossible to marshal them in training – much less when they are fighting. He hates being stuck in an armoured vehicle. One bomb and there will be sixteen dead. 'Shitty odds,' he thinks.

Inside his Mastiff, Adamson feels safe. Sweat pours down his face and he pulls his body armour away from his chest to get some relief from the soaking hot pressure which is, literally, cooking his liver and kidneys.

The company crunches to a halt and sets up a desert leaguer in silence. No lights are allowed, no cigarettes; nothing to give away their position to Taleban dickers, as the trucks are arranged like a circle of wagons. The Americans take their vehicles and set up an outer perimeter of sentries.

Nick Calder is called to Richmond's Mastiff. There is intelligence that Mullah Sheikh and other so-called 'High Value Targets' are all staying in one compound on the edge of Kats. 'D' Company have been given orders to put together an assault and an arrest (or kill) operation called a 'snatch'. The colonel's plan is to smash into the compounds with the Mastiffs, leap out, and attack the local Taleban commander. Calder is less enthusiastic – the whole thing is going to have to be planned and executed in just a few hours, and in darkness. While most of the rest of his troops are trying to get some sleep under stars so bright that they seem to hum with energy, he begins putting his battle plan together. Then, just as quickly, the snatch operation against Mullah Sheikh is called off – Nick has no idea why. But he is glad to roll onto the ground and grab a few minutes' sleep.

You get two kinds of sleeper in a desert leaguer on the eve of battle. The lucky ones, men like Strawman whose heartbeat doesn't seem to get above a resting thump, chuck themselves down and quickly slide down into a slow-breathing deep sleep. One officer in Musa Qal'ah became notorious for this. He was once found spread-eagled with his legs sticking out from under a Land Rover and it was assumed he'd been run over and was dead. Someone shook him and he emerged with an oil stain on his chest which had been quietly catching drips while he kipped. Strawman and his eight Afghans slept as if the brown rocks that dug into their hips, knees and shoulders were made of orthopaedic foam. But until you are so tired, or so battle-hardened, that you have ceased to care, you will most likely lie sweating on your back, staring into the noisy starlit sky, and occasionally slip into an anxious hallucinogenic half-sleep which jerks you awake every few minutes. You're being bruised by the desert floor and in the morning someone is going to try to kill you.

What rest that can be had is short lived. The company is up before dawn and is ordered back into the vehicles for another two hours before being dropped off north of Kats, in a wadi bed, which will shield their movements from dickers. Grabbing their weapons, twenty-four-hour rations, water and ammunition, they head off in two columns down either side of the wadi. They can hear the sound of battle further south where the Afghan and British units have managed to sucker the Taleban into a fight. They can hear heavy weapons thumping and the crashing crack made by mortars in the distance.

'D' Company's commander orders the Mastiffs to stay out of sight. Then he deliberately marches with his infantry into what he hopes will be waiting Taleban. This is what he's trained for all his life, but it's still weird. 'Here we are. We're the bait in our own trap. Not many people walk through the countryside hoping that someone will shoot at them,' Calder thinks.

He tells Adamson and the other platoon commanders that the moment the British are attacked the Mastiffs will roar forward and pour fire into the Taleban positions. Strawman is happy with the logic. He is also comfortable with the brigade's policy of ensuring that there should be an 'Afghan face' on operations, which will build the confidence and the reputation of the Afghan Army. But with eight men attached to Adamson's 10 Platoon and another eight with 11 Platoon, that is all the Afghan faces that are available. This means that when it comes to a fight, the Afghans and their Royal Irish mentors will be on point – the juicy first bite in the baited trap for the Taleban.

The company slowly rounds a bend to the left which takes the wadi slightly south. Razza spots a dicker kneeling down by a wall with a walkie-talkie radio in his hand. He and Strawman kneel and shoot at him, but he scuttles to safety in a nearby compound. Adamson sees Razza firing without aiming properly and thinks: 'They're using their guns like carnival air rifles.'

Nick Calder watches, transfixed, as three RPG warheads roar over the heads of 11 Platoon and explode 50 metres away from him in a splash of dust and shards of hot metal. Machine-gun bullets are starting to cut through the air and he is surprised to find himself thinking: 'This is just like training, only real. Real bullets and real bombs, but there's no big deal – in fact it's fun.'

Already under attack from the British and Afghans to the south of the village, the Taleban are now fighting to their north. Their already semi-hysterical tone on the walkie-talkies switches to near panic. They are yelling that the 'Infidel are coming from the north! From the north!' The sporadic staccato of rifle fire quickly builds into a crescendo of Taleban RPGs and machine guns as 'D' Company close in to the east side of Kats. The government troops, who are leading the way, are caught in open ground. Strawman yells at them to get moving. 'We've got to get into cover or we're going to get cut down!'

They need no second cry from Strawman. They rush about 150 metres towards the Taleban with Strawman's long arms herding them towards the first of the high, thick, mud compound walls. The rest of the company are strung out behind, still in the wadi, and take what cover they can find.

Strawman sees muzzle flashes from a compound straight ahead of him on the edge of the wadi and turns to tell Razza. He is thumped onto his back. Everything goes black. Then brown. As he comes around from momentary unconsciousness there is silence. He is coughing and his lungs smart at the chemical mix of dust and cordite. Someone is shouting into this blanket of grey. He can slowly make out a distant *zip zip* noise and one of his Irish mates is shouting at him while he feels his arms and legs; he knows he's been hit. 'Strawman! Strawman! Are you alright?'

'Yes mate,' says the Mancunian-Irish boxer. 'Better get the boss up here.' Somehow Strawman and Razza, who is beside him, have survived an RPG blast. Strawman's hearing returns suddenly as if someone has maliciously turned the volume up. Bullets are flying everywhere as Adamson, the platoon commander, charges forwards so that Strawman can show him which compound he is going to attack next. The two of them put their heads around the southern corner and can clearly see a Taleban gunman in a window; orange flashes and puffs of smoke leap through the frame. The air snaps above them. Strawman grabs Adamson and drags him behind the wall. Their faces are blasted with dirt torn out of the wall from exactly where Adamson's head has been.

'Nice one Bud. That was a bit close, ay Boss?' says Strawman.

Nick Calder immediately orders the Mastiffs into the fight. They roar straight up the wadi towards the Taleban. He stands and watches them with fascination as if he were leaning forward in a chair watching the TV at home. Strawman can hear bullets bouncing off the sides of the beasts. Dong! The Mastiff at the front is hit, broadside, by an RPG which splashes uselessly into the bar armour. The creature rocks slightly, then angrily swivels its gun turret onto the window where the gunman had been, and pours fire through it. Strawman can hear the sound of two-stroke motorcycles coming from just behind the Taleban front line. He knows they are being used to evacuate the dead and injured and to ferry men and supplies about. 'I hope you got fucking pounded and are now flopping around on the back of a bike, dead,' he thinks.

Calder has to react quickly if he wants to keep the initiative he has just won from the Taleban. The textbook would demand that he stand back to identify enemy firing points and then attack them. His instinct tells him to charge. So he does. Both 10 and 11 Platoons are ordered to attack and clear the Kats compounds. The Mastiffs will give fire support from the edge of the village and follow the wadi as it kinks south. With the Afghan Army leading, the compounds are quickly cleared. The dicker who was spotted earlier is seen again, and he's still on his radio. This time he is shot dead by a British soldier, 10 Platoon's Sergeant Andy Haigne.

Adamson is delighted – the platoon's first 'kill'. He is catching up with 11 Platoon who had just whooped with delight. Two Taleban, attempting to flank them to the right, had been spotted when they came over the crest of a small rise. They had been sawn in half by bursts from two General Purpose Machine Guns, which troops call the Jimpy. It can fire at a rate of 1,000 rounds a minute, that's sixteen bullets of 7.62 calibre a second. These details matter. In the 1990s the British Ministry of Defence ordered all infantry regiments to give up the Jimpy in favour of what it called a 'Light Support Weapon'. This was no more than a rifle with a bipod firing the same 5.56 calibre rounds that the ordinary soldier carries. It was useless because it could not fire as far, or as fast, as the Jimpy.

The first few seconds of a battle are often the most important. This is when one side or the other fires so many bullets with so much accuracy that the enemy is forced into hiding, dying, or giving up and running away. The Parachute Regiment never gave up its Jimpies. And now no infantry unit in Afghanistan would survive a day without them. They might each weigh about 26lbs and their belts of ammunition often add a couple of stone to a soldier's backpack, but machine gunners worship the weapon. So when 11 Platoon saw the two Taleban thrown into the air and torn to pieces by the machine gun, they were chuffed.

The platoon push deeper into the village with covering fire from the Mastiffs which, impregnable to the Taleban weapons, are able to carve straight up the wadi bed and shoot into the Taleban firing positions revealed by the smoke and dust kicked up by their guns. Strawman and his ANA rush ahead and break down the doors of another set of compounds; Adamson follows across some open ground to keep them under his control. A voice pipes into the earphone held to his head by a thick elastic band.

'You're under effective enemy fire, boss,' someone says. He looks down and sees the ground dancing sand and stones. He sprints as hard as he can to the other side of the open area and dives into cover while a Mastiff swings its black top gun onto the Taleban's position, spits out grenades the size of yoghurt pots, and tears the Taleban gunman to ribbons. Adamson can hear the cries of wounded and frightened dogs and other livestock above the almost overwhelming roar of battle. 11 Platoon charge on through shoulder-narrow alleyways and over walls, trying to trap Taleban die-hards into a last stand. But the highly experienced guerrillas, whose leaders fought the Russians, quite probably in Kats itself, are keeping their own fighters on the move and withdrawing ahead of the rushing British troops.

11 Platoon crash through the village clearing compounds. The US Marines drive alongside them in their squat wide-bodied Humvee jeeps. They have heavy machine guns and grenade launchers on top which swivel right and left as they drive south along the wadi, hoping to cut off Taleban who are being forced out of the compounds by the Jocks.

The ground rolls up to the right where the wadi bed turns left towards the centre of Kats. As Strawman runs forward to join the Marines with his Afghan troops, Adamson follows with his men; again the ground around him is torn up by machine-gun fire. Taleban rockets are shooting overhead. The white vapour from their tails weaves a grid in the sky above the heads of the Marines who are firing back at a group of compounds tucked into a wadi tributary. Four Marines creep forward and fire short bursts from their rifles from the brow of a hillock into the compound. One of them makes a throat-cutting motion to his neck and signals that they should pull back behind the crest, because the volume of rounds coming back at them is too great. He then signals to Strawman that an RPG might be used to arc over the brow and into the Taleban's firing position. An Afghan RPG gunner is called forward while the two British soldiers join the Americans in trying to force the Taleban's heads down long enough for the Afghan soldier to get a shot in with his own rocket.

Wearing no helmet or body armour, just his green uniform and beret, the Afghan soldier runs into the path of the Taleban bullets, hoists his weapon to cries of 'RPG *hoooah*!' from the Yanks, and squeezes the trigger. The compound to the left is no more than 200 metres away, with its downhill corner facing the gaggle of foreigners and Afghan troops. Four mulberry trees, planted on the near side for shade, are now being used as cover by the Taleban gunmen. Before the Afghan gunner's rocket grenade explodes an American cries out: 'You missed the mutherfucker.' A moment later it detonates – harmlessly and at least 50 metres beyond its target in the desert. Coughing and momentarily blinded by the dust and smoke churned up by the outgoing RPG, the Marine rate of fire drops and immediately the Taleban fill the air with their own bullets. They are kicking up thick fountains of dirt a metre in front of the Marines. The American equivalent of an RPG is known as an AT-4. It's what in kids' comics is always called a 'bazooka' – a disposable tube housing a rocket designed to kill a tank. The Marines fire two at the Taleban compound, and miss both times.

Sergeant Razza, the former Taleban Uzbek, has seen enough failed efforts with rockets. He emerges from behind a Humvee and calmly walks into the enemy's bullets which are slashing through the air around him. He turns his grenade launcher on its side while he adjusts its sights, then puts it on his shoulder, takes aim and squeezes the trigger. He rocks back and then forward as the high explosive warhead roars off like a mini jet, and slams directly into the ground at the base of the Taleban firing position, destroying it completely.

Adamson is excited. Now he wants to assault the compound just as he was taught in the Welsh Brecon Beacons, straight after graduating from Sandhurst earlier in the year. He rushes back down the hill to give Quick Battle Orders. One section attacks the compound. Thump, crackle, thump, crackle. Two grenades are thrown, and then followed up with a burst of fire as the Jocks charge into the compounds. The corporal leading the section prepares to go into another building when a whole family emerges – mother, father, teenage girls and two younger children – all of them crying and holding up their hands. The interpreter working with the British yells at them: 'Get down, get down, they are fighting, they are fighting. Get into your house or behind a wall, there is too much fighting.' The Jocks are amazed that any civilians are hanging around. The family is stuck like toddlers trapped between snarling dogs in a municipal park.

'You're safe now. Don't worry, we're not going to hurt you and we're really sorry about fighting near your house. We're here because your government wants us to help get rid of the Taleban. Have you seen them? Where did they go?' says Adamson.

'They ran when you attacked. We don't know anything. They came this morning and told us to stay in our house and keep quiet – that is all we know,' the father replies.

'Please stay off the streets, go back into your house,' Adamson says, trying to sound comforting to a family to whom he had, inadvertently, brought abject terror. They nod and walk back into the room where they have been hiding. Adamson turns his attention back to 10 Platoon.

A search of the compound turns up a machine gun, two AK47 rifles, grenades and a box of ammunition – but there is no sign of the Taleban team that have been using the equipment. The gunmen slipped away while the Jocks were dealing with the terrified family.

Orders come in to search a suspected factory for IEDs in compounds to the west. This time they find nothing except ripe fruit hanging heavily on carefully irrigated and manicured trees, figs and apricots which are immediately stripped from branches and stuffed into mouths. 10 Platoon find another small but beautifully kept compound to base themselves in for the day and the rest of the night. It is newly wired, has an indoor toilet, a garden with red and orange roses in full bloom, and intricately tiled walls. Given the savagery of the fighting it strikes Adamson as bizarre that there could be this much peaceful luxury anywhere in this landscape. Was this the home of a drug lord? A successful farmer? A businessman? He thought the decor was a bit '1970s Glasgow', but somehow he was touched – the owners' pride in their house and garden seemed to close a cultural gap between them and the British soldiers.

The owners had obviously been away for about a week. The grass was getting long. Their fruit was ripe for harvest and was now running down the chins of the Jocks and government troops. Maybe the family had been driven out by the Taleban; maybe they were all dead? 'We'll never know,' he thinks and takes a walk around his men.

They are shattered. They have been fighting since first light and are badly dehydrated. The Afghan troops could not be persuaded to carry water with them, and so are suffering the most. Two of them have to be tossed into a river to cool them down and Razza, who has run himself into the ground, passes out and is quickly evacuated back to the American truck.

The southern half of Kats has now been cleared. While 'D' Company rest in more comfort than they have enjoyed for weeks, Richmond calls Nick Calder to give him orders for the next phase. Sitting in the shade of a balcony he tells Calder that he wants 'D' Company to drive north through the rest of the compounds then into the fields and ditches beyond. The Mastiffs and US Marines will be waiting in the north to shoot Taleban flushed out by the infantry.

As the notorious British Bowman radio system works only occasionally, the colonel decides to walk north about 100 metres with the rest of his team, including Calder, to liaise with the US Marines. The Marines are on a piece of high ground overlooking the northern half of the village. Often quick on their triggers and keen on using staggering amounts of firepower, Richmond wants to make sure that they will know exactly where British troops are at all times.

The only way to do this is to point it out on the ground. Crunching up the track, Richmond marvels. To his right, desert rolls away to infinity. To his left the desert stops at a road running north to south. One side is dust, the other vivid green fields. He scrambles up to the Marine position. Part of it is a graveyard with burial mounds undulating behind a low stone wall. He joins the Americans, explains how he wants them to drive their Humvees north now, and wait for the Taleban to be flushed to them like driven pheasant. The Marines are cooking their boil-in-the-bag meals by putting them on the sizzling roofs of their vehicles. Richmond decides to stay on this rise in the ground to conduct the next part of the battle. He is close enough to be able to see what is going on. He will be able to send runners to either 'D' Company or the Marines, if – as is likely – the Bowman packs up. Most importantly, he can make tactical decisions based on the fine details of ground truth. A commanding officer will always want to be physically among his troops when his battle group is fighting, and channelling every moment of training over a twenty-two-year military career into reality.

Calder and other members of the headquarters staff are chatting and looking east and north into the wadi. Suddenly they are face down in the dirt and pressing themselves hard into the mounds of earth on the graveyard. Bullets are fizzing and zipping among them. Someone spots a Taleban firing point in the compound due north and a group of officers transformed into riflemen blast off dozens of rounds. It was as Richmond was collecting his map and getting up to take a closer look at the ground in front of him with a pair of borrowed American binoculars that he felt a thump in his leg.

Calder looks back at his boss. The man who has for the last eighteen months overseen every day of training, who has hardened and polished the battalion like a master forger, is standing on one leg. The other looks like it has fallen off a shop window mannequin and got stuck in its trousers; it is flapping and swinging about.

'My Sunray is down! My Sunray is down!' Nick sends the message over the radio net. ('Sunray' is the call sign given to every officer in command.) When a major like Calder says it of his colonel, hundreds of men feel for a moment as though they've lost a parent. For a few seconds they are rudderless and flounder, before someone takes over. In Kats the job falls to Major Andy Thomson, an Oxford mathematics graduate, the senior officer present and a battery commander with the Royal Artillery. He has satellite radio communications to stay in touch with artillery guns miles away and already has an intimate understanding of how the whole battle group is laid out and running.

Calder has confidence in Thomson. But he is stunned. What had been fun has just turned ghastly.

Richmond is lying in a heap. Above him US Marines are firing their .50 calibre machine gun. Empty brass casings, hot, and weighing close to half a pound, are cascading from the gun and down the side of the Humvee. Richmond is batting them away from his smashed leg and looking around for help.

A Marine and his operations officer, Captain Alli Hempenstall, rush to Richmond. During a brief lull in the shooting he can hear them discussing how they will move him.

'Let's just grab a corner each.'

'You touch my fucking legs and I'll personally shoot you.'

They laugh, grab him under the armpits and drag him to safety behind the vehicles where a medic comes to treat him. Richmond had no time to train with the 2/7th Marines before they joined his war in Afghanistan. And he is relieved to find that they follow the same sort of medical procedures as he has been trained in. They give him a shot of morphine, but still the pain is incredible. His leg is soaked in blood; he can feel the splinters of bone moving around inside his muscle. A tourniquet is pulled hideously tightly around the top of his leg and bandages wrapped around the holes. He's attached to a splint which is a length of branch torn from a nearby tree. It sticks out almost a metre beyond his foot.

'Yaaagh. That's my fucking leg. Watch my fucking leg,' he screams. Soldiers keep tripping over it as they rush into cover behind the Humvee and out again to shoot at the Taleban. Every time they do so it causes Richmond such an explosion of pain that he thinks he has been shot again.

Now, worse, a doctor is approaching. 'That's a surgeon's saw. It's shiny and short and he's spinning it about in the light and coming to chop off my leg. Oh, Jesus, no. Surely not?' The doctor bends over the wound and Richmond lies back – he cannot bear to see his leg cut off. There is a brief shooting pain, then the sound of sawing but no change in the steady agony. Then the doctor stands up.

'There we are. That should be better,' he says and raises his hand. In it he is holding two foot of wood which he's amputated from the branch with the silver surgeon's saw. Richmond is dimly aware that fighting continues in the background.

A Predator drone has spotted, and is tracking, the movements of the group of Taleban that shot Richmond. An F16 jet is also patrolling nearby. The Predator fires a Hellfire missile into the group, probably killing one or two. But the explosion is really intended to point out the target for the jet – which then drops a 500lb bomb on the enemy.

'Bombs away,' comes over the net. 'Bombs away!' men shout to one another, incredulous that they are hearing Biggles language – an anachronism in action. There is a wait of nineteen seconds before anyone can hear a plane. Nineteen seconds seem like a big margin for error. No matter how great the pilots are, for nineteen seconds you take shallow sharp breaths in through your nose. You don't know whether you'll be celebrating, or vaporised by your own side. For nineteen seconds you wait for the microsecond scream of a coming train as the bomb tears through the air. If you can hear it, you will live.

Down where the Taleban have been gathering, beyond a cluster of mud houses so pristine they look like a Greek adobe village tumbling down towards the Aegean, an orange flame flashes straight into the sky. It bulges out like a pumpkin and marshmallows smoke and dust. The Jocks are thumped in the chest by the blast 500 metres away. Their mouths are wide open to equalise the air pressure between the inside of their heads and the shock wave. If they don't their eardrums will burst and bleed.

'Fuuuuck me. Jesus,' someone whispers.

'Yahey!' say others.

'Watch your fucking arcs. Keep an eye out to see if anyone survives. Watch your fucking arcs,' a section leader is bellowing. Someone giggles. But it is a weird, nervous, giggle: a 500lb bomb on top of a handful of Taleban; there will be nothing left of them – nothing at all.

There is. The Predator spots survivors from the bombing as they are running towards the main Musa Qal'ah wadi. The F16 strikes again, and again there is cheering from the Jocks and the Afghan soldiers. More Taleban dead. Intelligence officers quickly pick up that several mid-ranking local Taleban leaders are thought to have been killed – although there is no sign of either the bomb-making factory or the medical centre that was believed to be in Kats.

Richmond hears the explosions as he is being loaded onto a stretcher and carried to a Pinzgauer four-wheel-drive ambulance for the most agonising ride of his life. Every undulation, every bump, causes his leg to move, grinding in the pain. But, he thinks, 'at least I'm in an ambulance and on my way out to a helicopter landing site well away from the fighting'. He hears the aircraft approach; someone throws a cloth over his face to protect him against the flying shale and dust. Someone else jabs a needle into him and he is now relaxed, dreamy, almost comfortable, among friends, and on a train.

Thomson knows that the battle group is exhausted. Two men have been evacuated as heat casualties and many others are starting to show the signs of severe dehydration. Kats has been cleared. Taleban have been killed, though accurate numbers will never be known. Any plans the enemy has of taking their fight into the town of Musa Qal'ah itself have been badly set back. With no prospect of holding the ground they have just taken because there simply are no troops to do it, Thomson gives the order to rest and withdraw back to the District Centre.

5

BLIND

I sit in a chair drenched in an oily flood of acronyms. Outside, in the squeaky corridor, bureaucrats are generating reports. They walk briskly from office to office, extravagant plans pour out of printers. A great air of purpose is generated by a £30 million budget for 'Reconstruction and Development'. But I am chewing on the insides of my cheeks to stay awake. The lieutenant colonel has taken time away from his other jobs to explain to me what is going on in the world of Security Sector Reform. He's handsome, tall, charming, with a twinkle of dash. He's very relaxed, has an easy-going smile. I don't want to be rude. I focus hard on his eyebrows, that way I'll keep up with him, appear to stay interested.

'I've got command of a company of 5 SCOTS here in Lashkar Gah, another company of 5 SCOTS in Fob Delhi down in Garmsir, my own guys from 2 SCOTS in company strength in Kabul – and the whole of the 23 SAS Squadron, which is based in Lahskagar and Musa Qal'ah, is also under my command. That's not too complicated. I can cope with being the commander of Battle Group South and of all retraining of Afghan police and army in Helmand. The problem is arse itch,' says Lieutenant Colonel Nick Borton.

I sit up with a delighted, uncomprehending snigger. 'Arse itch?'

'Not arse itch – ARSIC – Afghan Regional Security Integration Command. For the police and army training I have to answer to ARSIC, which itself answers to Sea Sticker Alpha.'

'Huh?'

'CSTC-A, the Combined Security and Transition Command-Afghanistan, which is based in Kabul. It has command and control over the 2/7th US Marines, who are also doing police mentoring and training in Helmand. And ARSIC is in charge of our own 23 SAS, who are also doing police training and mentoring. Frankly it's a bugger's muddle. Although we're part of 16 Air Assault Brigade, anyone doing police or army training isn't under the brigade's command. The Royal Irish Regiment, and the 2/7th US Marines do not come under British command in a British area. They come under ARSIC command out of Kabul – even though they're supposed to be working with us, or in fact are indeed us. ARSIC doesn't have a clue about what its own plans are supposed to drive. So it's a fucking mess that we sort out on the ground.

'And, what we're doing is really nurturing an armed militia through a counterinsurgency, not creating a police force,' he adds.

It's baffling – he's basically telling me that he works for his brigade commander, Mark Carleton-Smith, and two other different chains of command in Kabul – and the people he's working with – the US Marines – are also on their own.

'Sorry about the PowerPoint presentation, you did well not to slip into a coma. If you had, I'd have hidden you behind the fridge. Let's get a brew.'

We wander off to meet the officers and senior non-commissioned officers of 2 SCOTS. There's a small buzz going around. There are rumours and so-called intelligence reports that Marjah, a town the size of the Snake's Head, about 15 kilometres west of Lashkar Gah, has been 'coming under Taleban influence' since the insurgents were driven out of Garmsir.

'We can't do much about it now anyway,' says Borton. 'We don't have the manpower to go in there.'

A couple of weeks later Nick Borton is rescued from worrying about Marjah, Garmsir, and Lashkar Gah. The never-ending hassles of trying to persuade members of the Afghan National Police to switch from preying on the local population and serving as the armed thugs of drug *khans,* to being salaried servants of the state, are over. He is landing in a choking cloud of brown dust which rams its way into his nostrils and ears. He steps off the back of a Chinook and when the dust clears finds himself in a world painted in an infinity of brown.

The desert is a burned pancake to the west. There are some tan-coloured mountains to the far east, north and south. He feels like he's landed in a science-fiction film about a lunar station and its inhabitants, long forgotten and abandoned by a heartless mother earth. A group of men emerge out of the brown background dressed in desert combats. Their faces are heavy with dust which hangs from their eyelashes. The only colour in the landscape is in the rims of their sun-baked eyes which look like they've been coloured in with red felt-tip pens. A mini tornado sweeps through the Fob. Borton and his party cover their faces and mouths. Experienced inmates of this purgatory of dust ignore the swirling powder. Someone closes one nostril with a finger, takes a deep breath, and blasts a plug of muddy mucus out of the other. The snot plug vanishes into the brown talc at the man's feet. Fob Edinburgh, logistics base, artillery base, and baking hell, is a desert encampment. It is rumoured in other Fobs that there's a female medic at Edinburgh who strips to a bikini to sunbathe. But no one here's interested – this is a place that takes the man out of human.

'Christ.'

'Hello, sir! Great to see you. Don't want to chivvy you too much, sir, but we've got to get a move on, got to get to Musa Qal'ah as soon as possible,' says one of the dust men. His teeth flash with a smile, his hair is probably black, and I can tell from his easy manner and accent that he's probably an officer. I'm thinking: 'How long can it take, 7 kilometres, the sun is barely up, it can't take as long to go 14 kilometres. Surely.'

'Gordon! Splendid. Off we go then, into the back of the wagons?' says Borton. He's delighted to find that he's being ferried to Musa Qal'ah by his own men of 'B' Company of 2 SCOTS, the Royal Highland Fusiliers. He hadn't expected to see them for most of the tour. Now he can settle back into the armoured vehicle and enjoy what he hopes will be a short ride to the DC. He is going to take command of Battle Group North, to replace David Richmond, who was injured and evacuated back to Britain only yesterday.

'It could take us a while to get down to the DC. We came up pretty fast and that means the Taleban will know we're going back and they'll probably lay some IEDs for us. So we'll have to Barma all the VPs [vulnerable points] along the way. There's not much to do except sit that out,' says Captain Gordon Muir.

Operation Barma is a lifesaving chore. It involves nothing more than a couple of people walking in front of the vehicles, sweeping the ground in front of them with metal detectors. If they find anything suspicious, they call for the IED disposal team, who dig the suspected bomb out. These teams are run ragged across the whole of Helmand. Waiting for them to come and sort out a suspected bomb can take days. Still, the armoured personnel carrier isn't too uncomfortable. Someone has thoughtfully put some water bottles in the air-conditioning vents. I squeeze a cold meal of pasta and tomato slush out of a rations bag, and wash it down gratefully with cold water.

Across from me, Borton is alternately fidgety, and then silent, then close to anger as we find we're stuck behind the Barma team, in a tiny blind spot about 50 metres from a British sentry post at Observation Point Himal. A stretch of 10 metres of the dusty road is obscured from the OP by an overhanging rock. And that is where the Barma team think they've found a bomb.

'Call it in, mark it, and let's get the fuck on with it or we'll never get there. And I want to know how it is possible for the Taleban to lay a bomb, literally, under the noses of our troops,' Borton snaps. It's a full four and a half hours before we pull in to the Musa Qal'ah DC. We've been travelling at 1.5 kilometres per hour. No wonder Borton and the brigadier say the British efforts are being crippled by the inability to move around the province.

It's now eleven at night and still boiling hot. Borton is met by his new battle group's staff, Alli Hempenstall, operations officer, Olly Dobson, adjutant, Jules Kilpatrick, signals officer, and Jason Calder, 'D' Company commander. The battalion's second in command is Nick's older brother, Jason. There's a tall beak-nosed SAS lieutenant colonel called 'Rob' who hovers silently in the background, and a senior SAS NCO, a cockney who could be anywhere in age between thirty-five and sixty. He appears to be made mostly of biltong and moves about the operations room in short crab-like darts.

Borton is shown to a bedroom in the back of the building housing the operations room. It has no windows, a small fan, and a cot. Until a couple of days ago it was where Richmond had slept. 'Christ, I'm glad I'm not stepping into an actually dead man's shoes,' thinks Borton.

In the morning he has to take over Richmond's battle group: 1,200 men and women, spread over a vast area of desert. The headquarters and main infantry element are all Argylls, men who have been trained and turned into a fighting family by Richmond, who is now no doubt lying in a hospital bed in Selly Oak, in great pain, and filled with longing to be back in Helmand.

The fan clatters, spreading hairdryer air around the room. Borton wakes, soaked, and in a puddle of sweat which has gathered in the bottom of the nylon cot.

Morning 'prayers' – the commanding officer's morning briefing, is run by Jason Calder while Borton sits in. The Royal Regiment of Scotland is two years old. Its five battalions have been brought together under one regimental cap badge. But each is still a tribe with traditions and cultural behaviour defined by their original regiments: the Argyll and Sutherland Highlanders, the Royal Scots Borderers, the Royal Highland Fusiliers, the Black Watch, and the Highlanders.

The Argylls, who are now sitting around the big oblong table, traditionally wore kilts. The Highland Fusiliers, Borton's regiment, used to dress in trousers – trews which they were very proud of. Argylls were recruited from the Western Highlands; Fusiliers from closer to Glasgow. They are different military clans and have been forced into the amalgamated 'SCOTS' only in 2006. This has meant a loss of the tribal language and plumage which sets the British Army regiments apart. The Highland Fusiliers lost their trousers and now have to wear kilts.

When they join their regiments, British soldiers believe they are doing so for the rest of their military life. They learn the history of their units off by heart, and the symbolism of every thread of ceremonial dress. In the Argylls, apparently, senior NCOs and some officers can be found searching the countryside for road-kill badgers; their cured heads are hung from sporrans – quite why has not been explained. But anyone who might try stopping them should remember their battle honours stretch back through Iraq, Korea, two world wars, the Boer War, and to Balaklava, where they held the 'thin red line' against repeated charges of Russian cavalry during the Crimean War.

Borton sits silently through the briefing. He's not felt any tension among the officers of the Argylls. Puzzlingly, there is a sort of exuberant energy in the room. A bit like a prep school classroom. Two of his most important staff have seen to that, by trying to sabotage one another's first briefing with the new CO. Hempenstall, the operations officer, in charge of planning future fighting, speaks from

a clipboard on which Jules Kilpatrick, the signals officer, has written
'Call Me Sailor Boy' in huge white letters. Kilpatrick, meanwhile, is
sucking on a water bottle which is inside a wet white sock to keep
it cool. Hempenstall has drawn a penis on the sock with a black
marker pen.

Borton pretends that he has not noticed the pranks, makes a
brief speech about how honoured he is to be taking command of
his friend David Richmond's battle group, and then plunges into
more detailed briefings. He has US Marines from the 2/7th in Now
Zad and Musa Qal'ah, but not technically under his command.
He has a half squadron of 23 SAS and a company of Royal Irish
Rangers, who are mentoring the Afghan Army and manning the
patrol bases which picket the outskirts of Musa Qal'ah. He has a
Warrior company from 5 SCOTS and a Mastiff company from 2
SCOTS.

And he has the added problem of Mullah Abdul Salaam, the
district governor. This former Taleban leader is reputed to guzzle
anti-depressants, by the handful. Borton has been told that the
mullah cannot be trusted, that he looks like a pantomime genie,
complete with thick eyeliner and sandals that curl up at the end;
and that his militia, all members of his Alizai tribe, are accused of
extorting money from civilians in the town's bazaar. Numerous
members of his council are related to members of the Taleban, or
suspected of being Taleban members themselves. But he has the
backing of President Karzai. As a Taleban turncoat he has an iconic
status for the whole of Afghanistan. Borton isn't looking forward to
meeting him.

'So, what's he really like?' he asks Justin Holt as they wade through
the grey dust and up the small hill inside the DC to Salaam's 'White
House' for a security *shura*. Holt, the Foreign Office-appointed
Stabilisation Adviser (Stabad) is moonlighting. In real life he is a
lieutenant colonel in the Royal Marines. He's been seconded as
a Stabad to Helmand, and then assigned to Musa Qal'ah. 'You'll

have to make up your own mind. He's certainly entertaining,' Holt chuckles.

Holt likes Borton immediately. The tall good-looking Highland Fusilier is much like Richmond. He has a habit of rubbing his hands together when he gets excited. 'Anyone who can do that, grin like a happy schoolboy, and still command hundreds of homicidal Scottish clansmen is going to be good news,' he thinks.

When they arrive at Salaam's meeting room Holt removes his shoes before entering. The chamber is a long, tall concrete box. It is pleasantly cool. Large pillows have been laid against the walls and a tray with tea and small glasses is waiting in the corner nearest the door. Holt and Borton are waved to the back of the room and Borton pauses briefly, looks down at the miles of laces in his boots and elects to keep his footwear on his feet.

'Would you tell the governor that I have to be ready for action,' Borton says to his translator, and then collapses backwards onto a cushion. He wonders how his hosts have managed to make this simple room so comfortable, while the British accommodation is so ghastly.

'Sir,' says the translator. 'This is a very important meeting. There are top officials here from Lashkar Gah, from the provincial governor's office. They are here to improve the relationship with the district governor and ISAF.'

'Aha. Does that mean they're going to read him the riot act?' Borton whispers into Holt's shoulder, just as the governor appears in the doorway wearing golden curled slippers. The Mullah's feet, which bulge over the sides of the slippers, are decorated with filigree patterns in henna. He's wearing thick black eyeliner. Long dyed black hair tumbles from beneath a shimmering jet-black turban. Everyone stands to greet him. Borton is introduced to the governor and the representatives from Lashkar Gah. An elderly man with straggly hair and an unruly beard sits down opposite the mullah, with Borton to his right.

Dispensing with the typically long introductions and praise poems which usually begin such meetings, the man from Lashkar Gah breathes in slowly until the room is silent.

'Now we'll get to business. Would everyone please introduce themselves as we go around the room . . . Right, now. Let us hear from each of the branches of the security services here. Afghan National Army?'

Major Zangay, the operations officer of the Afghan government *kandak* (battalion) slowly folds his fingers together and leans slightly forward from the waist until he looks like he might topple onto his chin.

'We have clear objectives and clear orders. It is our job to bring security here for the civilians. We are doing that with men spread over nine bases around here to provide an outer cordon to stop the enemy from coming into Musa Qal'ah. We are trying our best to bring security to Musa Qal'ah. But we are having problems controlling the entry of people into the city who have weapons but no papers identifying why they need to be carrying weapons.'

He's now staring sideways at Mullah Salaam whose militia has no uniforms but insist they are policemen, and have been causing trouble in the town.

'If my people see civilians with rifles then they must ask them what they are doing with a weapon. If civilians with guns are allowed to move in the city without ID then the enemy can use the same technique to get into Musa Qal'ah.'

Mullah Salaam squeezes his mouth into a pantomime pout and flicks the carpet hair back and forth by his right knee. He reaches into the pocket of his *shalwar kameez* and pulls out a small ring of keys.

Major Zangay goes on: 'I haven't been to a security meeting or met the district governor [Mullah Salaam] since last winter [when the city fell to ISAF]. The only reason I am here is to make him look good, make the police look good and to make the army look good.'

One of Holt's British bodyguards emerges from the blinding light outside through the curtains across the door. 'There's an IDF [indirect fire] alert. We need to get into hard cover.'

'We are in hard cover. There are two floors of concrete above us. Let's carry on,' says Holt. 'We are all working closely to protect the people of Musa Qal'ah,' he adds – hoping that Mullah Salaam has quickly forgotten the very obvious complaint levelled at his thuggish militia.

This isn't going well. The Afghan Army do not trust Mullah Salaam. To them he's a Taleban 'traitor' and could turn on the government as easily as he turned on the Taleban. The government officers believe he is certain to be talking to his former friends in the Taleban. Most of the army officers are former members of the Northern Alliance, they're ethnic Tajiks and Uzbeks, with strong tribal animosities to the Pashto of the south, whom they consider mad savages. Meanwhile Salaam's police are out of the control of any government agency. And the one man who might be able to hold them in check, another local militia leader and Mullah Salaam's rival, Haji Koka, is away training with his own 300-man militia.

'We are here to support the army, the police and the NDS to ensure the security of Musa Qal'ah to enable Mullah Salaam to continue his governance here in Musa Qal'ah,' Borton says to cheer the mullah up. Salaam meanwhile is coquettishly fingering a curl of his luxuriantly coloured hair around his ear. Everyone seems to think that this is their chance to tell the man from Lashkar Gah that Mullah Salaam is a nightmare and that it's time he was replaced.

The man from Lashkar Gah looks straight at the army commander and tells him: 'You must keep Mullah Salaam informed of all operations so that when he's asked from higher offices about what is going on he will be able to answer. He is the man responsible for this area. It's been six months since Musa Qal'ah was liberated from the enemy but Mullah Salaam hasn't submitted any reports because, he says, you won't tell him what's going on.'

Mullah Salaam works his keys through his fingers, like worry beads, while looking straight ahead of him, slightly over the heads of his guests. He stops fiddling when his fingers find what looks like a tiny silver spoon.

Major Zangay replies: 'We can tell Mullah Salaam about the planned operations but we can't about the ones that are reactive – like last night when Satellite Station North was attacked.' I recalled being woken up by the crash of RPGs about a mile away and standing on the roof of the District Centre watching tracer arc back and forth across the valley. It could have been beautiful were the fireworks not lethal.

The man from Lashkar Gah goes on: 'All the people involved in operations should be kept informed. ISAF should use the experience of the district governor. He was here before and defeated the Russians. He is very well known to the people in this area and it would be good to listen to him.'

Mullah Salaam looks at the ceiling while simultaneously bringing the little spoon up and gently inserting it into his right ear. His pinky finger is daintily pointing in the air. Holding the little tool as if it were a tiny watercolour brush, he rotates it gently around inside his auricle.

Major Naim, the NDS chief, throws his lot in, or appears to. He actually manages to say nothing. His job is as much to spy on Mullah Salaam as it is to spy on the Taleban. 'I know a lot about who the Taleban are, and who is backing them, and who supports them. Recently we stopped twenty foreigners trying to get into Musa Qal'ah – this is a dangerous situation.'

The man from Lashkar Gah says again: 'You must share all your information with Mullah Salaam.' Major Naim smiles enigmatically.

Then the local prison director pipes up: 'We jailed a man with 60 kilograms of opium resin last week – and then he was released [by Mullah Salaam]. There were no documents and no charges. I actually don't know who anyone is in this room because we haven't met before. This is my first time ever at one of these meetings and I don't know what is going on.'

Asking the translators to preserve the dignity of Afghans in front of 'these *kufar*' (foreigners) Mullah Salaam tells them to stop translating the disagreements.

Now the mullah extracts the silver implement from his ear, briefly inspects it, and with a satisfied grunt, wipes it on the leg of his white trousers. He pops the keys back in his pocket. He opens his palms to the heavens and mutters a brief incantation in a low whisper. His eyes pop open like a gypsy woman hamming up a possession in a seance. Borton is goggle eyed and reddens. His eyes flicker to me and I openly smile back. This has the desired effect. Borton is now coughing hard to try to suppress his laughter. Holt is also smiling and nodding like a madman to try to stop the giggles from spreading.

'The army has no place in the bazaar. Leave that area to my police. Here, I speak for the President. In this area the order of seniority is: President Karzai, then provincial governor Gulab Mangal, and then in Musa Qal'ah – me.

'The army and the national police have no roles in the bazaar – that is the area where my police will patrol. The foreign troops must plan all of their operations with me and I will approve them. They must also stop releasing my prisoners from the jail.

'Why do the British here not want to trust me? I was in the Taleban but I left them to serve my people and the government. I know a lot about what is going on here and yet no one wants to ask my opinion?'

Borton replies while Holt nods: 'We very much appreciate what you have said and what you have been doing for us. May we suggest that we have a regular weekly security meeting and that we stay in close touch? If you have concerns please do not hesitate to raise them with us at any time.'

With that, the security *shura* breaks up. Glasses of tea are cleared away. Borton can't wait to get out.

'Blimey. Thank God I've got you as the Stabad to soak this up,' says Borton to Holt.

'Well, he's our man here. He's got to be. He's got iconic status with the President and he's the only Taleban we've managed to turn. So we've got to make it work with him.'

'But that ear thing. That ear pick. That was incredible,' says Borton. 'Still – I liked him! Tells it like it is – I think we'll get on fine.'[2]

The next day I arrange a private meeting with Mullah Salaam. He still looks like a panto villain and has some bizarre personal habits. But so what? This is a very far-flung dust-blown medieval land, dependent on the production of drugs; a place that has been torn up by war for decades. This isn't Europe and Salaam isn't a candidate for Suffolk County Council. And there is something about him that seems anxious to do the right thing. Of course he wants to survive and you would be amazed if he wasn't playing both sides. The trick will be to make him feel that he is – really – on the same side as the British. If not, he will sell them out.

It would be easy to underestimate the mullah because he looks odd. But lunch with the mullah holds out the promise of fresh flat bread, stewed meat, tomatoes, okra, drinking yoghurt and, above all, fresh fruit; water melon, grapes, pears, and pomegranates. The British lunch in Musa Qal'ah is the same, the same every single day. Pasta sludge with chicken and mushroom sauce. Or, a bag of some kind of Chinese-sounding meal which promises mushroom and noodles – but is woody and tastes like creosote.

At lunch I cannot hide the yearning I have for nourishment. Salaam's eyes sparkle with amusement. I lunge shamelessly into bowls heaped with ripe tomato and cucumbers which, somehow, have been chilled.

---

2 Lieutenant Colonel Borton got over the initial shock of Salaam's habits and worked closely with him over the coming months. 'I enjoyed a very close relationship with him which worked out for both if us,' Borton says.

His story is typical, except that at forty-six, he's lived longer than the average Afghan male by three years. He has three wives, one died a few years back. And seventeen children.

'Wow. How many sons and how many daughters?'

'I have seventeen sons, and ten daughters. Three of my sons died or I would have twenty children,' he explains. Female children therefore, literally, don't count.

He was just eighteen when the Russians invaded Afghanistan in 1979 and immediately joined the mujahideen. 'We fought them at first just with old hunting guns and petrol in bottles which we would light and throw on their soldiers or their tanks. Then we started getting guns from the US, from Britain and from Pakistan. I've been fighting almost non-stop from that time until now. Eighty members of my family have been killed.'

He rose to become a local commander and leader of his Alizai tribe. When civil war tore Afghanistan apart in the early 1990s he was drawn to the Taleban who promised to end banditry. 'There was peace in every part of Afghanistan where there were Taleban in charge. It was very good with the Taleban. But they did not have the support of the foreigners and so they were toppled. Al Qaeda was not part of the Taleban but they paid the price of allowing al Qaeda to be guests here in Afghanistan. After 2001, when the Taleban ran away into the mountains, things got very bad.

'As the years went by it was clear that the Taleban fighting the government were not real Taleban – they were just thieves and foreigners. We should not call them Taleban. We should call them criminals. I am a Taleban – but I am not a criminal. Afghanistan is at war because its neighbours in Russia, Uzbekistan, China and above all in Pakistan don't want there to be peace here.

'Pakistan is the biggest enemy of Afghanistan and most of the Taleban fighters we have here are Pakistanis. They are too hard on the people to come back to power, that will never happen,' says Mullah Salaam.

Outside there's the metallic crack of a rocket landing nearby. 'I know the people firing those rockets. I do, you know. I was in the Taleban so of course many of them are my friends. I speak to them often on the telephone. I try to persuade them to support the government. But they are too corrupt; they are making money from the war.

'Why don't the British talk to me more? Why don't they want to trust me? I can help them if they tell me what they are doing, I can advise them.

'I can tell you now that the Taleban are moving into the villages south of here. They will try to cut the roads. Their leader is Abdul Barri, I know him well. I spoke to him this morning,' he says.

He waves me to the door of his office. I squeeze past his favourite son, Tubeh, a boy of about fifteen who appears to have been inflated with a pneumatic pump.

'Look at the flags when you go outside. See if you can notice anything interesting about them,' the mullah adds – then he winks.

Overnight Borton is told that Major Naim of the NDS has agents to the south of Musa Qal'ah. They are reporting that the Taleban have taken over Dagyan, about 4 kilometres away. The Taleban, it turns out, have infiltrated close to the District Centre.

They have been flying flags as aiming points for their rockets. They've also closed the road to Musa Qal'ah. Just as Mullah Salaam had warned.

Corporal Jamie Dougal is pissed off. It's an hour before sunrise – the only time when the heat eases and a light breeze strokes his face and he can slide into a comfortable sleep on top of his Mastiff. The truck has become a home. There's a good stash of porn crammed under the radio equipment in the back. The driver has his bed in the crawling space between the cockpit and the rear. Water and rations are shoved between the bar armour and the bodywork outside. Staring up at the sky he thinks it would be nice just to

have a day to give it a deep clean, dig all the sweaty gunge out of
the seats, blow out the air conditioning so that it doesn't puff that
jet of hot dust into your face when it's switched on, and find a bit
of padding to stop your back slamming into the metal edges of
the turret every time the monster lurches over a bump. But no.
Borton has ordered a reconnaissance patrol down to Dagyan and
Yatimchay, Jamie is up.

There's a brew on, quick orders from the boss, then he's up in the
gun turret behind the .50 calibre still rubbing his face and digging
the bits of hard mud out of the corners of his eyes, where it's coagu-
lated and dried overnight. Four of the trucks shoulder their way
through the chicane at the entrance to the DC, and out into the
Musa Qal'ah wadi.

Everyone feels it. The moment you pass through those gates you
feel a sharpening, a needle prick of danger. But you also feel taller,
free. You can actually see the country you are in once you are beyond
the 'Hesco' walls, made of giant wire barrels filled with dirt, which
encircle the camp. Four metres high, they stop people from shooting
in, and everyone inside from seeing out.

Jamie can see a local Afghan, a '*chogie*', is up early. He has parked
his Toyota Corolla, the ubiquitous car of Helmand, on the edge of
the river which runs across the gravel on the far western side of the
wadi. Jamie watches him though his binoculars, wondering if he's a
dicker. 'If he is, can I shoot him? No,' he thinks. The last three IEDs
that have been found in the wadi have all been radio controlled. 'Is
this fucker going to try to blow us up?' Jamie looks closer – making
sure that the man isn't merely going through the motions of cleaning
his car. The man is working hard and not rubbing on a part of the
car that's already clean.

'Still, fucking early to be out washing your car.'

The right of the wadi is pretty. The desert flows down from the
east and spreads out into green gently cultivated fields. When the
wind is in the right direction, there is a ghost breath of air which has

been cooled as it passes over the water. There's a whiff of woodsmoke in the air. Now the cockerels are starting to crow.

Jamie is in the second wagon. There is a *whoosh*, a crash, and the Mastiff rocks to the side – it's been hit broadside by an RPG. Jamie's knees buckle in a reflex and he drops from his turret down into the belly of the truck. He jumps straight back up as if spring loaded. He gets his gun firing to try to force the Taleban out of the game. He can see the smoke trail from the rocket which has just hit his vehicle still hanging in the air. He fires bursts at where it vanished into a tree line – the .50 calibre leaping like an unruly pony. A trained sniper, he takes great pride in using the .50 calibre as precisely as a surgeon. The gun has a three-times magnification sight. An odd dark shape appears in the bottom edge of the screen and begins to fill the view-finder, fast.

'RPG! RPG! It's coming right at my fucking head. RPG!' Jamie yells and again flops down into the Mastiff. The blast of the rocket knocks him onto his backside. It fills the turret with marshmallow-thick, acid-smelling grey smoke. The rocket has shredded the day sack he had clipped to the side of his wagon with some food and other goodies in it. He puts his head up for the third time and glances at the back of the truck.

'I kill Taleban. I fuck kill fuck Taleban,' yells the Afghan army officer who had jumped in at the DC with a backpack full of his own RPG warheads. Short and powerfully built with a body pockmarked by the battle scars of past campaigns, Captain Zain is the commander at the southernmost outpost of Musa Qal'ah, Patrol Base South. His base, known as 'the Chinese Restaurant' because of its inexplicably oriental portico, is now visible about 800 metres off to the east. The Afghan officer is forty, but looks fifty-five. He's been fighting for most of his life. A former member of the Northern Alliance, he'd fought the Taleban in the Panjshir valley, north of Kabul, and since 2001 had been chasing them across the east and south of the country. The day before this operation he'd been complaining of homesickness. He hadn't seen his wife or three daughters for four months. He was pissed off that at his relatively advanced age, he was on the front line of yet another war. His face has a long scar which runs along his jawline back from his chin.

Zain's eyes are shining wide. His face is covered with what looks like soot and his teeth are shining. He is staring up at Jamie in his turret and reaching back into his pack to grab an RPG warhead. 'I kill Taleban. Look! Fuck. Faaauuuck!'

The rocket shoots out of Zain's launcher in the back of the Mastiff. The air seems to get sucked clean out of Jamie's head with a gigantic pop, and the rocket disappears towards the muzzle flashes of small arms which are coming from a sort of badger-hole bunker. The rocket goes into the hole then explodes with a *hump* sound. Jamie is struggling to clear a jam on his .50 calibre. Zain fires another rocket, then another. Behind the main line of Taleban positions, he can see a motorbike traversing the scene through billows of smoke. 'Watch! Fuck! Watch!' Zain is giggling and yelling.

He fires again. The rocket smokes away apparently into thin air. The motorbike vanishes in a crack, flash, and jet of unexpectedly black fumes.

'Quality mate. Fucking quality!' one of the Jocks shouts.

Rifle bullets are plinking uselessly off the sides of the Mastiff. RPG rockets are now being fired in volleys from the Taleban trenches on the eastern side of the wadi. A dozen rockets streaking towards the British trucks look like an enfilade of cannon firing broadside from a galleon.

One or two of the Taleban positions are blown up, or shot to pieces, and their inhabitants killed. But after forty-five minutes the two sides are at stalemate. It's impossible for the Mastiffs to assault any closer to the Taleban positions and root them out. The Taleban, meanwhile, are finding it equally difficult to destroy the bar-armoured Mastiffs.

Corporal 'Lachie' MacNeil and private Nick Whelan moments before they ran into a group of Taleban fighters. Nick was injured when he was blown up by an IED a week later.

Lieutenant Jim Adamson poses in a field of marijuana. The heavy crops in the Green Zone forced young men into hand-to-hand combat note his fixed bayonet.

Colour Sergeant John 'Strawman' Brennan, 1 R IRISH, on patrol north of Musa Qal'ah formed a close bond with Afghan soldiers but would later find their performance disappointing.

Lieutenant Colonel Nick Borton took over Musa Qal'ah at twelve hours' notice after his friend Lieutenant Colonel David Richmond was shot in the leg by the Taleban. Borton won a DSO for his service in Afghanistan.

Lieutenant Colonel David Richmond, CO 5 SCOTS, was the first British commanding officer to be shot on operations since colonel 'H' Jones was killed in the Falklands in 1982.

Major Harry Clark, 'B' Company commander, 5 SCOTS, found himself surrounded and fighting every day for almost a month in Nad-e-Ali, close to Helmand's provincial capital, Lashkar Gah.

'C' Company 2 Para's Lieutenant Nick Mys (left) and Captain Josh Jones before setting out on patrol. Jones's 'buggers' grips' are beginning to flourish.

The intense fighting around Sar Puzeh lasted seventeen hours. Here 9 Platoon sergeant Ruby Connor slumps asleep during a brief lull.

Frank 'the Yank' Ward, grew up in America's mid-west, dreaming of being a British paratrooper and sniper. Slightly wounded in action, he got to live that dream in Helmand.

An opium processing laboratory over-run by 2 Para during a seventeen-hour battle on Operatio Oqab Talander. The fierce resistance from insurgents lead many to question whether the British were fighting drug militias or the Taleban.

Fresh from Sandhurst, Second Lieutenant Alexander 'Beatie' Barclay won an MC for leading hi platoon in the rescue of Garrie Wallace and two others during an ambush in Nad-e-Ali.

ance Corporal Steve Lewis, 2 Para, dispatched seven Taleban fighters on a single day during peration Oqab Talander and recorded thirteen confirmed 'kills' in 2008. The blow-up rubber x doll was used as a decoy in the snipers' nest on the roof of Fob Gibraltar.

orporal Matthew 'Des' Desmond, 2 Para, killed a wounded insurgent who had reached for the d holster Desmond is holding up during Operation Oqab Talander on June 24.

A Grenade Machine Gun manned by the Pathfinders at dawn, screening the turbine convoy as it drove through the Gorak Pass on Operation Oqab Tsuka.

The 120-vehicle Combat Logistics Patrol, to move the hydro-electric turbine and its parts through 180 kilometres of enemy territory, a top secret deception plan which saved dozens of British lives. Here the convoy passes through the Gorak Pass escorted by an Apache helicopter.

Major Joe Fossey (centre, kneeling) gives an orders group during a rest on Operation Oqab Tsuka. SSM 'Paddy' Beattie is to his right, next to sergeant Gaz Jones, and WO2 'Moxy' from the bomb disposal team.

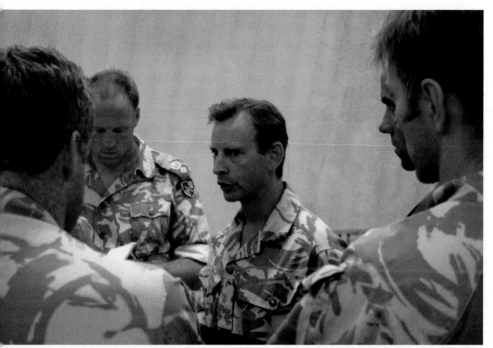

igadier Mark Carleton-Smith gives his commanding officers a final pep-talk before Operation qab Tsuka. Lieutenant Colonel Joe O'Sullivan, CO 2 Para is in the background.

Seaking helicopter re-supplies Queen's Royal Lancer's Vikings on Operation Oqab Tsuka.

Sergeant Chantelle Taylor. Although a medic, she expected to be patrolling and fighting with the infantry and probably killed a Taleban fighter near Marjah.

Corporal Garrie Wallace immediately after he was rescued by Beatie Barclay. Wallace, a reservist, saved the lives of two men by his calm and quick thinking when his vehicle crashed during an intense Taleban ambush. He did not expect to survive.

So the British call in fast jets. 'Bombs away! That'll fucking show them,' someone shouts as the first jet roars overhead. There's a brief scream, a percussive smack sound, then the ground erupts like a small volcano – 100 metres too far south, harmlessly in the wadi.

Another bomb is ordered up. The plane roars again, the bomb comes hurtling down; one or two Jocks think they catch a glint of it flashing past and it screams into the ground with a smashing sound and a small pop of smoke. It's a dud. 'Blind! Last drop was a blind!' the forward air controller calls to the aircraft on his radio. The plane returns.

The Taleban are still shooting at the Jocks, which cheers the Jocks – they don't want the Taleban to run away before they can be turned into flying mush by the bombs. Another one is dropped, again it screams, another little pop. Blind! A fourth finally manages to hit a major Taleban firing position. There is a brief lull in the shooting, which gives the Jocks enough of a sense of achievement to withdraw back to the DC.

But now two unexploded bombs containing 1,800kg of Triniton high explosive are lying buried in the wadi gravel, inside a village controlled by the Taleban.

'If that explosive ends up in the hands of the Taleban they'll be able to build the mother of all truck bombs. They could ram our gates and blow us all to hell. Still, the good news is we know where the bombs are and we know the Taleban will be interested in them. So we can, er, kill two birds with one stone – so to speak,' says Borton as he gives instructions to his staff officers to draw up plans to get the IEDD (bomb disposal) teams into Musa Qal'ah immediately. He plans to send the whole battle group back down to Yatimchay to secure the bombs, blow them up, and get out.

Spy planes have already filmed two groups of people who have been digging the sides of the holes left. They can be seen using shovels and picks, digging into the river bed that has swallowed the bombs. Borton is under intense pressure from Carleton-Smith's staff. The explosives inside the bomb, they are saying, could end up anywhere in Afghanistan. If they were used in a spectacular attack – like blowing up the provincial governor and ramming the gates of the US embassy – the whole Afghan adventure would risk 'strategic failure'.

And the Taleban, the Afghan NDS intelligence network tell us, are feeling delighted with themselves after ambushing and driving off the British 'tanks'.

There's more news from another *shura* with Mullah Salaam. A mother with a three-month-old child was killed two nights ago, during the small skirmish outside Satellite Station North (where a platoon of Afghan army soldiers is being mentored by a handful of Royal Irish rangers). Now the family has come to the elders of Musa Qal'ah seeking help – there's no baby formula in the town, they say, and a wet nurse cannot be found. The elders tell the British military liaison team that the baby is crying too much, and they will kill it rather than endure the racket. There's a stunned silence. Everyone wonders if this is a sick joke. An urgent request for baby formula is put through to Lashkar Gah.

As I walk away from the meeting a young corporal stops and asks for a light for his cigarette. 'When you get out here – the reasons for being here get all blurred. We have to ask ourselves "Would that woman be dead if we were not here?" And "Who are we to impose our way of life on a people whose culture has not changed for 3,000 years?"' He draws in a long deep lungful of air. 'Still, when you get into a firefight and the adrenalin starts pumping it's like no other drug in the world could compete. You feel like you're running slowly but in fact are sprinting like an Olympic athlete. So in the end, it's just about having fun.

'Move fast and stay low', he adds, tossing his fag into an empty ammunition tin, and wanders off – whistling.

Early the next morning 'B' Company of 2 SCOTS are up, again, in their Mastiffs, and 'D' Company of the Argylls, or 5 SCOTS as they don't like to be known, are crammed into the backs to provide dismounted troops. The plan is to drive straight back down the wadi taking the same route they did the day before, and 'advance to contact' – head straight to a fight – with the Taleban. The Argylls will then jump out of the back of the trucks, overrun the Taleban positions, and secure the missing bombs. The engineers will come in and blow them up – there's no sign yet of the bomb-disposal experts. So ordinary engineers, who have at least been trained to get rid of unexploded ordnance, are now expected to destroy the bombs. Apparently there's a technical safety requirement to be 1,000 metres from these things when they go off. The British and Americans are going to be only 200 metres from the detonation.

'You'll not be getting out of those trucks anyway, sir,' Corporal Scott Cox, the commander of one of the Mastiffs, tells Lieutenant Jim Adamson. 'Not, that is, if ya' want to live that long. The fucking Taleban are going to light us up like fucking Christmas trees.'

'We'll see, we'll see. Let's see if they can handle an attack from us Jocks, eh?' says Adamson, without conviction. He's heard the overnight stories of the Napoleonic volleys of RPGs. Charging into well-prepared positions across open ground isn't how he wants to spend his morning, he thinks, as they head back down the wadi.

Adamson can't see much of what is going on. 'Contact Left! Contact Left!' the top gunner in the turret cries out. Rockets are again slamming into the sides of the Mastiffs and roaring overhead. The top gunner with the .50 calibre gets a stoppage. Lance Corporal Jamie McCleary jumps up to give a hand. The gunner is struggling with the gun – and tears the whole firing mechanism clean out of the gun's belly as if he was gutting a chicken. The handle and firing mechanism hang uselessly in his hand. He giggles and smiles wide – 'What can ya' say except "fuck this for a game of soldiers". This is fucking pish, boss,' he laughs. Grabbing his Minimi, the Jimpy's little brother, he slots it into the turret and starts firing into the puffs of RPG smoke and the dust kicked up by Taleban machine guns about 600 metres away to the east.

With his ears straining against the noise outside, Adamson is anxiously listening for the order to wrench open the doors of the trucks and charge the Taleban positions. 'I fucking hope it doesn't happen. It fucking better not happen,' he is saying inside his head. To his men, though, he is brimming with enthusiasm and laughing encouragement. When, finally, he gets word that a full-frontal assault against well dug-in positions is off the cards, he can resist temptation no longer and, grabbing a Jimpy, pops open the escape hatch at the back of his wagon, and begins spraying bullets into the Taleban lines.

The 2/7th US Marines are part of the convoy that's getting splashed with rockets. He sees three rockets slam into the side of the Armadillo, which doesn't have bar armour. 'Christ. I don't think they'll last long in there.' There's a sudden *whoosh* close to his head and he twists to watch a rocket explode 25 metres behind him. 'What the fuck?'

The rocket came from the west, from the opposite side of the wadi. The Mastiffs are now being enfiladed from both sides. Then an onrushing train howl of mortars wipes out any thought. Turret gunners are sprayed with gravel. The American Armadillo's front two wheels are shredded. Adamson's Mastiff races forward with four others to encircle the US marines in their truck, and their lightly armoured Humvees. Three Americans have been wounded, one in the foot, another in the guts, and one has a cut hand.

Corporal Scott Cox, the commander of Adamson's wagon, clambers out into the mayhem of screaming men and mortars. His driver backs up to the stricken Armadillo. It has a built-in solid double tow bar. Cox attaches it to the Mastiff. Mortar bombs are landing all around. There's yelling and Adamson can hear almost nothing but the sound of his own gun, which he's using to try to hit the mortar crews. They seem invisible but are somewhere to the west. His platoon sergeant, Billy Carnegie, has got out of his vehicle to help move the injured Americans to safety in the Mastiffs. The Marine on the stretcher appears to have wet himself. A dark stain spreads across his hips and crotch and soaks into his tan-coloured camouflage uniform. But it's not urine, it's blood. He's got a bandage on his stomach and has been given morphine. He's making his stretcher crew giggle as they sprint through the flying rubble because he's saying 'I love you guys. I just love you guys,' in a Californian stoner's drawl.

The Armadillo's tow bar snaps after about 15 metres and flops uselessly into the dry river bed. Scott Cox is out again. He runs through explosions down the length of the Mastiff to get the rope which he has coiled on the front of his own vehicle. Bullets are making *ping* and *tink* sounds off the sides of his truck – he's between his wagon and the enemy who have spotted him. He uncoils the thick ship's rope, gathers it quickly into his arms, and charges towards the Armadillo. The ground at his feet seems to foam with the tiny explosions of dust from bullets. He ties the Armadillo to the back of the Mastiff, leaps back in and gives the order to move.

The Jocks can see the blackened and relieved faces of the Americans in the back of the truck. In the front seat the driver and commander mouth their thanks and give a thumbs up.

'Wankers. Wankers,' the Jocks respond. 'This is quality. We've got better kit than the Yanks. That's a fucking first – and probably last,' they say as the Mastiff effortlessly drags the 22-tonne American truck, ploughing a two-foot deep furrow up the wadi all the way back to the District Centre.

As the Marines limp in with a Humvee also in tow, Jamie Dougal is grinning like a cat. Men come up to him and slap him on the back. 'Nice one mate. Saw that. Confirmed kill. Nice one.' He's got his own back for yesterday. He'd shot a Taleban at around 700 metres with his sniper rifle and seen him collapse motionless to the ground.

But, the unexploded bombs are still there.

6

GYPSIES

The hard black plastic flap of a door slaps open. A pair of blondish filthy spectres emerge out of the hard light into the air-conditioned cool of the operations tent. Both matted creatures have white grins. The taller one wraps a long arm around Captain Mike Nett (not his real name), hooking him in close and, like a lover, puts its lips to Nett's ear. With Eartha Kitt relish it tells him: 'I've-been-shitting-in-a-plastic-bag.'

Then it crushes him to its chest in a bear hug. Nett's breath is forced out of him with a *huuugh* sound. He staggers back spluttering, and retches.

'Christ! Fuck. Oh God. Yeeuck. You fucking stink, Rachel!'

Corporal Rachel Worthington (a pseudonym), and her team mate Staff Sergeant Sam Black (also a pseudonym), are part of an informal elite. You find them in small silent clumps waiting for lifts on helicopters, snoring, slumped back against their webbing, their helmets cradled in their laps, their heads back and mouths wide open. Their hair spikes out in all directions, glued with filth. You can see their skin through their worn-out trousers; their faces are caked with old dry dirt and burned to leather. Their shirts are soaked in salt. They are the gypsies of Helmand.

Much like the indigenous *kuchi* desert nomads you come across in their apparently random black-tented camps scattered around the desert, no one knows much about them – they're not part of a major tribe or even a well-known clan. They come, do their mysterious thing, and then vanish back into the dust. They're never around long enough to make friends. When they have to stay overnight they're nodded towards a few broken cots that collect the dust which blows in through the flapping sides of a listing 'transit tent'. Without them hundreds of British soldiers would be dead.

There are very few IEDD teams in the whole of Helmand, an area of 58,584 square kilometres, almost twice the size of Belgium. Taleban bombs are hidden in the shale of the river bed, under bridges, paths, in ditches, at the bottom of flights of stairs, at the corner of buildings – anywhere a foreign soldier might tread, kneel or sit. Every time a device is found an IEDD team is sent to get rid of it. It takes around three years to train an Ammunition Technical Officer (ATO), or Ammunition Technician as the non-commissioned officers are known. We know them as bomb-disposal experts – they're the people you see in movies battling the wits of the terrorists who've booby-trapped the booby traps that trigger bombs. In Britain they've had to deal with the work of the Irish Republican Army, in Iraq with Hezbollah and Iranian-trained experts who build radio- or mobile phone-triggered bombs that can tear a tank to pieces.

In Helmand their enemy is less sophisticated but brilliantly ingenious. Bombs are fashioned from homemade explosive – a mixture of aluminium and other stuff which looks like coal dust, artillery shells, and mortars. They are hidden in sandbags or crammed into pressure cookers. Some are simple – a Taleban bomber hides behind a wall or in a tree, waits for a soldier to get close and pulls a string to set it off. Others are detonated with remote-control buttons from a car's locking system or a cell phone. Most, probably, are what are known as PPIEDs – Pressure Pad Improvised Explosive Devices – which are Victim-Operated Explosive Devices. Two boards with electrical contacts, which are kept apart by nothing more than soft foam, are connected to a hidden battery and the bomb. When someone treads on or drives over the boards, they are squashed together, an electrical circuit is completed and the device goes off. On a road the bomb might be a metre or two from the pad, so that when it detonates it doesn't just blow up under the engine but under the cabin – killing as many people as possible. They can be linked in a daisy chain of devices; many have anti-lifting triggers intended to catch anyone trying to dismantle them, or extra triggers, fake batteries – any number of tricks to try to make sure that the ATO taking that lonely walk out to disable a bomb is doing so for the last time.

Rachel, Sam and Nett's reunion is in the headquarters of Helmand's Joint Forces Explosive and Ordnance Disposal Group. All of the experts who stick their fingers into bombs come from the 11 Explosive Ordnance Disposal Regiment. Divisions of rank are mostly ignored and their wives are all close friends back at their camp near Oxford where – because of the secrecy of their work – they are seldom acknowledged as local heroes. More often teenage hoodies try to pick fights with them or spit on their uniforms. Their work is secret because they can undo years of terrorist planning for a spectacular orgy of bloodshed with a snip of pliers. Sam and Rachel have been out for fifteen days non-stop. They can't remember how many different Fobs they've visited but they do know that over the last three days they've disabled nine bombs. These included a group of five IEDs which were found a five-hour patrol into desert hills, in the midday sun. They discovered two of the five bombs while they were disposing of the other three.

'Good drills, good drills,' says Sergeant Major 'Moxy'. A round-faced ball of a man with a forward-tilting walk and darting movements. He's trained every single soldier, of every NATO nationality, that has passed through Camp Bastion in how to find IEDs. Searching for the hidden bombs is known as Operation Barma, wherever and whenever it happens. Inevitably it's given birth to its own verb 'to barma', past tense barmered, present continuous: barmering. Whoever you are, you will not escape Moxy – day or night, and whatever the weather – he will have you nervously sweeping the ground in front of you with a metal detector, then face down in the sand, gingerly flicking away crumbs of desert until you find what he's laid for you. He uses deactivated real bombs and other bits and pieces he has collected from the IEDD teams in his purpose-built 'Barma Lane' at Bastion. If he thinks you're not taking him seriously, he'll arm the bombs with giant bangers. 'I haven't, yet, got anyone to actually piss themselves,' he says with a chuckle.

Moxy's burned, pale complexion makes him look like he's been boiled and that he's about to burst with anger. In fact he's in a state of almost permagiggle. Not yet qualified to disable bombs, he's a former paratrooper and knows that his teams are kept going, and kept alive, with a constant stream of bad jokes. These have been a mainstay of the bomb-disposal clan since it was created during the Irish Troubles in the 1970s and '80s. Back then the operators, as the people who disable the bombs are known, were anonymous, their faces hidden by masks. Usually the public attention would be drawn to a police or engineer team which was securing the area around a device. 'The lunge' was the one way that the IEDD specialists could have their moment of glory. They had to remain anonymous but they could enjoy some private notoriety inside their own organisation for 'the lunge'. The trick, after taking some piece of killing technology to pieces, was to walk away but make sure that you stay in the frames of press photographers – and then lunge with one leg as if you were stepping over an enormous and unexpected puddle. If you could do so while holding a toolbox, so much the better. If you got your lunge into the papers, you were a hero among your comrades – and you owed the mess a crate of beer.

There's no particular type of individual who is drawn to dealing with ticking bombs. Some are quiet and shy; others big and bold

– none more so than Sergeant Major Gaz O'Donnell. He has the shimmering stage presence of Freddie Mercury, and looks like an overgrown Asterix. He has a pop star's grin and he knows, you know, he knows it. He takes every opportunity he can to get his shirt off. Most people waste away in Helmand. As the weeks go by their eye sockets get bigger and darker, you can see collar bones sticking out of their T-shirts. But not Gaz. When he's not in the field, he's on a sunbed, or in the gym, or crunching fresh fruit and salads in the Camp Bastion cookhouses as if his life depends on it – which in many ways, it does. The result of this combination of ultra-danger and super-healthy living is that Gaz's eyes have a disconcerting shine. He loves the media and the media love him.

Already the holder of a George Medal for extravagant bravery defusing bombs in Iraq, he is rapidly becoming a totemic figure in Helmand. He has no false modesty. He knows what he does is exciting and sexy – that, in part, is why he does it. He chats with visiting journalists in a slow hypnotic Edinburgh burr and is full of easy friendship and jokes. Topless and throbbing with testosterone on his way back from a gym session he stops to talk with a female journalist in Lashkar Gah. His stories told, and the woman gaga and churning with visceral desire, he takes his leave with a brief handshake, walks twenty paces and subtly flexes the muscles across the top of his shoulders making his 'Living the Dream' tattoo jump and shudder.

Mullah Salaam's in Lashkar Gah seeing a doctor arranged by ISAF. He's complained vigorously of pains in his liver, his feet are swollen and a bloated purple colour, and his stomach is rock hard.

But something's gone wrong at the police station. Justin Holt is called to go up the hill to the jail opposite the White House. Tubeh, Mullah Salaam's fifteen-year-old son, whom everyone including the Afghans, calls Tubby, has stirred up a major storm among the British.

A member of the Mullah's militia, whom he insists on calling

'police', has been arrested by the real national police. The militiaman was browsing the bazaar when he came across a stallholder
selling sunglasses. When he was quoted the going rate of the Chinese
designer knockoffs he apparently didn't haggle but beat up the
shopkeeper. Major Naim reported him to the British who insisted
that the militiaman should be arrested. It was important, they said,
to get Mullah Salaam to understand that his men were not above the
law.

Tubby was outraged. Leaving his sisters and three mothers at home,
a plush and heavily guarded villa next to Mullah Salaam's office,
he marched into the jail and ordered the release of his clansman.
The British were not informed but found out later in the day when
they attended the weekly security *shura* and saw both Tubby and his
henchman sitting on the sofas tossing raisins into their mouths.

'There is someone sitting here who should be in jail. He's
committed an offence in illegally releasing a prisoner who was facing
charges for assault in the bazaar. Don't you think that he should be
returned to prison? People can't just release others from prison when
they have no official status,' says Holt to a room full of nodding
turbans. An elderly man with a white beard that looks like spun silk
strokes it thoughtfully then grins with delight. Everyone seems to
agree and so a police lieutenant is summoned to take Tubby and his
friend to the lockup. It's a walk of 15 metres. They pass a cell which
houses a lunatic howling from one barred window. Policemen lounge
in flip-flops drinking tea and tearing off chunks of naan bread. The
lieutenant in charge isn't happy – he starts asking for paperwork, a
charge sheet, witnesses. He is gripped by a desire to be as scrupulous
as possible with the Mullah's son.

An empty cell is being swept out by a junior policeman especially
for the boy. Cocking his head to one side and smirking, he throws
his chin up and attempts a swagger but produces a hip-swinging
mince into the cell. Holt calls for another *shura* of elders in a few
hours.

'This is a delicate case and you should give it careful consideration to decide what to do with Tubby until his father comes back and can exercise his proper authority,' says Holt. There's more nodding and smiling and he's quickly ushered out of the *shura* room.

A couple of hours later he's called back in. 'Sir,' says a very tall elder with a thick black beard, who has managed to fold his legs under him as if he's got an extra joint, 'we have spoken with Tubby. In fact we gave him a good beating and he cried like a baby. He should have learned his lesson.' At the back of the room three men in black turbans nod seriously and mutter to one another under their breath. They have thick, hardened farmer's hands and are younger than most of the others.

Mullah Salaam is due back the next day. What started as an attempt to get a teenager to behave himself is turning into dangerous show-down in which the government authorities, and the Brits, could be caught in the middle of a tribal squabble they would never understand. The beaten and humiliated Tubby is released into house arrest and told to wait for his father.

When Mullah Salaam returns he sets about Holt quickly. Calling him to his office, there is no offer of tea, no biscuits or sweets. No sign of hospitality is shown.

'I am not happy. When you came here I thought that we would work together very well. But you put my son in jail. The PRT [in Lashkar Gah] apologised for this, even senior British Army officers apologised for this,' says Salaam, who is puffing hard and appears to be in some pain.

Holt replies: 'Your son was put in jail because he illegally released another man from prison. That is not acceptable to the security *shura*.'

'You do not have the power to do this. I'm unhappy – my enemies have heard that Mullah Salaam's son is in jail and this has shamed me. When you took him to jail my wives and the children were left without a man in the house, they were crying. The

Taleban – everyone – knows that my son was in the jail and they were laughing at me. You have knocked my turban off. You are here as an adviser not a judge. I would not endure the shame you have brought me if you made me King of Englandstan.

'You must understand that people plotted to put my son in jail to shame me . . . This is a plan by my enemies in Musa Qal'ah and terrorists who want our relationship to fail. That is why they wanted to shame me.

'But we will try to forget this if you can try to make sure that you are only an adviser.'

Holt nods, smiles, and produces several bags of mineral supplements and special teas which his wife, a nutritionist, says will help ease Mullah Salaam's liver and blood pressure complaints.

'Governor – my wife sent these out to you after I described your symptoms and the drugs you were taking here. I hope you don't mind. She sends you the very best wishes for a full recovery and suggests you take this tea twice a day.'

'You are very kind. She is very kind. Please thank her for me,' the mullah says – but nods abruptly and signals with a backhanded flick towards the door that the meeting is over.

Two bombs large enough to flatten a city block and kill everything inside a 200-metre radius are still sitting, unexploded, in a village where highly organised and well-trained Taleban are in charge. They've twice ambushed the SCOTS and, while being raked with heavy weapons from the Mastiffs, they have proved capable of dropping mortars with precision. No one's quite sure why the bombs didn't go off when they were dropped by the jets on Yatimchay.

In the Musa Qal'ah operations room, plans are being quickly drawn up for what could prove to be a ferocious battle to take the village, and get rid of the bombs. This being Afghanistan, though, there are always back channels being worked in secret. So Major Naim, the head of the local Afghan secret police, is trying to do a deal with the Taleban. Communicating through Mullah Salaam and the elders from the security *shura*, who make no secret of their contacts with the Taleban, a message is sent to the enemy: 'Let us come down and disable the bombs without a fight – they pose a danger to both sides and above all to the civilian population.'

After a few hours Holt comes into the operations room and takes Nick Borton, the commanding officer, aside: 'no deal'. Borton has been the battle group commander for five days. Since he arrived his battle group has been ambushed, he's ordered a counter-attack on the Taleban, two bombs have vanished, and now he's going to cancel a night air assault by 'D' Company on a different target and switch the whole plan to overrun Yatimchay. He has to get rid of the unexploded bombs.

At 0100 hours 'D' Company will fly in two Chinooks to a desert landing about 5 kilometres southeast of Yatimchay. They will then hide out in dead ground (out of sight and sound of the village). The Mastiffs will again run the gauntlet down the Musa Qal'ah wadi as a deception to draw Taleban fire, so that 'D' Company can attack from the south, clear through the village to the site of the bombs, and provide security for the IEDD team which will dispose of the troublesome ordnance. Nick Calder, who will lead 'D' company, is blank-faced. He's nodding and jotting down notes as if he is facing a maths test.

Gaz O'Donnell has come with his team, a Conventional Munitions Disposal Team, under Sergeant Chris, and a search team led by Lieutenant Dominic. Gaz has two children by his first marriage and one with his second wife who is due to have another in three weeks. Getting rid of the air-dropped bombs would normally be a job for Chris because it's a conventional weapon; but Gaz has come along in case it's already been booby-trapped by the Taleban, and Dom is there to secure the area and search for other devices which could be planted to trap the disposal teams. 'It's all about layering the risk – our job is to assess the risk and then lower it.'

After Borton has given the orders they sit around having a smoke and a cup of tea. Chris's only real concern is that he's 'going to get bitten by a snake. But so long as the enemy aren't left hanging around it should just be a question of digging down to the bombs, setting our own device to blow it where they are, and then getting away to a safe distance before it all goes up.'

'And if something goes wrong?'

'Then we're all in the kill zone.'

0345 hours. The order comes: 'Company on the move.'

In the back of a Mastiff, which is going to be bait, there's the artillery and forward air controllers. The turret is being manned by a lad known as 'Shakin' Stevens' because although he's deadly calm when firing his .50 calibre, his legs vibrate like tuning forks.

Adamson and his platoon are excited and have hardly slept. Taking off from Fob Edinburgh out to the west in the desert they bunch up, filling the red deckchair-like benches that swing down from the sides of the Chinook. The howling engine makes it impossible to talk. But they're pretty sure that the landing won't be 'hot' – the Taleban won't actually be waiting to cut them to pieces as they charge down the tailgate. Still, once you're in the aircraft that's it – you're stuck and there will be no steady build-up. None of the infanteers' hard-learned sixth sense for danger is any use when you're dumped, disorientated, and the scream of the engines fades to either desolate silence or the sickening swarm noise of bullets.

'D' Company charges out of the backs of its two Chinooks, into a merciful and absolute silence. They can see the straight-edged tops of the compound walls like ruler lines against the moonlight. Women and children have been seen fleeing the village into the desert, they're told; a sure sign that the Taleban are waiting for them, waiting to kill them and trap them in the bewildering mess of identical alleys and ditches which run through Yatimchay. The Jocks' ears are straining for the sound of a rifle being cocked, a safety catch being switched to fire. The landscape, seen through night vision goggles (NVGs), swims in front of them in shades of soupy green, streaked and smeared with a ghostly white when the goggles pick up a light source. Until recently, British NVGs were almost all monocular and soldiers rarely get to train with them – so, robbed of depth perception, they stumble into one another and walk into walls which appear further away.

Calder sends one platoon to the south of the town to clear the compounds along the wadi, another will plough straight through the middle of Yatimchay, and the third in the west will provide support. They go stealthily at first, moving so fast that Calder is afraid they're being dragged into a trap by the Taleban. He radios to Borton to suggest that he's likely to arrive at the site of the unexploded bombs ahead of schedule.

'Bloody hell,' says Borton. 'So much for us in the Mastiffs being the deception. Nick's racing through Yatimchay. Step on it everyone or they'll be left there without support from us.'

He's excited. This is his first battle group operation in Musa Qal'ah. He woke up feeling nauseous. But now the machine is grinding away and he has no time for stomach problems. He's been struggling to communicate with his own headquarters in the Musa Qal'ah DC. As his Mastiff approached Yatimchay he'd prayed that he'd be able to control the battle group and talk to brigade headquarters on his Bowman radio equipment. 'BOWMAN' was known as 'Better Off With Map And Nokia', when it was used in peacetime exercises. In Helmand it was more often known as 'shitcom'.

In February 2007 the House of Commons Committee of Public Accounts said: 'In some areas, most notably the radio provided for the dismounted infantry, the equipment delivered failed to meet the requirements of the users even though it met the requirement in the contract.' In other words no one bothered to ask the infantry, who would be carrying the Bowman, what they needed from a radio system. If they had they would have been told that the very heavy batteries had no visible charge level meter. That when the batteries discharged fully they had to be sent back to the manufacturer for repair. And that the Bowman is less effective in most environments than the sort of walkie-talkies you can buy at Currys for fifty quid.

Today Bowman is failing again. The Mastiffs pull up in the wadi outside Yatimchay. The river bed here is as wide as a motorway. A stream about 10 metres across runs down the east side. There's no sign of the Taleban. The villagers clearly believe there will be a bloodbath and pour out of their compounds – some picking their way over the river west into the desert. The Mastiff top gunners watch them intently through their NVGs. They're dissecting the movements of young men among the refugees – looking for an unusual gait, or a long object which could be a weapon concealed under a blanket thrown over a shoulder. Dickers are spotted on the edge of the desert fizzing back and forth on their motorbikes like warrior ants taking messages to their bosses. But otherwise there is silence.

Nick Calder, communicating with Borton via the Musa Qal'ah headquarters on the artillery network, is approaching the site where the bombs landed. It's about 50 metres east of the wadi's edge, and about a hundred from a farmer's compound. In another ten minutes he declares the area secure. Dom then emerges from the back of a Mastiff with his search team that spreads out with their metal detectors and begins shuffling towards a crater. Calder's infantry, tucked into ditches and lurking behind trees, face out towards the village. They wait for the inevitable whistle of bullets which will signal the Taleban ambush that they are convinced they've walked into.

Gaz, Dom, Chris and the rest of the disposal team appear nonchalant. Nick Borton is watching them from the top of his Mastiff as they get closer to the hole where one of the bombs splashed through the river gravel. A stillness grips the Mastiff company who are watching – horribly anticipating a gigantic explosion which will vaporise the bomb disposal team. Chris now makes the lonely walk up to the crater. He's calm but sweat is cascading down his face. He wishes he could take his helmet off – 'it's not going to save my head if this bastard goes off', he thinks. As he gets closer he sees that the sides of the crater have been excavated – shovels of sandy mud and shale have been dug out – the hole looks like a small mine or a very wide well.

'Fuck me, no. No! They've gone and got to the bomb before we have – it's gone. Oh, Jesus,' he thinks as he looks around himself hopelessly like a man in a car park who can't find his car.

Then he looks closer. There are no drag marks. No one could have got the bomb out of its hole without scraping the sides. The Taleban might have snuck in and dragged it away, but a 2,000lb bomb would leave a trail. There's nothing. Better news too is that the search team can't find any evidence of a second blind drop – there is only one unexploded bomb. 'How the fuck can you not tell the difference between a bomb that goes off and one that doesn't,' Chris thinks as he patrols back to the Mastiffs to get some rope. He cannot see the bottom of the hole and cannot find the bomb. So he is going to drop down the 4 metres into the hole to poke around.

Still no Taleban. Chris returns to the hole and is lowered in: it's deliciously cool in there and a metre deep in water at the bottom. There is a slight dampness in the air and a musty clay smell. If the shooting starts up top, Chris will be safe, he thinks. His daughter is just short of her sixth birthday. He is playing lucky dip in the mud of shingle with a rod and a spade, prodding through the mess looking for the bomb. He figures that since the Taleban, or whoever's been digging for the bomb, have not blown themselves up then he will be reasonably safe. Still, when you're searching through debris like this the only nice surprise is when nothing happens. He finds hard bedrock, but no sign of the bomb.

Now, thigh deep and bent double in a hole where above him the so-called 'war on terror' has raged in earnest for the previous two days, Chris begins to dig at the side of the well wall where the shale is softest. He thinks that perhaps the bomb has squirted sideways. Nothing.

He spends the next five hours looking for a bomb that didn't go off, and now cannot be found. It's nowhere – vanished. No one has got it. It has somehow buried itself under Yatimchay. Gaz O'Donnell, who, although a warrant officer, is the senior expert present and therefore in command of his superiors when it comes to getting rid of bombs, is desperately trying to raise brigade headquarters on his satellite radio. He suggests dropping a missile fired from the Guided Multiple Rocket Launch System down the hole. Through a broken line he manages to get the message that brigade don't like the idea – there's too much room for error. Using Bowman, at a range of about 200 metres, he tries to relay this to Nick Borton. But Borton cannot hear a thing and so, along with his tactical headquarters, including Major Andy Thomson, his artillery battery commander, he clambers out of his Mastiff to get a closer look and talk through the options with Gaz.

Thomson is rolling his eyes – the last time he went on the ground with his CO, David Richmond, his boss was shot through the thigh. Borton has been ordered to stay out of trouble. 'Your instructions are not to get shot,' Mark Carleton-Smith told him when he set off for Musa Qal'ah. It's incredibly hot, as usual. Climbing out of the Mastiff they feel suddenly very short – like someone who's been in the saddle all day and dismounts to find he's no longer eight feet tall. Their legs are stumpy. The first few steps in the gravel of the river bed are wobbly and palsied as the ground slides under their feet. Aside from the low steady growl of the Mastiff engines, there's silence.

'Right – we can't raise brigade and we can't talk to each other on

Bowman so we'll do this the old-fashioned way – face to face and take a decision on the ground.

'Good spot for an ambush this, no?' Borton says to a tolerant smile from Thomson as they stumble over the river bed and up to the hole where the bomb has vanished.

'Right – here's what we'll do. We'll fill it in with a big fucking blast that makes the Taleban believe that we've blown the bloody thing up. Give me a bloody great firework and make sure no one can ever dig this damn thing out. Can you do that Mr. O'Donnell?' says Borton.

Gaz nods, Chris goes back into the hole again, packs plastic explosive into the sides of the hole, and they all take cover behind an earth wall about 200 metres away while the fuse burns. There's a crack. Grey rubble shoots in a cone-shaped jet of smoke into the sky and blooms into a mushroom cloud.

'D' Company are then ordered to walk back to the DC through Yatimchay – and are given lifts in a shuttle of Mastiffs since the Taleban appear to have vanished. Not a shot is fired.

'What an incredible faff. About two hundred men, a night air assault, a deception that used us as bait. The Taleban knew we were coming, they knew where we were going, and they knew we would have to be there for some time. We know this group is well trained, their drills are exceptional. It's great that we got the job done with no casualties. I just can't figure out why the Taleban didn't attack. Perhaps they saw the size of the force and just bailed out. Bizarre,' says Borton later over dinner in the Musa Qal'ah cookhouse.

There's no sign of fresh food but there is tinned fruit. I notice some soldiers are picking out the cubes of pineapple and crescents of peach, and chewing them one by one, slowly. It's the only food that has provided their teeth with any kind of resistance for weeks.

On 8 September, I sat with Gaz O'Donnell at Camp Bastion outside the headquarters of the 11 Explosive Ordnance Disposal. He had his shirt off, as always conscious of his steadily bronzing torso. And we were enjoying a chat about the birth of his son Ben, eight weeks earlier.

'Does him coming along make you want to slow down? Give up the active part of the job and switch into training?' I asked.

'No chance. I would not dare. This is what I do, it's what I am, how I am defined and how I define myself,' he replied.

The son of a middle-class family from Edinburgh, Gaz had played lead guitar in a variety of bands around Scotland and 'enjoyed the weed a little too much during my well-spent youth'. In the army he found an even greater drug and a bigger thrill than being on stage – defusing bombs. He was never afraid. The intensity of the battle of wits between him and the bomb maker, mixed with the knowledge that he saved many hundreds of lives, combined with the fame and gallantry decorations his work brought, proved a narcotic mix. On 10 September it killed him.

Mike Nett, the operations officer, was called to Musa Qal'ah that night. Someone had to take over Gaz's team and finish the clearance of bombs which had been found hidden in the wadi about 6 kilometres from the DC. The team was close to collapse, and close to refusing to go out on the ground.

Losing Gaz had seemed inconceivable – he was indeed like Asterix, indomitable. His legendary bravery, his George Medal in Iraq, meant that he was almost a fictional character – and therefore immortal.

Nett took them all back out to the scene of Gaz's death. He crawled forward to within five metres of the site where his friend had died where another device had been found. He slowly worked the dust from around it to try to find if it was connected to a detonating cord which would lead off into the buildings and shrubbery to his left. He found a battery – then a second battery (one was a dud, meant to mislead the technician into thinking that if he took the one battery away it could not be detonated). He found an anti-tank mine buried about two feet under the ground and began to lift it.

Resistance. There was an anti-lift device under the mine. Maybe that's what killed Gaz.

7

PAYBACK

24 June, Sar Puzeh

Arms are thrown across faces. Men hunch and brace against the hurricane of sand and gravel blasted at them by the departing Chinook. They tuck themselves into small folds in the desert so as not to silhouette themselves against the night sky. The radios are silent. It's 0315 hours. Tracer rounds from a Taleban heavy machine gun chase the disappearing helicopters through the air. The howling of the aircraft engines vanishes and the dust settles around 'C' Company 2 Para. As their hearing returns, the soldiers recognise the *woosh*-bangs from RPGs which have smashed uselessly dozens of yards away to the east.

A road, about 500 metres to their west, draws a thick marker line between the rubble of the desert and the fertile Green Zone. Shown as Route 611 on Afghan maps, the road follows the Helmand River from south to north. The Taleban shooting is coming from the Green Zone in the village of Sar Puzeh.

'This would have been fucking ally [cool] a month or two ago – real bullets being fired at us by real people. Now we just watch them like a firework display,' thinks Des Desmond, who has been put in charge of a section from 9 Platoon, to cover for corporal Paul Lloyd who's been sent back to England for medical treatment (he knelt on a drug user's syringe left in a field).

During the briefings before the operation Des kept a private tally of the numbers of Taleban that are thought to be in the area: 'We know there is going to be massive resistance. Using the Taleban maths there are 250, which really means about 100 of them. And we have a company so we're pretty matched – not great odds,' he thinks as he stares out into the gloom through his NVGs, watching the tracer rounds – white streaks burning across the landscape of the green screen of his eyepiece.

Des doesn't need to be there, but he personally approached Nick Mys and asked to be included in the operation. 'Me and my big fuckin' mouth,' he mutters to himself, and smiles. Two men, Jeff and Jay, were killed while he was acting as 8 Platoon's sergeant. The blind rage and lust for revenge he'd first felt has mutated into something different. Something colder, sharper.

Adam Dawson, 'C' Company's commander, has been waiting anxiously for Joe O'Sullivan, the 2 Para commanding officer, to land. The moment Dawson gets out of the Chinook and tries to communicate on his Bowman he finds it has lost all of its pre-programmed encrypted frequencies. It is useless. He sends runners to link up with his platoon commanders, Murray McMahon and Nick Mys. The company is almost deaf: 80 per cent of the radios have 'dumped their fill' – their memories have been wiped. Dawson guesses that the Electronic Counter Measures on board the Chinooks, used to frustrate missiles fired from the ground, have somehow scrambled the radios' software. Whatever the cause, this is catastrophic.

An assault by air at night relies on speed and surprise. Now darkness is dissolving rapidly – and the Taleban know the British are on the ground. There is no surprise and the British attack is on hold while the company scuttles about trying to restore communications.

There is no way to fix the radios because the company's 'fill gun', a gadget that looks like a big TV remote which reloads the frequencies

into the Bowman sets, has also been wiped clean. Dawson prays that
O'Sullivan will have the equipment. It will soon be light and the
Taleban gunners will quickly become more effective.

Three quarters of all the radios on the second lift in have also
dropped their fill – they are useless. But at least the artillery team
with O'Sullivan have a fill gun, which is run around the whole battle
group to restart the radios – until it also collapses. The battle group
has completely lost the use of more than a quarter of its radios. And
the mucking about has cost the company valuable time – around
thirty minutes. Nick Mys has only one working Bowman radio in
his whole platoon and will have to rely on the short-range Personal
Role Radios, a short-range network usually linking just a platoon,
that each soldier wears to stay in touch with his comrades.

A sudden ugly screech fills the air. Des, Murray, Nick, all of the
little dark lumps scattered across the landscape overlooking Sar
Puzeh, instinctively crunch up. No one can get used to the sound of
a vicious, gleeful, angry, open-mouthed serpent-cum-train charging
out of the sky; anyone who doesn't crouch and tremble for a second
is probably mad. It turns your stomach. Bile shoots into the back of
your throat.

When the rocket explodes a nano-second later, harmlessly a few
hundreds metres away, it goes off with an anti-climactic crash. But
adrenal glands have gone off like a bomb inside every soldier's body.
It makes them shake and feel a delicious, absolute clarity and power
– and snarling rage. They feel like leaping to their feet and using a
machine gun like a hose against the shadows in the village below –
shouting 'Fuck you – you missed.'

But nobody moves.

There has been talk for over a year about a secret operation to take a
gigantic turbine from Kandahar to the hydroelectric power plant at
Kajaki. The plant itself is in government and ISAF hands – although
the frontline is little more than a couple of kilometres from the

turbine hall. The dam was built in the 1970s by the US government and it provides power for all of southern Afghanistan, including the city of Kandahar. Washington and Kabul are determined to double the power station's output by adding another turbine – a housing for it was constructed when the station was first put up. It is a hole waiting to be filled. The Americans and Karzai's government want to show that they can, and will, improve the lives of ordinary Afghans.

Getting a turbine up through the Helmand valley, which the Taleban control, will be seen as a major coup for Karzai. The Americans want to show that the foreign troops, who will deliver it, are a force for good in the country, and that the Taleban offer only a return to pre-industrial darkness. The turbine move will have strategic value at least, as one of the biggest publicity stunts NATO has ever pulled off, and one day it might even be seen as strategic progress in what was turning out to be a bloody year for ISAF.

But to drag the turbine, the transformers and the cranes needed to get the turbine into its cradle at Kajaki, will take hundreds, possibly thousands, of troops. They will be like slow-moving ducks in a fairground shooting alley. As they crawl north, the Taleban will sow mines, IEDs, booby traps and horror along the route. Above all, there is only one known route from Kandahar to Kajaki: the A1 road running west from Kandahar to Gereshk, then due north up the 611 to the dam. The Taleban knows it, everyone knows it. As a consequence many in the British Foreign Office think that moving the turbine will cost too many British lives to be justified.

Some of the British think of the turbine move as General McKiernan's *Fitzcarraldo*. In Werner Herzog's film a fictitious Irishman has a 320-tonne steamship dragged from one Amazon tributary to another, across mud and hills, in order to export rubber, make a fortune, and build an opera house with the profits deep in the jungle. It is a tribute to man's refusal to allow ambition to be undermined by the facts on the ground. Advisers in the Foreign Office believe that the idea of moving the turbine through a war zone belongs firmly in the realms of fantasy. The British want General McKiernan to postpone the turbine move until the Helmand valley is secure. The plan to move the turbine, which could result in a large number of British deaths, is being described by senior British civilian officials as 'totally mad with the potential to destroy domestic public support for our presence in Helmand' – it could be a public relations disaster.

Bizarrely, no one actually gives the British commander an order to plan for how to move the turbine hundreds of kilometres through Taleban country, though he knows that orders might eventually come. In the chaotic command structures of ISAF there is a general assumption that the order has been given. Carleton-Smith decides he'd better begin an intense period of careful planning and prepare himself for a last-minute instruction. So he orders Major Y to draw up a series of plans in Lashkar Gah.

The Major disappears into the brigade's conference room for long periods and emerges exhausted. Three walls of the headquarters conference room are covered in military hieroglyphics. Some of his team's best efforts, when fed into a computer simulation, predict that more than fifty British soldiers will perish if they drive the turbine up the 611. Carleton-Smith and his chief of staff send Major Y back to his white boards. Around the headquarters the turbine move is being dubbed 'Operation Certain Death'.

No NATO force has travelled the full length of the 611 since Mark Carleton-Smith drove it in 2005, three years earlier. Predator, Reaper, and other planes equipped with spy cameras, are being tasked to film the road. Engineers are taking the results, turning them into three-dimensional images, and then working out where the road will need to be repaired, or rebuilt. It will have to carry a convoy of around a hundred vehicles, four of which are likely to weigh over 100 tonnes each. The convoy will move at about 4 kilometres an hour – if it is lucky. But this is guesswork. There is no substitute for 'getting eyes on' – taking a look.

Which is, partly, why 'C' Company and the 2 Para Battle Group headquarters, plus a platoon of Afghan National Army and their Royal Irish mentors, find themselves huddled on a hillside in a notoriously dangerous part of Helmand.

All through June, the brigade's operations have been part of what is called Operation Oqab Talander – Eagle's Thunder. The idea is to capitalise on the operations in May by launching unpredictable attacks on Taleban concentrations up and down the Helmand valley. Isolated British District Centres and Fobs are strung out like a necklace of pearls along the valley. The hope is, one day, to link them into a constant ribbon of territory under Afghan government control.

In fact the Taleban appear to be taking the initiative – forcing British troops to react to their moves. At Garmsir, the Taleban chose not to fight too hard. At the end of May, during their last air assault, 2 Para found that 300 fighters who had been expected to be in the Regay Villages in the southern end of the Musa Qal'ah wadi, chose to hide and watch, rather than fight and die. Then the Taleban struck with the 'successful' suicide attack against 'B' Company at Fob Inkerman which killed three paratroopers. Four days later the insurgents killed another two paratroopers in the slick ambush at Fob Gibraltar. At the same time the Taleban blew up the gates of Kandahar's prison, releasing over 1,000 men, including hundreds of their own fighters. The Islamic insurgents even managed to shoot David Richmond, a British colonel, that day.

Then three days later the Taleban killed three SAS soldiers as well as the first British woman to die in combat in Afghanistan. No one knew how many Taleban had been killed over the last few months – the Americans said they killed 400 at the Snake's Head. But the numbers of Taleban dead were meaningless. The insurgents had driven Helmand onto the front pages of the British newspapers with the total British death toll passing a hundred – ninety-five of whom had been killed since January 2006. In Britain former army officers and political pundits were beginning to question why British troops were fighting, for the third summer running, in Helmand. And ask what was the strategic logic which could justify the deaths and horrific injuries.

This morning, Joe O'Sullivan's battle group has been told to discreetly reconnoitre what appears to be a bridge or culvert which crosses under the 611, just outside the small village of Sar Puzeh – to see if it could bear the weight of a turbine convoy.

Over the previous months American secret agents and Special Forces soldiers have been making overtures to the local tribes in the area, the Alikozai and Barakzai, to try to persuade them to switch sides – or at least stop supporting the Taleban. It was hoped that they might be 'turned', like Mullah Salaam in Musa Qal'ah. But the talks have failed. So now, in addition to inspecting the road, O'Sullivan's 'mission intent' is to take his battle group into Sar Puzeh, along with the ANA and NDS agents, and try to make contact with local elders. The hope is that a show of force will reassure anti-Taleban leaders and frighten others into backing the Karzai government. If the Taleban are around, then they will be destroyed or driven away.

This is another 'hearts and minds' operation, even if it is now hard not to see every boy in a field, or old man taking tea, as a dicker, every 'fighting age male' as an enemy. Joe O'Sullivan, the commander of Battle Group North – the 1,200 soldier unit which includes his own battalion, 2 Para – will have to manage and channel his paratroopers' rage. He has an imposing physique and a brusque manner which sometimes chafes – but no one doubts his competence. For two years before his arrival in Afghanistan he hardened and honed his battle group to prepare them for the ferocity of the fight which he knew lay ahead of them in Helmand.

Platoon commanders had been seen staggering about in a hallucinogenic haze of exhaustion, talking to shrubbery, on exercise. He'd chucked problem after crisis, and piled drama on chaos for them.

He'd made his company commanders refine and rehearse their tactics and battle plans until they felt he was almost bullying them.

But he had known that, when 2 Para hit the ground in the Upper Sangin valley, the battalion was going to be fighting with relentless intensity.

'I am not out to win a popularity contest. I see it as my moral duty to ensure that my battalion is as tough and well prepared as is humanly possible. If that means I don't give everyone a pink fluffy feeling – I'm sorry, but so what?' An enormous man of some six foot four or five, he cannot help look down on most people, literally. A habit, born of shyness, of half-closing his eyelids when he speaks makes his subordinates sometimes feel that he is sizing them up, as a meal. Those who know him well, say he is a 'much nicer man than he realises'.

Five Paras have died under O'Sullivan's command in June. The airborne brigade have lost twelve soldiers since the start of May. The colonel can see and feel the anger and frustration in his troops. Their faces have tightened up, their lips are pursed as if they are preparing to spit. They have been quieter over the last few days, nervous energy burned off in relentless knee jigging and foot tapping. They want payback – they want to get out and kill.

He's shown his own frustration and anger. He's barked at the brigade headquarters down the secure phone line from his operations room in Sangin: he demanded an explanation as to why Jay and Jeff had not been evacuated by helicopter. The brigade headquarters have nicknamed him the 'Gorilla of Sangin' because of his aggressive approach. This morning, his guts are churning. He has diarrhoea.

Mys takes his platoon to the northern edge of the Sar Puzeh to survey the bridge while McMahon and 7 Platoon head for a spot about 100 metres south, just across the 611. It is around four in the morning. The occasional burst of speculative fire is still coming from the Taleban Green Zone; fighters are trying to get the British to shoot back and reveal their locations.

'Dickers!' says Mys over his Personal Role Radio, the platoon's
short-range radio network. 'They're dicking us for sure – if you can
identify anyone watching us and helping the enemy – shoot them.'

Scrambling down towards the village using his NVGs, Des's
breathing sounds like a steam engine. Dickers are trying to make out
the British who are camouflaged against the hill. When they pop out
from behind walls and around corners they looked almost comical
through his green vision goggles – they remind him of characters in
Space Invaders, the video arcade game of his childhood. '*Deh-deh-
deh-deh, deh-deh-deh-deh, dededede, dededede, ddddd.*'

Adam Dawson, the company commander, spots movement in the
door of a mosque on the east side of the 611 road, about 500 metres
away. The building has two prominent minarets. A man emerges
from the building, looks around him for less then a second, and
then casually raises what looks like a pipe to his shoulder. RPG! He
fires. The fat warhead appears as a black lump chased by a bright
light. It sails harmlessly over 'C' Company's heads. Another guy,
possibly the same man, is back in the doorway with another rocket.

'Q, Q, quick, get the sparkle wand on him and tell the Apaches
to get rid of him. Now. Now. Now,' Dawson whispers to Corporal
Quentin 'Q' Daniels, his forward air controller.

Q fumbles for his high-powered laser torch. Invisible to the naked
eye it can point out a target to the aircraft as accurately as putting a
finger on his temple. Q points the torch straight at the middle of the
RPG gunner, who has the weapon on his shoulder. He is scanning
from side to side in the general direction of the British but unable
to pick out a proper target. The gunner is thrown backwards – his
arms and legs fly off, then the farting sound of the Apache cannon
reaches Dawson.

Des leads his section towards the road and across it. He can make
out alleyways and compound walls ahead of him and there is the odd
burst of fire over his head. The reconnaissance of the bridge is over
in less than five minutes. The 'bridge' turns out to be nothing more

than a large culvert which takes rainwater from a wadi under the road. The concrete tube will support a convoy, the engineer decides, and 9 Platoon moves quickly to screen the west. But by the time Des crosses the road and heads into the compounds he feels like his spine is crawling with spiders. He doesn't want to show his section that every cell in his body is telling him that something is wrong, but it is all wrong. The map he is squinting at through his green NVG monoscope is a crisscross puzzle of white stripes. His section moves a few yards south then hit a dead end; they shuffle back to the road, turn right and right again and plunge back right back into another maze of alleyways into the Green Zone.

Up on the higher ground, the Fire Support Group, commanded by WO2 Michael 'Weasel' Williams, silently scrambles south to provide covering fire for the platoons in the village, with Javelin rockets and Jimpy machine guns. The Taleban spot them and shoot at them, over Des's head.

Des sees the group of Taleban on a building to his right: they're blasting away with a machine gun and single-snap shots at Williams and his men. Williams presses on, leading his men to where they can get a better view of the ground below them. The first spills of sunlight from beyond the horizon across the Green Zone are turning the black night sky a deep, unending blue. The stars have been switched off. The sergeant major knows that the Taleban will soon be able to see all of 'C' Company and the advantage of their night vision goggles will be lost. He clambers up a ridgeline which runs east to west, giving him a perfect perspective to the south. As he crests the ridge and takes a stride beyond it, bullets tear up the ground at his feet and drive the men behind him to take cover. Lance Corporal Gary Houldsworth is close to him, also exposed on the Taleban side of the ridge. He immediately dives onto the ground and begins firing back into the gloaming with his SA80 rifle. Williams goes down on one knee and slumps forward.

Gary continues to fire into the Green Zone. He can hear Williams swearing, a good sign. An officer comes charging across to try to pull the sergeant major into cover. Weighed down with a Bowman radio, six litres of water, ammunition, rations and body armour, the officer can't move the wounded Williams. Houldsworth can see him struggling. A small lip of dirt on the slope is giving him protection from the bullets; they sound like swarms of bees around his ears and are kicking dirt into his face. He gets to his feet and charges back up the hill. He can hear the single-shot snaps of rifle rounds whipping past him. An RPG bursts above his head; shards of metal *whuck* into the ground around him; a thick black acrid smudge of smoke wraps around and chokes him. He grabs Williams by the top of his shoulders and digs his heels into the earth and hauls. Using the muscles in his thighs he tears Williams back over the brow of the ridge, into safety on the lee side, away from the bullets. He rips off the sergeant major's shirt and body armour to look for the wound. He finds a small puncture just above the Osprey body armour, 4 centimetres above Williams's right nipple. Turning him over he runs his hands over Williams's torso but can find no exit wound. He rips open a field dressing. A medic crawls forward to them and applies an Asherman Chest Seal, a valve dressing to treat a 'sucking chest wound' and prevent a collapse of the lungs, over the hole.

The medic's hands are slimy with blood. Williams is reported as a 'T1' – a high-priority medical emergency for evacuation.

Then the medic sits back on his heels and looks at Gary. 'Sorry mate. He's gone. He's T4.' The evacuation is called off; there is nothing they can do and no point calling in a helicopter to collect a dead body.

There is a stunned incredulous silence. A sergeant major – a senior non-commissioned officer, the glue that binds an infantry unit together – dead? Impossible. But there he is. The ebullient flat-nosed and round-faced little Welshman, Cardiff City's most devoted fan, dead at forty, and now lying in a dip of desert by the side of the road.

Mys and his platoon have moved about 50 metres into the

compounds of the village on the west side of the 611 to provide
McMahon's platoon with flank protection as they are bounding
south down the main road. But he quickly finds that, with the
Bowman radios mostly down, he risks losing control of his men in
the densely built-up landscape. He orders them back closer to the
road. As he turns around he catches sight of a gunman who pops
into an alleyway just off to his left. Mys shoots him. The gunman
falls forward and slightly to his left, disappearing back into the alley
with only his lower legs sticking out. Someone rushes forward to
drag the body back into the alley and check if he is dead – but Mys
calls him back. There is no time to search the corpse. He can hear
gunfire from what seems like dozens of different places and he needs
to keep his guys on the move.

'Leave him,' he orders. 'Ruby, on me.' He calls his platoon sergeant
Ruby Connor over for a face-to-face chat.

'Listen, you know that when the platoon commander is getting
the first rounds down it's going to get tasty. This is going to be a
major fucking fight and we need to keep everyone sharp. Spread the
word that this is going to get busy.'

Moments after, Des gets back to the edge of the 611 and sees
another Taleban fighter emerge into the road about 50 metres away
from him. Des swings his rifle up into his shoulder and fires a quick
burst. The gunman spins. Des sees his shirt explode out the back
where his rounds have ploughed clean through him. The fighter
flops into a ditch out of sight and is left where he fell.

Less than a year earlier, Tim Duncalfe left the University of East
Anglia with a degree in Modern History and immediately joined
the Territorial Army's 4 Para. As a reservist he could have waited
until he was called up for the war. Instead he passed through basic
training and P Company, the Parachute Regiment's harsh selection
process, volunteered for Afghanistan, and found himself the lead
scout in Des's section as they cross a field to the east of the 611.

Bullets are still flying over their heads towards Williams's fire support group. Most of the shooting is coming from the roof of a compound. Tim spots a man in a dark outfit slip off the back of the building and begin to run towards them. Another section of British troops is about 100 metres southwest, and the insurgent is clearly trying to get into a position to either attack them, or call fire down onto them. Then the man vanishes. And reappears from a hidden ditch about 20 metres in front of Tim. They are both amazed by the sight of one another. Tim – tall, blond, curly headed and middle class, the descendant of the farming community of Shropshire – is now face to face with a Taleban in a green *shalwar kameez*. Tim fires a three-round burst which knocks the man backwards. He lies in the ditch.

Tim is stunned, shocked at the speed of his own reaction, momentarily unable to comprehend what he's just done. Des comes charging up from behind and says he will go forward to search the body because Tim faces an awkward move across the ditch to get to his victim. Des slings his rifle across his back and, because of the cramped conditions, takes out his Sig Sauer 9mm pistol. He approaches the body with the pistol held out in front of him like a New York cop searching a room, and sees that the Taleban has an ornate holster hung across his chest. The Afghan fighter moves his hand suddenly across his body towards it. Des fires three times into his head, spattering the dust behind.

'That's as close as I ever want to get to a fucking pistol duel,' he says.

Des assumes he has killed a commander because he was carrying the unusual holster, and the bandolier was full of bullets, although the Russian-made Makarov pistol had a clip that was half empty. The bandolier is an indication of rank.

'Only a commander would be so cocky as to care more about looking tough than having his weapon properly loaded,' Des says as the section presses on into the maze of compounds. Later on that day, when he hears about Williams's death, Des is convinced he's

killed the man who'd been behind it. 'I reckon he's the cunt who
was dicking and spotting for the gunmen who killed Weasel. We got
fuckin' payback.'

Nick Mys has received the news of Williams's death over the
company net but keeps it from his men. The sergeant major had
been a very popular figure and he doesn't want his paratroopers
to begin the day downhearted. Most of the Taleban shooting is
coming from the south and west and he is now directing Apache
attack helicopters onto the targets. The great black dragonflies
hang overhead threateningly, filling the valley with the sound of
their steady *wack-wack-wack* rotors. On Mys's command they
swoop in low and then stop, appear to rear like a horse, and fire
their cannon.

Mys knows he should not keep Williams's death from Ruby –
that would not be right: Ruby had worked with Williams for years
and they were close friends. So he calls the tall red-headed sergeant
over to him: 'It's Weasel. He's T4. Sorry mate, really sorry. Keep it
to yourself for the time being,' says Mys who, at twenty-four, is six
years younger than the sergeant. Ruby nods briefly. 'Cheers for that,'
he says, looks down briefly, then jogs back to the platoon.

It is now daylight and already the heat is starting to invade the
men's bodies. But the initial bout of killing has fired them up.
Leapfrogging one another as they pound through the compounds,
the Paras giggle as they pass one another, saying: 'Living the fucking
dream mate – living the dream. Get some! This is fucking mental –
fucking the real fucking thing, ay?'

After 9 Platoon have been fighting through the compounds and
Green Zone for about two hours Nick Mys is called to meet up with
Adam Dawson, the company commander, and Murray McMahon
of 7 Platoon. Murray is ordered to take over the clearances through
the Green Zone while Nick crosses the road onto high ground and
into a cluster of compounds on the edge of the desert. McMahon
is excited and desperate to get into the battle. He charges off with

his platoon back the way that Mys has come out of the Green Zone, down a tight little alley with mud walls on both sides.

Mys's snipers, Frank Ward and Steve Lewis, are the first to get to the edge of a compound, about 50 metres up from the main road. Bullets continue to crackle from Taleban positions across an open field to the southwest and another to the northwest. The sniper pair are sitting on an earth bench watching the pyrotechnics as if they were in a municipal park. Bits of the compound wall are flying off. Bullets are hitting all around them with a spitting sound. Des thinks they are going to get shot.

'I don't want you two sat outside here unless you're happy with it,' he says as he ushers the rest of his section through the compound doorway to safety.

'It's fine Des mate – we're fine here,' says Steve.

A flash to their left. There is a bulge in the air. A crackling noise and a rushing sound. Steve and Frank look at each other, then look back to the front. Their heads follow the RPG as it roars past about 10 metres away and explodes to their right. They turn back to one another again.

'Oh-Fuck-In-Hell!' says Frank, and laughs.

Steve is flat on his stomach looking down the 12.5-times magnification sights of his L96A1 rifle. It fires rounds which can kill at 1,200 metres or more. It is the closest military weapon to the sort of firearm used to stalk red deer in the Scottish Highlands, which is where Frank and Steve have done some training. The sudden and unpredictable movements of a wary stag offer snipers the opportunity to test and hone their hunting skills for the time when they will be called on to shoot people. In Scotland, though, they're not allowed to shoot at moving deer, and not at ranges much over 300 metres. 'The stalkers don't want to have to track a wounded animal for miles and miles and put it out of its misery if we fuck up. So they're pretty easy shots – when someone does fuck up though it's awful – the deer is in pain and the sniper is told to fuck off away down the hill and never come back,' says Steve. The penalty for a screw up in Afghanistan is, of course, more severe.

Frank swings left. There is a streak of smoke hanging in the air which leads straight back to three men who are sliding backwards off a wall. Frank opens fire with his Minimi immediately, killing one of the RPG team. The others have ducked before Steve can get a round off. But he chuckles happily without moving his eye from the scope. It is like a cartoon. He can see a hand clutching an RPG warhead emerge above a brown wall and reload the launcher. He is delighted as the launcher bobs along for 20 metres behind the wall and pauses. Then it dips towards Steve. The gunner emerges into Steve's sights with the RPG on his shoulder ready to fire. Steve squeezes when the fighter's face is in the centre of his sights. The rifle punches into his shoulder. He sees the face wobble with the impact. Half of the head vanishes out of the circular frame of his sights. The RPG falls back over the wall and disappears, briefly. Seconds later it is up, bobbing along the wall again. Steve watches it until it stops, and repeats his technique – shooting another Taleban fighter in the face.

'Looked like someone bounced a football off his head, the way it snapped backwards,' Steve says.

Steve and Frank both have had what polite company would describe as 'troubled' younger years.

Frank 'the Yank' Ward, twenty-two, was born in Switzerland to a British father and American mother. As a young child he spent a few years in England before the family settled back in the States, in Spring Lake, Michigan. He'd wanted to be a sniper since he got his first pellet gun for Christmas aged twelve. As he grew up he graduated to bigger weapons at the local shooting ranges. 'I always wanted to be the best, the pinnacle, and that meant being a sniper.'

Powerfully built and, like a lot of snipers who spend months training in camouflage, covert observation and insertion (creeping about unnoticed), Frank is quiet. At fifteen he'd fashioned a branding iron out of some metal he found lying around at home into the word 'WARD'. He heated it in his mother's gas oven. When licks of smoke were curling off and it throbbed red, he pressed it against his left shoulder. The smoke from the burning flesh smelled of roast pork. Then, he heated the iron up and branded his other shoulder. 'I must have kept it on too long or pushed down too hard,' said Frank: the brands don't say 'WARD' or anything else – they're just a mass of scar tissue now.

Frank joined the British Army because he feared he'd lose his British passport if he became an American soldier. He also wanted to do SAS selection. With just two years' service in the Paras behind him, he's young to be a sniper. The Sniper Platoon mostly draws its recruits from more seasoned soldiers. He is the 'number two' in the sniping pair – usually the junior slot – responsible for ranging the targets, working out wind speed, humidity, temperature – anything that can affect the trajectory of a supersonic fragment of metal. Heat, or high altitude, thins the air and will make a bullet fly straighter for longer distances. But if you're using a sight you've zeroed in England at sea level, you're going to shoot over a target in high, hot Afghanistan. A side wind will blow a bullet off course, or far enough off course to miss over 700 or 800 metres. Afghanistan is, in many ways, a sniper's war. Most insurgent attacks are conducted by a dozen men or less who can tie up a whole company and draw helicopters and jet aircraft into the battle. If a sniper can kill or injure two or three, he can immediately drive down the ability of the Taleban to suck energy out of the British.

Steve and Frank are doing what they are trained to do: as they put it, it's their 'job to kill people and there's no other way of saying it really. Of course we're glad when we get a kill – it's what we do.'

There was a time in the British Army when you could join and serve out a full twenty-two-year career and probably not hear a shot, let alone fire one, in anger. There were tours in Northern Ireland to give the experience some edge. The death toll there of 726 British soldiers was spread over thirty-eight years. Northern Ireland claimed a total of around 3,700 lives. But however horrible and dirty the campaign against sectarian terrorism became, it was never a war.

But since Tony Blair's premiership, with his interventions in the Balkans, Sierra Leone, East Timor, and wars in Iraq and Afghanistan, it is a certainty that soldiers will do what they are trained to do – to go to war and kill people. And if you happen to be a sniper, you train harder than most to become very good at taking life.

Steve, twenty-nine, was a dustman near Newcastle for six years before he joined the army. He'd wanted to join at twenty-one but he'd had to wait.

'I'd done some jail time and if you do more than twelve months in the nick then you've got to do a five-year probation period.'

'What were you in for?'

'Burglary.'

'Right.'

'And arson.'

'Arson?'

'Yeah. Innocent.'

'Of course!'

'It was good fun actually working on the bins. Kept me fit. But at twenty-one life was getting a bit grim. I was on the drink constantly . . . I had to wait until I was twenty-three to join – the offence was committed when I was fifteen. A stupid kid really. But once I was in I never looked back. I love it, I love the army. It's a good life. I'm keen as fuck.' He is now married to a policewoman.

Steve shot his first human being early in the tour. He keeps a record. A Taleban sniper was shooting at a British patrol a few kilometres north of Fob Gibraltar. Frank used a range finder and plotted the Taleban sniper at 730 metres. Steve could see him lying on a roof with a Soviet-era Dragunov rifle, which looks like an AK47 with an extra long barrel. Steve shot him in the head. 'There was a bit of disbelief to start with, it was like you say, exhilarating. Yes it was good. I mean the head shots are a bit better, especially when it's close range . . . I'm saying "good", does that mean I'm sick or what? They'd do a lot worse to us if they got hold of us.'

'But it's not the sort of thing you want to boast about – not even to your mates in the army. If you were a civvy and you killed people you would go to jail. We do it because it's the job and we take satisfaction from the fact that we're killing people who are trying to kill us. Even so, like, if you talked about it much people would want to avoid you – they'd think you were weird,' Frank adds.

After spending weeks at war in one another's company, Frank and Steve (who is a vivid redhead and is known as the 'Ginger Nasty') are starting to look quite alike. They both have grown sideburns and Edwardian moustaches which frame their mouths. They have close-cropped hair, powerful noses beneath intense frowns, and crystal blue eyes. They look like birds of prey.

'Come on and fight us. Come out if you have the nerve. You say you're the big fighters – then come on out and prove it. We won't run away. Come and make yourselves martyrs – you feeble little boys and women.' The pitch of the NDS agent's voice is piercing, even without the distortion of a megaphone.

Dawson watches the agent standing in full view of the Taleban about 50 metres away from him – closer to the enemy machine guns and RPGs. Dressed in green combats and wearing a black belt with a pistol hung on it, the agent paces back and forth between broadcasts, clearing his throat, spitting and composing his next stream of insults. The rounded edges of the roof facing the Taleban puff little spurts of brown dust at the agent's feet. Dawson can hear the air crackle around the mad Afghan with his megaphone. RPGs roar past him – some explode in the air above him leaving that black smudge everyone now recognises.

'You shoot like women. You are chickens. You are goats. You aren't proper soldiers, you aren't warriors. You don't dare come and fight us but shoot from miles away – you shoot like women, like children. Are the guns too heavy? Are you getting tired and hungry? Come and fight us like men, come out and fight us, you women.'

Dawson finds himself involuntarily hunching when the rounds look especially close to the NDS agent. He is meeting with Joe O'Sullivan and they can hardly communicate over the din of the shooting. After initially catching the Taleban unprepared the insurgents now seem to be moving back in some kind of order. There are blood trails but no bodies left behind as Dawson and O'Sullivan advance; this means that the Taleban are still able to evacuate their casualties and are probably going to coalesce around a front soon. And at this rate of fire the company will be needing an ammunition re-supply within hours.

'It's not going to be over in a heartbeat, and I doubt at this point there's going to be any outreach and sitting down at a *shura* for tea with the locals,' Dawson says. O'Sullivan agrees.

The colonel has just returned from trying to have a discreet crap behind a wall on the side of the road. He was squatting when a burst of Taleban bullets tore above his head causing him to wobble dangerously backwards.

'There are more dignified exits for a commanding officer than being shot into your own shit,' he'd thought at the time and is still smiling as he returns to Dawson, when there is a burst of fire from their left. Dawson can just make out the smoke of one of 9 Platoon's Jimpies. Lying in the road are two Taleban fighters, in four pieces.

George Ford's been in the paratroopers only since the beginning of the year. He'd finished his basic training and P Company, and was posted to the war in Afghanistan before he'd had the chance to complete his jumps course and get his wings. Dawson, his company commander, and Mys, his platoon commander, are delighted.

'He's only just old enough to buy a drink and get married and he's out here fighting and doing as well as any man twice his age. Fantastic,' says Dawson.

Mys adds: 'Good one Fordie. Keep watching your arcs.'

These men seem almost blasé about killing. They are much older and tougher than they were a month ago, and three hours into a battle that is getting fiercer. They have been running and fighting non-stop since before dawn. The race through the compounds, the sudden fire-fights, the constant incoming bullets and rockets have been driving the precious adrenalin through their veins like a hydraulic pump. There is none of the shakes and panting that goes with the fear and thrill of the first few times that young men try to kill each other.

'This,' Mys says to himself. 'This is proper war.' It's what he'd always wanted.

He breaks into a big compound just to the east of the 611 with very high walls. There are hypodermic needles everywhere.

'Look out lads – make sure you know where you're sitting down or kneeling, there's needles all over,' Mys says over the PRR. A handful of local people stare at him as he approaches the compound. A couple of men stand in a doorway; they look terrible – their skin is drawn tight, their eyes are red-rimmed, yellow, and glazed. 'Junkies! Fucking junkies? I come thousands of miles to fight a war and run into a bunch of junkies!'

The compound is a bit bigger than a tennis court. A carpet about 5 metres by 3 has been rolled out on the grass of the compound. Around it lie pairs of flip-flops and sandals. There are oval-shaped metal plates full of sweets in plastic wrappers and the locally made sugar candy which smells of cardamom. Whoever has been sitting and chatting here, and drinking the tea that is still hot, has run away without their shoes. Great lumps of what look like molasses are wrapped in clear plastic bags. There are dozens of 200-litre drums filled with a brown sludge, bags of chemicals, strange still-like equip-ment. 9 Platoon has found a huge opium-refining laboratory. Earlier in the day, sections reported moving through compounds they said looked like they were full of drugs. There was enough raw material here to refine millions of pounds' worth of heroin.

'Lads – don't interfere with the drug stuff. That's for the local police and the NDS. We're not getting into the drug eradication business. It's strictly off limits to us,' he orders. The Afghan secret police are following up behind the Paras; they will burn the drugs and blow up the laboratories.

Mys's platoon finds drug-refining chemicals and sacks of opium in about four compounds. Sar Puzeh, it turns out, is a major drug-production centre generating tens of millions of dollars' worth of opium and refined heroin. It is no wonder that militia groups are protecting their businesses. The question no one has time to ask is – Who are the British fighting? The Taleban? Drug lords? Both?

McMahon's 7 Platoon are rushing south through the Green Zone on the west of the 611 road. Lance Corporal Tel Byrne, twenty-four and from Blackpool, spots a compound with high walls about 50 metres across open ground. Taleban are on the right, somewhere; rockets and machine-gun bullets are whipping about the platoon.

'Boss, that compound over there – I want to get in there. It will give us mega arcs. We will be able to see right across the Green Zone from there,' Tel says.

McMahon raises his eyebrows. Tel is only a young 'lance Jack', a lance corporal, who has not been in command of a section for long. Now he is volunteering to take his men directly into the enemy's line of fire.

'Okay, we'll give you covering fire,' says McMahon.

Tel and eight men rush across the open ground as most of the platoon's guns are turned in the direction of the Taleban. In Vietnam the Americans called the sudden use of guns, fired in unison into the jungle until their barrels were burning hot, 'three-minute madness'. McMahon's platoon give it about thirty seconds – enough for Tel to get across the open ground and up against the compound wall. As he turns the corner of the building a Taleban fighter pops out from behind a tree. The insurgent raises his AK47 with one hand and fires a burst of rounds which go up the wall between Tel and Corporal Mick McFadyen, another sniper. Tel stares straight back at him and shoots him eight times, killing him instantly. The fighter slumps forward onto the ground, where he will stay for the rest of the day. Tel runs on.

He knows he has to keep his men moving or they could be cut to pieces. There are eight other Taleban, also in the tree line by the compound. They are now running about and looking desperate – some are already wounded. Tel's men shoot them all. They then discover that the entrance to the compound faces directly into the main body of the enemy.

'What's the score there?' asks McMahon over the platoon's radio net.

'I'm getting in the compound. I'm going over the wall.'

It looks about twelve feet high. Private Simon Broth volunteers to go over. He needs both his hands to get a grip on the top of the wall, so he leaves his SA80 rifle and checks his pistol is ready. Two men get under his feet and shove him straight up the side. His fingers dig into the earth of the wall – it feels like scratching a school blackboard. He swings his left leg as hard as he can up, and plummets over – grabbing for his pistol as he falls hard onto his feet and steadies himself against the inside wall. Holding the weapon in front of him he thinks he saw someone disappear out the door. In any case there is a brief haunted silence before Tel lands next to him. They quickly clear the compound but find no Taleban.

They discover a two-storey-high tower used for drying grapes, its walls a lattice of brick and air vents – providing a perfect firing position. 'Right let's get the snipers and gunners up there now. Fantastic arcs,' says Tel – and charges up into the tower. It is a decisive moment.

In 1999, US Marine general Charles C. Krulak wrote of how,

in modern warfare, decisions taken by corporals, the lowest rank of non-commissioned officer, could have strategic consequences: a corporal who ordered troops to open fire on civilians could risk causing public support for a conflict to collapse. Now, in the Green Zone in Afghanistan, it meant that a young corporal (a veteran of two tours of Iraq and one of Northern Ireland) had made a tactically brilliant decision to occupy a compound which helped secure the area for the whole battle group.

McMahon comes up to the wall. 'Christ, I can't believe I sent them over this,' he thinks as he scrambles over it himself. But the risk has been worth it. He sends Corporal Clint Pretorius, a tall thirty-one-year-old South African originally from Durban, to the neighbouring compound – a task which involves another sprint across open ground under fire – and a third section to take over another with arcs straight down south. It is about noon. They have been fighting for more than nine hours. Now they have a location they can defend.

Tel and Mick McFadyen are delighted with their eyrie. They can see Taleban about 350 metres to their west, running back and forth along a tree line, which will certainly be planted along a ditch, giving the enemy a ready-made trench to fight from. Bullets are constantly shooting well over their heads, aimed at the other British groups on the high ground behind. RPG rockets are also roaring past, heading the same way. Tel's Minimi gunner, a Liverpudlian with Chinese roots, Wayne Ho, has joined them in the tower. They nod and grin at one another.

'This is fucking mustard this. Fucking perfect. Nice spot, perfect arcs, bit of shade, bit of ventilation – and none of them know we're here!'

Four Taleban directly in front of Tel's section run out of the tree line. As they emerge Tel can see that they are hiding their rifles and an RPG behind their backs. They are heading out to try and flank where the platoon has recently been – unaware that they are being watched through binoculars and a sniper scope. As always, Taleban fighters seem to know the British rules of engagement – or hope that they do. They assume they will be safe if they have no visible weapon, which is true. They do not realise that since they are armed, have emerged from an enemy position, are advancing on the British, and their comrades are still shooting, they are 'fair game'.

'Mick, let them get a good 100 metres or so, so that they are clear of any cover, and then drop the second one in the line. I'll take the rest,' says Tel.

Mick waits. He picks his target – a man striding across a field of poppy stubble. His scope so magnifies his target he feels that if he reaches out beyond the barrel of his rifle his fingers will feel the insurgent's brown tunic. His white skull cap is traditional among the Pashto peoples of southern Afghanistan. But it is poor camouflage. He has a long-barrelled weapon of some kind on his shoulder. Mick fires. The man flops instantly to the ground as though his bones have melted. Mick knows the fighter is dead. Tel sets his SA80 rifle on rapid fire and sprays the other three – two fall dead and a third scoots off out of his arc – but into Wayne's sights – and is cut down. Then Mick spots another fighter running off to his far right. He is wearing a light blue, almost turquoise, turban and matching *shalwar kameez*, a white undershirt beneath it. Hanging down his side he wears an AK47, with its butt sheared off. Mick fires again. The man falls – but isn't dead.

'Lower body shot,' Mick mutters. 'I bet that fucking hurts.'

The fighter's legs appear to be useless; he is trying to pull himself back towards the cover of the tree line and ditch with his hands, keeping low and using the ploughed soil to hide from Mick – who fires again, and again. Still the man slithers, leaving a thick brush stroke of blood in his wake.

'Don't think he will be much good to anyone, so in that respect – job done,' Mick says.

In the macabre brutal logic of infantry war, it is often better to wound than kill. A dead man is mourned, but he cannot scream or shit himself in fear and pain. But a gut-shot soldier with his entrails hanging out will horrify his comrades; his yells will cut through to their own visceral terror, and four men will be taken out of the battle to get him to where he can be safely treated. Yes. A sniper might not aim to maim – but he knows that it's a 'good thing' when he does.

McMahon soon joins Tel in the tower, where they remain for the rest of the day, alternating the Jimpy and Minimi gunners and shooting at shapes that are picked out along the tree line. No one knows how many more Taleban their platoon kill; but the numbers mount steadily, the bodies lying baking in the sun.

Across the road, 9 Platoon have set themselves up in three little compounds in an area marked 'London' on their maps. The fire support group are further up the side of the hill overlooking the road – and getting most of the incoming fire as a result.

Steve Lewis and Frank Ward are the first into a derelict hut. To get to it they have to sprint about 50 metres across open ground which the Taleban rakes with machine-gun fire. They set off at a slow jog for the first few paces.

Then the bullets started smacking into the ground at their feet in front and behind. 'We fucking took off. I reckon we cleared that 50 metres in about two seconds,' says Steve, panting and laughing.

They dive through the door of the smashed little compound and find they have the protection of four walls, no roof, but one of two small holes which look out over the Green Zone and to the south. Taleban fighters are visible about 300 metres away. The ground falls down a grey shale embankment to a group of three buildings. Steve puts his barrel up to a hole in the wall about 6 inches across. *Snitch!* A bullet spits into the mud an inch or two from the hole. A Taleban sniper, and a good one at that, has spotted them. Frank and Steve scour the landscape below for any

sign of a gun being fired – most often the Taleban give themselves
away with the blue-grey smoke from oil burned in the barrels of
their weapons. There is nothing.

Through the rest of that day Steve shoots another five people.
Frank 'gets a few' with his Minimi. And the Taleban sniper keeps up
his work. He fires at anyone passing the window on the wall which
faces his way. The British soldiers inside react like kids baiting a
poisonous snake with a stick – the thrill of being shot at and missed
makes them giggle with relief when they dive past the window and
the bullet flicks past them.

'You either love it or hate it!' says Steve, laughing at Des Desmond
who's almost got a bullet in his brain.

Adam Dawson and Joe O'Sullivan set up their field headquarters
between 7 and 9 Platoons on the 611 road itself. One or two local
people, including a doctor who runs a pharmacy, peers out at them
from behind the steel shutters which protect the local shops lining
the road. Vegetables are piled high in wooden trays. The officers
look longingly at peppers, onions and tomatoes, football-sized
cabbages, water melons and green pyramids of limes. Dawson's 'C'
Company have not had any fresh food for weeks. Paratroopers who
live on a diet of red meat and carbohydrates when in Britain are
now craving the crunch of a fresh lettuce leaf. Food talk has replaced
pornographic reveries back at Fob Gib, where Britain's shock troops
torment each other with recipes for stir-fried crab in oyster sauce,
garnished with lemon grass, bamboo shoots and water chestnuts.
Anything that gives resistance to teeth, anything you can actually
chew, anything that isn't the reddish-brown pasta-based pulpy mess
that they've been living on.

There isn't any chance for them to enjoy the fruits of Helmand.
The Taleban are continuing to attack with a dogged ferocity that
means they are continuing to die. The tree line opposite 7 Platoon is
strafed again and again by American fighter jets, and then pounded
with artillery. Nick Mys sees eight insurgents run into a compound

south of him, and drops 105mm artillery shells on them, smashing the building to rubble and dust. An hour later another eight armed men take up positions in the mess the bombs have left behind. Mys gives a repeat of his fire orders to the gunners, who pound the remains of the building with the men inside it.

The Apaches are firing everything they have on board. Their 30mm cannon and Hellfire missiles tear into buildings and the FL-7 rockets, which fire flechette darts, attack men hiding in trees and crossing open ground. The battle group is killing relentlessly. From the British point of view it is turning out to be a 'great day'. By mid-afternoon the Taleban attacks begin to subside.

O'Sullivan decides that there is little point in trying to cross the Green Zone to the west: the aim of disrupting the Taleban has been achieved and there is clearly no chance of political dialogue. The mid-afternoon resupply of ammunition and water, which has also taken Sergeant Major Williams's body back to Camp Bastion, has exposed how vulnerable Chinooks can be to Taleban fire. When it came in to land every gun in the valley seemed to have been turned on it. It had pulled away, jinked hard in the air, and then landed very quickly inside a compound with its rotors barely clearing the surrounding walls. And this had all been achieved courtesy of a section of Royal Irish Rangers who secured the landing site by brazenly enduring Taleban machine-gun fire.

The intense resistance of the Taleban in this drug-rich area tells O'Sullivan that more re-supplies will be essential. But this means that the Chinook will have to land actually inside the Green Zone – with an unjustifiably high risk of being shot down. Furthermore, O'Sullivan doesn't have enough troops. He's been evenly matched in numbers for a day. But if he stays on for longer the Taleban could easily call more men in from the north and south and might fix his own forces where they are – forcing them into a long defensive fight. Or he could push on south and recce another bridge or culvert – but he knows his troops are exhausted.

Late in the afternoon O'Sullivan decides to call on the Chinooks to pick them up. He identifies a new landing site east in the desert. But the RAF prefers to land close to where they had dropped 2 Para that morning.

The battle group first tries to take a new track into the desert to reach the landing site in the north, but it quickly becomes clear that the quad bike can't get across the endless ridges and wadis, leaving O'Sullivan little choice but to order a march straight back north up the 611 for 2 kilometres.

Mys's platoon is screening the western edge of the track. Ruby Connor is the last man in the whole battle group.

'I'm hating this. This is fucking shit. I'm hating this,' he says to himself as he stares out into the thick foliage and blank compound walls to his left, convinced that Taleban gunmen will ambush the company when it is at its most vulnerable. Everyone is exhausted. They have been in a constant fight for seventeen hours. Had their tab along the road not been so dangerous, and their adrenal glands not squeezed a last few drips of the precious stimulation for fight or flight, Ruby is sure the men would be starting to collapse. They scour their flanks and breathe in short shallow gasps, waiting for the first shots and a terrible, terrible ambush.

Dawson is anxious too. This extraction is entirely against the military grain. They are going back over their own routes, and back to a landing site the enemy has already identified as a target. Why would the Taleban let them get away with this? He turns off into the desert with Mys's platoon following, pestering the young lieutenant almost constantly. 'Last man off the road yet? Last man off the road?'

Ruby makes the right turn and walks backwards into the desert, still convinced the Taleban will attack. The village is silent.

The Taleban, or drugs militia, are silent. The daring tab back up the 611 has caught them off balance and they leave 'C' Company to sit and sleep in the desert for three hours before helicopters come to collect them. The estimates of the numbers of Taleban dead vary between thirty and seventy, perhaps more. 2 Para have lost another soldier, but have taken revenge for all their dead that June.

8

WHAT GOES AROUND COMES AROUND

24 June, Fob Gibraltar

At first glance there's nothing about Captain Josh Jones that would
justify his nickname in Fob Gibraltar. 'C' Company's second in
command could have been a model for the Action Man doll. He's
very tall, he's dark, and classically good looking. He has cobalt blue
eyes, a broad chest, a triangular torso, and muscular thighs. But
when he pads from the operations room down to the 'desert rose'
urinals dressed, as always, in nothing more than a pair of blue swim-
ming shorts, the penny drops.

He has the camel-like gait of Jar Jar Binks – the clumsy gangling
part Rasta-cum-amphibian *Star Wars* hero. Nick Mys, the 9 Platoon
commander, chips in libellously. He claims that when he borrowed
Jones's car in Colchester 'he had a teach yourself Klingon CD still
in the player'. And so Jones is known as 'Jar Jar'. He denies learning
Klingon – the CD is part of an audio-book box-set version of the
Star Wars film trilogy, which seems odd enough.

'Actually I have been having Arabic classes. I'm more likely to
come across someone who speaks Arabic than Klingon. But come to
think of it, Klingon does sound cool. Maybe we'll have it as a family
language,' says Jones who refuses to wear shoes inside the Fob. 'Too

hot. I grew up barefoot in the Solomon Islands and the Australian outback. Bare feet are healthier.'

He's been a dustman, and a topless 'tequila boy' for celebrity parties around Europe with a leather apron and shot glasses to pour booze down the throats of braying women. To pay his way through law school he played bass guitar in a rock band that toured Europe. But the moment he qualified as a barrister, he joined the Parachute Regiment. And was the champion student on his P Company Parachute Regiment selection course.

'I saw the law offices and ran. I had to answer that call which brings us all out to places like this.'

His black Edwardian 'bugger's grips' sideburns are flourishing – three months into the tour he has become the spitting image of Harry Flashman. He even waxes the ends of his moustache into turned-up hooks.

While the rest of 'C' Company are north on Operation Talander at Sar Puzeh, Jones is left in charge of the Fob. He has what remains of 8 Platoon and a handful of medics, cooks and engineers to guard the outpost against attack. About 500 metres south, a platoon of Afghan National Army is being mentored by about eight Royal Irish soldiers. Their compound is known as the Witch's Hat.

Fob Gibraltar feels abandoned. The sangars on its corners are manned day and night, along with the operations room. Everywhere else is empty – anyone not on guard is lying in their cots, soaked in sweat, and dozing. In the hour before dawn, the heat in the air eases to around 35 degrees centigrade. Someone has tidied up the tea brewing area and put a fresh strip of blue paper towel down the middle of the long table where officers and NCOs usually gather to swap cigarettes and stories. The hot water urn is making a whispering sound as it starts to heat a new drum of water. The steady *thrum* of generators has been ignored so long it is unheard. A low doorway with a curtain for a screen opens into a mud-walled chamber about 3 metres wide and 5 metres long, with a high arched roof designed to draw some of the hot air up.

Jones is sitting in his blue shorts monitoring the company radio network and trying to work out what is happening to his friends up in Sar Puzeh. His legs are jiggling independently under the home-made wooden table while he works on his laptop computer. His legs stop moving.

He recognises Sergeant Major Michael Williams's zap number (an emergency individual code for use in reporting a casualty over the radio). He's relieved – at least Williams is T1 – wounded but needing urgent treatment and evacuation. Seconds later Jones exhales as though someone has squeezed all the air out of his thorax. He stares at the wall in front of him. Correction. A T4 casualty, not an emergency. Williams is dead.

A dismal paranoia descends on Fob Gibraltar. Williams was a sergeant major, the second they had lost in as many weeks. Was this a 'Jonah Fob' – jinxed?

The Taleban have been circling. They have been coming, unarmed, close to the Fob and making eye contact with the British sentries. Some smile, creepily. Mostly with the 'I'm looking forward to killing you' stink eye. The operations room has logged a steady increase in Taleban interest since the end of the poppy and wheat harvest at the beginning of June – which coincided with the Taleban defeat in the Snake's Head. The day after the suicide bombing of three paratroopers at Inkerman, two RPGs were fired into Fob Gibraltar, and a day after that a suicide bomber killed himself, but failed to kill anyone from 'C' Company out on patrol.

On 12 June, the Taleban had killed Jay and Jeff in an ambush. Eight days later an Afghan Army patrol out of the Witch's Hat was blown up by an IED, which partly detonated and caused minor injuries. Two days later the Taleban began to prowl around the Fob. There had been a steady rise in what the army calls 'Fighting Age Males' (FAMs) and 'Unknown Males' (UKMs) moving in groups. Some had even been seen patrolling much like their British enemies: spaced and walking in a line. And when a Russian-built freight helicopter flew into the Fob with supplies, they dropped to one knee. The group's leader went down the line talking to each of his men and looking towards the Fob. This was blatantly a reconnaissance and ground familiarisation tour by the local Taleban. They knew they would not be shot at if they were unarmed. The British soldiers sneered at them – but knew that an attack was coming.

On Saturday morning clusters of young men in dark clothing were spotted standing on three roofs about 500m to the northeast of the Fob. One was using binoculars to watch as the huge white Russian 'Hip' helicopter came clattering over the base to land. Another man was standing in a doorway, also watching, and speaking into a mobile phone, or walkie-talkie. When the helicopter took off two rockets streaked towards it from a hidden location about 800m north of the Fob, to the right of where the man had been standing. The rockets soared passed the aircraft and exploded harmlessly. Then on Sunday a man on a motorbike, who matched the description of a suicide bomber which had been sent out by intelligence agents in nearby Gereshk, crossed the bridge over a canal outside the Fob and drove past slowly.

Two different radio intercepts say that the Taleban are massing as many as seventy-five men to attack Fob Gibraltar, and plan to ambush a civilian convoy of trucks. In the afternoon gravel trucks which have left Fob Gibraltar are hit by a roadside bomb about 1.5 kilometres south of the Fob on the way to Fob Keenan.

At 0915 hours on the Monday morning, while the rest of 'C' Company are locked in their battle in the north, the 'Hip' arrives again. A small team off-load it while the rest of the Fob is ordered onto the walls to protect it. It disappears east across the desert, low and fast, climbing high to avoid surface-to-air missiles. Jones gets another message; another Russian helicopter is on its way. It lands at 0940 hours. There is a 'faff' – a chaotic unloading of the unexpected helicopter. It comes in heavily laden with engineering supplies. It is on the ground too long – ten minutes is plenty of time for the Taleban to organise someone to shoot it down.

A sentry looks north towards the top end of the Hammer's Handle and sees two Fighting Age Males. They are close to the building that was used by dickers the day before, when the helicopter was rocketed. One is watching the Fob through binoculars. The dickers are tucked under a tree, crouching in undergrowth. The sentry asks another soldier, who is manning a Jimpy, to take a look through his binoculars. The howl of the helicopter's engines behind them gets louder and more highly pitched – as it prepares to take off. Dust and small stones bulge in clouds away from it.

'Seen. Two males, one with binoculars. One in brown dishdash. Someone get me a range on that,' the machine gunner replies – another private goes to get a laser range finder. The two dickers are 535 metres away. 'Can I fire warning shots and scare them off?'

'Go ahead.'

The team can't see any other locals near the dickers. The machine gunner fires a burst to the left of the two men. The bullets kick up dust next to them; they get up lazily and wander away. A few seconds later they saunter back into vision and continue to watch the helicopter through binoculars as it takes off. Another burst is fired. This time the Taleban disappear. The helicopter takes off.

Half an hour later, Jones, who hasn't slept for twenty-four hours, gets a call from 'Amber 34', the Royal Irish mentor in the Witch's Hat. The Irish captain tells him there is a man standing at the gates of the Afghan Army camp: his wife has been shot in the chest and his daughter, about twelve, has been killed. A nasty crowd is building up outside and there is severe tension inside the camp between the Irish and their Afghan comrades. The Royal Irish captain is going to bring the family up to Fob Gib for treatment along with the senior Afghan officer.

'Jesus!' Jones pulls on his trousers, webbing and body armour, grabs his weapon and runs down to the gate.

The Afghan Army captain is shaking with rage. He seems to be having difficulty breathing. 'No respect! No respect!' he's saying with a snarl. The wounded woman is put on a stretcher and rushed up to the medical centre. Her brother goes with her.

'Don't touch her. Don't touch her,' he yells at the medics who are moving to pull back her blood-soaked shirt to get at the wound.

'If we can't touch her we can't make her better. We must, we must lift her shirt to treat her wound – she might die.'

The brother turns away in shame. He is shaking too. Jones calls a helicopter to evacuate her. At the gate the ANA officer and the woman's husband are waiting.

'You are killing our people! You are here to help the civilians but you are killing them. You have no respect. British soldiers have no respect,' the Afghan officer says in a cold voice.

Jones is stunned. 'We will investigate. We will look into who is behind the shooting. But for now we have to make sure that the mother survives, whoever shot her, that is our duty and we are glad to be helping.

'The Afghan army and the British must stay together. We must not argue. You understand this, we are allies – the Taleban want us to argue and have misunderstandings. We are going to do all that we can to help this family. We are not going to let them down. If we shot their daughter then we will have an investigation. There will be ways we can help the family,' Jones insists.

The Afghan officer claims that the Royal Irish mentors have not shown the wounded woman proper respect. When their medic treated her he'd cut through her shirt and exposed bare flesh. This is a big insult to the Afghan forces. 'We are living with the community and have friends, we're making friends, this has brought great shame on us.'

Jones is puzzled. The Afghan officer seems more angry than the man who has just had his wife and daughter shot – possibly by someone in the Fob. Jones turns to the husband – he knows he has to acknowledge that the British have fired and that it is therefore possible that a British soldier has killed his daughter. He knows that in the local culture he has to keep the honour of the British in the face of local custom. If there is an error, then the British would and should offer compensation.

The man, who appears to be in his fifties but is probably no more than thirty-five, is distraught. He speaks in short, clipped, dignified sentences, but tears roll down his face.

The Jimpy is a favourite infantry weapon. Now, it seems, it has been a liability: its rounds have torn into an Afghan family, who must have been somewhere behind the dickers.

'May I see your daughter?' Jones asks. He knows he will be asked by army investigators if he has confirmed the death. He also wants to pay his respects.

'It's the least I can do – come face to face with what he says we've done,' Jones thinks as he walks through the gate out to a white saloon car which is parked in view of one of the sangars, where British sentries are watching it down the sights of another machine gun.

Josh Jones's wife is a couple of months away from having their first child. He loves the uncomplicated joy of young children. Now, he is afraid. Afraid of what his soldiers might have done – and afraid of how he might react when confronted with a badly mutilated child. 'She might have half her head missing – stay focussed,' he mutters to himself, in a sort of prayer. The father opens the car's boot.

A black-haired child lies on top of the spare wheel. She appears to be sleeping serenely. There is a neat round hole in her right temple.

'Thank God,' thinks Jones. 'She has not been torn up by the bullet.'

'Please accept that we would never want this to happen. That if we did this it is an accident because the Taleban are in your village. We are here to help – not to kill children.'

The father nods – and they agree that he will return the next day, once he's buried the child, to discuss how he can apply for compensation. 'It is not your fault. It is the war,' the father says.

It is harder to get the ANA officer to calm down. He seems on the verge of changing sides – angrier than the father has been. But he agrees to return to the Witch's Hat, and leave the compensation negotiations to the British.

Jones walks back across the gravel and up the ramp past the Royal Marine and Paratroop Regiment's memorial. He turns right to go back to the radio room. He can understand that the Afghan officer is furious – he has a right to be. But the officer's resentment seemed to run deeper.

'Cake,' Jones thinks. The last time he'd seen this rage which verged on hate in the eyes of this officer – it had been over cake. He could hardly recall the details. Sometime, in the middle of May, Fob Gibraltar had taken delivery of about a dozen aluminium catering trays loaded with dry-looking pale brown sponge cake. The cooks had no idea why it had been sent, and no one wanted to eat it – so it was shoved into a refrigerated container, and forgotten. No one thought to contact the logistics headquarters in Camp Bastion to explain the cake. It was just cake.

But relations between the British mentors and the Afghan Army down in the Witch's Hat had become strained. The Afghans appeared reluctant to patrol: they were sulky and uncommunicative. The officers and senior NCOs looked at the ground and shrugged with surly indifference when they were addressed by an increasingly baffled group of Royal Irish infantry

'You've been stealing our food,' the Afghans finally snapped. 'We cannot trust the British – you have been stealing our food.' They were close to open revolt. The mentors had no idea what they were talking about – all rations were separate and anyway they had been giving the Afghans goodies from their own food parcels.

The ANA compound sits at the southern edge of the Witch's Hat, a cone-shaped cluster of compounds which juts into the Green Zone from the desert. Across the dirt road, which leads into the desert, a mud hut with an awning serves as a small shop selling cigarettes, batteries and biscuits. The Afghan Army compound over-looks a graveyard to its west and open fields to the north.

Supplies for the Afghan soldiers come very rarely. They seldom, if ever, get paid. The Royal Irish were living in three small rooms with the typical vaulted ceilings of the region. But everyone ate better in the Witch's Hat than the paratroopers in the Fob. They could buy local produce at the shop – and the British baked their own bread in an oven they made out of an old ammunition box.

'Our chain of command has told us they have delivered our cake but you have not passed it on to us. You have taken our cake.' This was weird – what were they on about?

The Royal Irish got on the radio to Fob Gibraltar: 'Have you seen any cake? The ANA wants cake.'

'Cake? Cake . . . ' Jones remembered. There were stacks of what looked like Victoria sponge in the container at the back of the cook-house. 'Must be Afghan Army cake!' An ANA patrol was invited to collect the cake and tensions eased – a bit.

More recently the Afghan platoon commander, a captain, and his platoon sergeant had got into a fight and drawn knives on one another. The mentors discovered that the squabble had been over the affections of a young Afghan soldier in the platoon whom they each wanted to use as a catamite. The platoon sergeant had won, and his officer's credibility with the rest of his men was blown.

Jones had quite enjoyed the many jokes about the cake but the trouble caused by the catamite had revealed deep problems with this unit of government soldiers. Now, with a dead child on the British conscience, he senses a darkness settling further over Fob Gibraltar, even as the sun reaches its breath-choking zenith and the mercury climbs past 50 degrees centigrade. He is getting radio messages that there is intense resentment of the British among the Afghan troops.

By mid-afternoon a crowd of about fifty – mostly men, farmers brandishing their hoes and spades – is gathering outside the ANA camp. The crowd tell the Afghan soldiers to abandon the British so that the Witch's Hat can be overrun, and the British slaughtered. The ANA sergeant is joining in with the demands that the government troops walk out of the Fob and leave the British to the mob. The mentors quickly pack and radio Jones to tell him that they are facing a mutiny inside their camp, and a hostile crowd outside. He immediately orders a doubling of the guard.

They can see armed men begin to mix in with the mob; others are handing out weapons. Jones orders eight men to form a Quick Reaction Force, in case the British mentors need to be reinforced, or rescued.

The Afghan sergeant and several of his men cock their weapons and point them at the British. Two of the Royal Irish mentors guarding the walls spot a pair of armed men in the crowd. They are giving orders and yelling for British blood. One opens fire on the camp – and both are shot dead. The civilians in the crowd scatter across the road. Some gunmen jump into pickups which race away past Fob Gibraltar. Others scatter into the buildings by the Witch's Hat compound – they've lost the human shield of civilians which has allowed them to get close to the ANA. The Royal Irish mentors put a heavy rate of fire into the Taleban firing points, just 50 metres away, and seize this moment to break out of the ANA camp.

At exactly the same time Taleban gunmen who had left the Witch's Hat earlier now attack Fob Gibraltar from the north.

The Quick Reaction Force crash out through their own gates and take up positions on either side of an iron bridge, which crosses a deep and fast flowing canal on the road down to the Witch's Hat, to give the Royal Irish some protection.

'Get anyone who can shoot a weapon onto the north wall. I want those firing points smashed,' Jones tells the guard commander.

The noise of the attack and the responses from the British are overwhelming. Medics, store men and signallers line up along the north wall looking out towards the Hammer's Handle. Bullet casings from rifles and the .50 calibre pour onto the floor of the earth rampart making it slick with brass. Taleban firing points are getting hard to spot through the smoke and dust. There is s a patch of open ground for about 50 metres, including the track leading into the Hammer's Handle, then a wall and beyond it more open ground in front of a cluster of high-walled compounds. A Taleban gunman can fire a burst, move location in a second, fire another burst, and make the British think there are dozens of insurgents out there. Outside the gates two Wimik Land Rovers fire their .50 calibre machine guns north up the road.

The Royal Irish turn up in what seems like just a few seconds. They are shattered and have the haunted, lost look of betrayal. Only one Afghan soldier has remained loyal – and he has come up to the Fob with them. When the Taleban opened fire down at the Witch's Hat, some Afghan soldiers had walked out of their camp; others simply watched the British fight. Only one tried to protect them.

Now, the Irish are safe from the troops they have been training. Jones is amazed by how quickly the Taleban have been able to exploit the killing of the twelve-year-old girl. They have infiltrated the crowd and reinforced their attack on the Fob, which is now thick with the dust and smoke kicked up by British guns. But the Fob is still under attack. Taleban rockets smash into its thick Hesco walls, and there are the explosive shudders of what seem to be Taleban mortars.

A private is part of the Quick Reaction Force which ushered the Royal Irish in. He is driving a Wimik which has a Javelin missile in the back. Realising that the machine guns are having trouble stopping the heavy wall of fire coming in from the Taleban, he tears up to the wall in the Wimik. He jumps on his brakes outside the Fob's welfare hut, just behind two other soldiers who are also rushing to the north wall, and loads the 30kg Javelin onto his back and races up to the walls to set it up.

A Taleban machine gunner has found his mark. His bullets are kicking up spurts of dirt and tearing the top edges of sandbags. The

British are being forced to keep their heads down – which is stopping them from shooting back effectively.

The machine gunner who'd sparked the incident by accidentally killing the child, walks into the operations room – he has bad bruising on his legs and backside. 'I've just been run over. I've been run over in the middle of a fucking firefight!' he says. He is led to the medical centre, next to the north wall where the private is setting up his Javelin.

The private spots the source of the machine-gun fire. The rocket leaps out of its tube and seems to shoot off far too high, pauses like a bird of prey hanging above its victim, and then dives onto the target. The private ignores the bullets. Peering through his Command Launch Unit (CLU) he can see two more machine gunners hidden behind a rise in the ground and camouflaged by shrubbery. The CLU's thermal imaging picks them out – they show up as psychedelic ghosts on his monitor, their gun barrels fire-red. Using the video-game controls which drive the Javelin, he puts a pair of brackets around one of the gunmen on his screen, which tells the Javelin's onboard computer to lock onto the target inside the brackets. The rockets are 'fire-and-forget': they track their target with an infra-red sensor in the nose cone, even if it moves. He pushes the firing button – out leaps the rocket. It seems too slow to fly at first, then it arcs quickly into the sky before doing another sudden dive. The Americans, who built the Javelin, call this sort of Javelin flight 'the curveball'. It is designed to slam into the turret, the weakest point, on a tank.

It explodes with a crack and flash of orange; a human being is turned into burned vapour. Cheers ring out across the north wall and British machine gunners turn up the volume on their own guns. The private fires a third rocket and the torrent of Taleban bullets falls to a sporadic trickle.

Six Taleban have been killed and another ten wounded in one day around Fob Gibraltar. But whatever the numbers of enemy killed, nothing can compensate for the collapse of the mentoring team, and a near mutiny by their Afghan trainees. If the Afghan Army had turned on them the British would have been massacred. Such a disaster would have caused an outcry in Britain and demanded an answer to the troubling question of why British soldiers are fighting and dying so far from home.

Lieutenant Colonel Ed Freely, the Royal Irish commanding officer, moved quickly to get the Afghan *kandak* commander into Fob Gib and on to the Witch's Hat first thing the following morning. He was escorted down by some of the Royal Irish mentors and a section of paratroopers. The troublesome sergeant was removed from his post and then the whole Afghan platoon was told it would be returning to Shorbak, the main ANA base next to Camp Bastion. There it will be broken up and its men dispersed into other units to prevent them stirring up trouble again. The Royal Irish mentors are also replaced – with a section of paratroopers loaned from Fob Gibraltar on a monthly rotation.

Jones is reeling: 'In the morning we lost Sgt Major Williams, his death hit everyone for a six. Then we may have killed a girl and shot her mother. And that is the first time that has happened in the AO [area of operations]. So we're the first Fob to kill a civvy. Then we have a fucking mutiny in the ANA Compound. Then we become the first Fob that has been proper fully attacked in the campaign. And then obviously blokes have been fighting for their lives out up in Talander. What the fuck can happen next?'

The machine gunner got an apology from the private who ran him over. But he wasn't listening – he thought he had accidentally killed a child. He was silent for days.

The brigade headquarters in Lashkar Gah maintains the clinical and unhurried air of good-natured competence, which it has gone to some trouble to cultivate. In the secret operations room, which occupies the walled-off left-hand corner of the headquarters building, real-time video-link black and white images of the fighting play out on flat TV screens on the walls. Sometimes you can see British troops and their Taleban enemies in the same frame. As images are piped into the ops room, small clusters of officers gather, clutching cups of coffee. Out in some far-flung corner of Helmand a Taleban leader's car explodes when hit by a Hellfire missile – there is a white flash on the screen: the car, which is now missing its roof, rolls on for 50 metres with dead and wounded fighters tumbling off the sides and back. The ground splashes, as if someone has thrown nails at the dust: an Apache is firing its 30mm cannon at gunmen running for cover. They vanish in a cloud of smoke.

Both sides look like children playing hide-and-seek. They scamper back and forth, creeping along walls, and crouch in ditches, waiting to give each other a fright. On other screens chatroom conversations in multi-coloured fonts reduce the details of a death or battle to a few bloodless military codes on J-chat:

'Zeus. Hotel 22 contact SAF, RPG.'

'Rgr.'

'EF grid 876445678864 PID 12 pax.'

'Rgr.'

'Request AH suppress grid 876445678864.'

'Rgr wait out' . . .

This translates as:

[Soldier:] 'Headquarters this is H22 . We're in a fight.'

[HQ:] 'Okay.'

[Soldier:] 'We've seen twelve Taleban at grid reference 87644678864.'

[HQ:] 'Okay.'

[Soldier:] 'Please send a helicopter to kill them.'

[HQ:] 'Okay – hang on.'

It is impossible to comprehend the heat, fear, hunger, hate, chaos, noise and horror of combat from the headquarters. Two army captains, men in their mid-twenties, monitor and run the moment-by-moment decisions which control the fighting. These battle captains sit at the centre of the blinking screens, live feeds from spy planes and drones, and ranks of telephones, parcelling out the small numbers of attack or rescue helicopters and artillery. They take decisions on which groups of men who are fighting in a world of dust and smoke will get help, and how much.

They carry the burden of watching their comrades fight, kill, and die through a virtual-reality filter of LED screens and text messaging. They work in twelve-hour shifts and when they escape the ops room it is only to sleep, eat, or pound around the track which runs inside the perimeter wall of the Lashkar Gah compound. Running and the gym is what stops people going mad in 'Lashkatraz'. Men and women grimly drive themselves to masochistic heights of self-flagellation on rowing machines. Their faces flush puce, their necks varicose, eyes bulge red, and salivary puke hardens white against their lips in the terrible heat. Then they shower and go back into the air-conditioned professional murmur of the headquarters, having briefly forgotten the guilt, and jealousy, that goes with not being on the front line.

June had been a terrible month. The J-chat screens flashed constantly with reports of TICs (Troops in Contact). The summer was known to be the fighting season. Road resupplies to the Fobs were getting more and more dangerous; convoys were getting blown up every time they drove north or south from Camp Bastion.

In May, Mark Carleton-Smith had predicted that the Taleban would try to 'fix us in bases and restrict movement and then pick us off with landmines'. That is exactly what had been happening. And with the access only to a handful of helicopters to use in surprise attacks, which had to be booked weeks in advance, Carleton-Smith was losing the ability to take the initiative away from the insurgents.

Many of the Taleban's leaders had fought against a far larger

Russian army in Afghanistan. The Soviet Union had sent a whole division into Helmand (more than 12,000 men) compared to the British who were fielding around 5,000.

'The people who've got their targeting squared away are the opposition – they've had more than twelve months to study our patterns,' Carleton-Smith told his senior officers in Lashkar Gah.

If the brigade was going to be doing little more than holding ground, or 'mowing the grass', then he wanted it to think hard about what it was doing, and what the consequences might be. From a moral and a political perspective.

'Our focus should be on limiting the tactical liability. We must ask ourselves "What do we achieve when we go out and risk young men's lives?" If we suffer casualties for no great effect here, there could be a very great effect on the home front back in the UK. Families will be shattered – and public support for what we are trying to achieve could fall.'

On 24 June, the Taleban, or a drugs militia, had chosen to stand and fight 'C' Company of 2 Para. Reinforcements heading for that battle were put in a three-point snap ambush when they came across 'B' Company on a patrol further south – forcing a two-hour fire-fight close to Fob Inkerman. The Taleban had exploited the killing of the child at Fob Gibraltar and nearly provoked a lynching of British troops by their Afghan allies.

June was supposed to be the month when the British stirred up the enemy, forced it onto the back foot, and weakened it for a final major offensive by the whole brigade in July or August. Instead there was now a steady stream of intelligence from the Afghan secret police and army that the Taleban were infiltrating Marjah – 15 kilo-metres southwest of the provincial capital, Lashkar Gah.

Privately, American officials and senior officers were becoming critical of the British effort in Helmand which, to them, appeared to be stalling. The Americans were tiring of the British telling them that they were experts at anti-guerrilla warfare because of their years fighting insurgencies in Malaya, Kenya, and Northern Ireland.

This frustration eventually boiled over in Kabul, where the US ambassador, Bill Wood, lost his cool during a discussion with Sir Sherard Cowper-Coles – the British envoy. Sir Sherard had referred to Malaya as a success.

'Sure – but you only won in Malaya through dumb luck,' Wood shot back.

The next day he wrote an apologetic note to Her Majesty's representative. But by then the gossip had already reached Lashkar Gah. But perhaps the ambassador had a point.

'We should guard very carefully against the assumption that because we're British we know all there is to know about this sort of warfare. It's not in our DNA and Helmand isn't Northern Ireland,' said Carleton-Smith.

But now he needed to grab the initiative away from the Taleban and to prove to the Americans that the British were not letting the Taleban run amok.

In Fob Gib, Josh Jones waits for the return of the rest of the company. He can hear the exhaustion in the voices over the radio he's been monitoring. He knows they will need cheering up – so he's got his wife to buy them a paddling pool on eBay.

'C' Company love the pool and get used to the pace of operations, which continue relentlessly, though closer to the Fob. Until in July, a patrol providing security for a bomb-disposal team to get rid of a device which has been planted on the road to the Witch's Hat is attacked at the main gate.

Pete Cowton, twenty-five, is killed five days after Operation Talander after he takes cover during a Taleban ambush about a thousand metres from Fob Gibraltar and stands or sits on a bomb hidden in a ditch.

Jason Rawston, twenty-three, takes cover during another ambush less than 400 metres from the Fob and is killed instantly on 12 September. He is shot in the head by a stray round from a Taleban machine gunner firing blindly through thick maize.

These deaths, combined with other casualties, Jones calculates at the end of the tour, mean that one in three members of 'C' Company who have been deployed to Fob Gibraltar on the ground have been killed or injured – a staggering statistic. The area under government influence around the Fob has not increased at all because, no matter how many firefights 2 Para wins, there are no troops available to hold the ground that is gained. This apparent futility has little effect on the troops though.

'We're bred to fight. It's what we do and what makes us tick,' says Adam Ireland – who never sleeps in his own bed but uses the cots left by men from his platoon who are on leave. He never explained why.

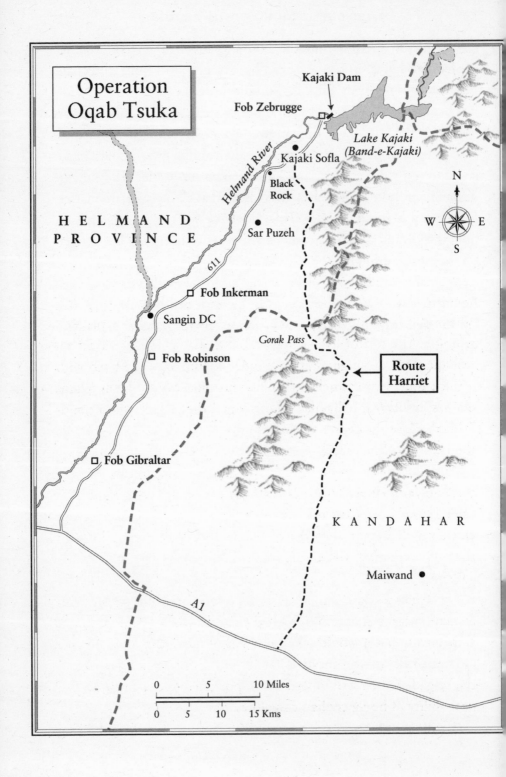

Operation Oqab Tsuka

Kajaki Dam

Fob Zebrugge

Lake Kajaki
(Band-e-Kajaki)

Helmand River

Kajaki Sofla

Black Rock

H E L M A N D
P R O V I N C E

Sar Puzeh

611

Fob Inkerman

Sangin DC

Gorak Pass

Fob Robinson

Route Harriet

Fob Gibraltar

K A N D A H A R

Maiwand

A1

| 0 | 5 | 10 Miles |

| 0 | 5 | 10 | 15 Kms |

N
W · E
S

9

EAGLES DARE

The brigadier is taking short notes; his handwriting is like type. He's sitting at the top of a U-shaped table in Joe O'Sullivan's 2 Para headquarters in Sangin. Purpose built in June out of Hesco with a thick roof, it still smells of freshly cut pine wood. A tall, plain-clothes, military intelligence officer with a thick black beard stands at the back of the room. Outside, running parallel to the building, the Helmand River races with silvery cool along a canal.

'Sir, we can try again and we will, but the bottom line is that, through both direct and indirect talks, we've drawn a blank. We can't buy our way up the Upper Sangin valley. The leaders and elders say they appreciate the offer but if we try to come through their territory then we'll be attacked.'

'Right.'

No one had said it would be easy. No one here was saying, with any enthusiasm, that it even looked possible. Mark Carleton-Smith is then told that it would take hundreds of men, that it would take days, a week, maybe more. That it would draw resources out of the brigade which would weaken important Fobs. That there is a probability of heavy civilian casualties.

'Right. Gentlemen . . . The Americans are coming! We risk being put in the corner, sidelined and forgotten. The Americans think we're wet and present only problems.

'I am not here to listen to how a mission is not possible. I want you all to take on board that it is our job to carry out the tasks we are set – not go on about how we can't do things. I want a complete refocus on finding solutions not problems. Find them.'

There is a short silence while this is absorbed. Exactly a week earlier Carleton-Smith had been showing frustration of a different sort. In Lashkar Gah he'd organised a war game using the plans, drawn up by Major Y and his team, to get the power plant turbine from Kandahar to Kajaki. The 3 July simulation had produced estimates that taking the turbine up the 611 road to the Kajaki dam could cost fifty lives and more wounded. The hundred-truck convoy would have four vehicles weighing over 100 tonnes each. There were 120 known points which would need engineering works, including sixty-seven culverts which would have to be rebuilt to carry the enormous weights. This would add up to a minimum of seventy-two hours of engineering work – most of which could be expected to be under Taleban fire.

The route north from Fob Robinson has the greatest density of IEDs anywhere in Afghanistan; it would take seventy-five hours to clear through the 'VPs', vulnerable points, where bombs were likely to have been hidden. This part of the journey would take the convoy past thirteen known narcotics processing plants, some of which were huge. There would be heavy fighting around these – 2 Para had just shown that on Op Talander at Sar Puzeh.

'We can pick a fight in the Upper Sangin valley. The question is why? Which fight do we pick? And what for? I still haven't seen an order that tells us to do this [move the turbine]. But if it comes we better be ready,' Carleton-Smith concludes.

In the week between the two meetings he has managed to divine that the enthusiasm for moving the turbine, immediately, is coming from the US ambassador, Bill Wood. The British ambassador, Sir

Sherard Cowper-Coles, and Hugh Powell, the newly arrived head of the British civilian mission in Lashkar Gah, are dead set against moving the turbine at this time. They see no point in risking British lives to take the machinery up the Helmand valley when the operation could be postponed until the road is secure. The idea of asking British soldiers to die fighting their way up the 611 is a political and moral horror for the diplomats.

'What would the consequences be for the families of the men killed on such an operation? And what would the justification be to the British people?' Powell asked his colleagues and military planners.

But Ambassador Wood, unaware of the high British casualty estimates, wasn't interested in British equivocation. He did think that the British were wet. Until recently American officials and military officers had been rather awestruck by the British Army. Its regular infantry units often beat American Special Forces groups in military endurance competitions. The sheer weight of martial tradition and pomp in an army which pre-dated America was intimidating. But since the British had been elbowed aside by the Iraqi Army, and their American advisers, in taking Basra back from Shi'a militants in March, and since British troops had been forced to negotiate a retreat from Musa Qal'ah in the face of a relentless Taleban onslaught in the summer of 2006, Britain's martial reputation had been badly damaged. Many American officers continued to admire the fighting energies of the ordinary, and badly equipped, British soldier. But they questioned the commitment of the British government to the Afghan war and therefore wondered what the point of having the British in charge of Helmand was – if the British force there was not resourced for victory.

Wood told Sir Sherard that the British objections to the turbine move showed prevarication and obstruction. He wanted it done, and done now. Sir Sherard hoped to pacify him with alternative proposals which could show demonstrable progress in Helmand. But the chances were that if the American said 'Do it', it would have to be done.

Carleton-Smith knew this. If the order to move the turbine came through, he would not be thanked for turning around and saying that it could not be done, or that the British Army wasn't prepared to take the job on. So in Sangin he issues his terse instructions.

Not only is the turbine move likely to mean that a lot of British troops will die – but he is under increasing pressure from Helmand's Governor Mangal, and the Afghan Army, to concentrate his forces on fighting in the south of Helmand. He is being pulled in at least two directions. He takes himself off for a swim in the icy waters of the canal at Sangin.

Jumping off a bridge overlooking the orchards – which had been on the front line in 2006 when the Paras were last in the town – he lets the current sweep him downstream. The cold water soaks up the accumulated heat and tension of the previous four months. Being picked up and carried is a delicious moment of surrender to the laws of physics. Just for a few moments he is not trying to direct and determine events. He can go with the flow, literally. He catches hold of a rope that dangles off a footbridge 50 metres downstream (if he'd missed he would have been swept into Taleban-held territory). And in one ape-like movement he swings his whole body onto the crossing.

Padding back upstream across the gravel for another go, he tells a friend: 'Most of my life here is spent fighting friendly forces – sometimes the Taleban seem almost incidental.'

Tom Neathway loves it. He's a bit jealous of the guys from 'C' Company at Fob Gibraltar: he's heard that they're getting into a lot of fights. Most of his fighting has been at long range on this tour. Still, he's happy. This is what he joined the army for – 'proper war fighting'. This morning the Afghan National Army is going to push forward while Tom and the rest of a British platoon sit hidden in a compound. If the Taleban attack the government troops, the British will 'smash them with everything we've got'.

Dan 'Brad' Bradley searches the compound thoroughly with his metal detector. The cluster of mud-walled buildings has been used by the British before: it would be an obvious target for booby traps.

'All clear,' he calls.

Two Jimpy gunners get onto a bamboo roof and set up their guns looking north. Tom walks towards a low hole cut in the wall which will give him good arcs for his sniper rifle. He can't get the rifle into position on its bipod because a sandbag is partially blocking the hole. He bends down to move it.

His legs are whipped backwards from under him. He's hit by the blast as if he's been rugby-tackled, head on.

'That's it. I've lost my fucking legs for sure,' he thinks as he flies through the air and flops to the ground. His left arm is hurting. He can wiggle his fingers. Good news. Turning his face sideways he sees Brad standing close by.

'Hey, mate – help me up can you?'

Brad stares back – his mouth is hanging open.

'Jan! Jaaaan! Jan!'

Lance Corporal Jan Fourie, the South African medic, comes charging over.

A foot. In a boot. Swirling in a white cloud. Major Joe Fossey sees the boot and sprints down an alley between two compound walls and bursts through a hole in a wall. He stops. Empty brass bullet casings are flowing in a golden stream down a wall on the far side from two British Jimpy gunners who have found Taleban targets. To their left is a hole in the wall. Under the hole is a crater about a metre wide. Next to it is a white and red mess of a man.

A medic is bent over the body. Jan Fourie's hands are scarlet against the ash-white coating of dust from the bomb. They are moving frantically, twisting the tension strap on tourniquets to stop Tom's blood from pumping into the sand. Two other soldiers are staring. Their faces are vaudeville-white masks; their eyes are wide and rimmed with red; their lips looks like bloody injuries against their waxen faces. Fossey can see they're in a bad state of combat shock as he runs forward to help with the torn man lying in the monochrome dust.

Tom, a sniper with 2 Para's Patrols Platoon, is lying face down. He is twenty-four. Both his legs are missing and so is most of his left arm, which is held on by rubbery white tendon strings. Joe snatches the tourniquet he wears on the front of his body armour and fits it to Tom's thigh. They roll him onto his back.

Tom slips his right hand into the front of his trousers. 'Thank fuck for that – I've still got a cock,' he thinks.

'Jan – check my cock's alright will you? I don't want to live if I haven't got a cock.'

Jan, an Afrikaner with an accent so thick Tom is one of the few in the platoon who can always understand him, has a quick look.

'No, my china. Your cock's fine.'

'I can't feel my legs,' Tom says.

'You're fine Tom – *lekker*,' says Jan.

Tom doesn't feel pain. He can hear that they are still under fire.

Two other soldiers help pick Tom up and they carry him to a quad bike which has been brought up to evacuate him back to a safer area. They can't strap the stretcher onto the back of the bike properly. So Jan follows behind – keeping his hand on his friend's body to stop him bouncing off into the dirt. The bike gets stuck against a tree. Tom can hear bullets whipping past. Jan stays with him.

Tom's mangled arm keeps sliding off and flopping around behind the quad bike. 'Fucking hell Jan – can you pick up my arm for me?' Jan puts it back across Tom's chest and when Tom grabs his left hand in his right, it's cold. It feels like it belongs to someone else.

Fossey goes back to the compound. One of Tom's body-armour plates has been blown off and is lying in the crater. What it's made of, and what bullets it can withstand, is a military secret, so it can't be left for the Taleban. It would take too long to clear a safe route to it. Fossey makes a bomb out of a ball of plastic explosive and a fuse. He tosses it onto the plate, backhand, like a French boules player. It lands dead centre. He walks away to take cover behind a wall. Thump. The compound shakes with the explosion.

They are about 2 kilometres from the Kajaki Dam and Fob Zebrugge, the British base there, which is run by 'X' Company of 2 Para. The compound was supposed to be an observation post, but the Taleban obviously saw the holes which have been cut for machine gunners and snipers before and booby-trapped the firing point which Tom selected for his sniper rifle.

The patrol had hoped to disrupt the Taleban around two villages, Bagar Kheyl and Machi Kheyl, either side of a wadi which drains into the Helmand south of the dam. The sortie was part of a relentless process in which British influence extends only as far as the soldiers can walk and fight – which is no more than 2 kilometres. Beyond that the river valley and desert is dominated by the Taleban. Insurgents have sown the route to the dam with bombs and mines. The defence of the Kajaki dam is a military ping-pong match and Tom is the latest British casualty. But he's not the last; not today.

Major Joe Fossey had taken over 9 Parachute Squadron of 23 Royal Engineers (Air Assault) a couple of weeks before the Sangin meeting with Mark Carleton-Smith. When the brigadier told his staff to find solutions, Fossey had moved quickly. He had felt an icy challenge from Carleton-Smith. He'd come up to Kajaki to see for himself what would need to be done to the road to squeeze the turbine into the cramped base which defends the dam against the Taleban. He knew that if the turbine was going to be moved then his squadron would be in the vanguard. He would be building the road and fixing the bridges, while the rest of the hundred or so trucks came along behind him.

On 20 and 21 July he'd inspected the route a couple of kilometres south down to the front line. Each time he was caught in a firefight with the Taleban. But he'd managed to measure the width of the road. He established that the southernmost British defences, a Hesco bunker, would have to be pulled down to get the trucks carrying the turbine along the narrow cornice, which runs along the base of a steep 1,000-metre escarpment to the ridge above.

Today he's chosen to go out on patrol because he has been stuck at the dam waiting for a helicopter. An extra engineer is always welcome – and his own men will respect him for sharing their burden. He knows he can't show he's as shaken as they are by what has happened to Tom. He picks his way carefully – placing his boots in the prints left by those in front – downhill towards the rendezvous point. It's best to follow the tyre tracks of the quad carrying Tom. Sometimes the wheel marks disappear on hard ground – that's when his foot hangs in the air while he chooses where to put it down. He walks with the exaggerated deliberation of a drunk.

Tom's blood has dried on Joe's hands. It's mixed into a paste under his fingernails. He can smell it evaporating off the front of his trousers and body armour. He feels heavy and sick. The black cloud of a headache looms in the back of his skull. They've been on the ground for hours. It's the middle of the afternoon and the air is so hot it's hard to breathe. Tom is carried, unconscious, into the Chinook. Fossey doesn't believe he'll live. He turns his face away from the dust blast at takeoff, and wonders if Tom would even want to survive.

Tom, the man with the schoolboy face, dies.

Twice. And twice his heart is restarted on the helicopter before it reaches Camp Bastion. Drained white by blood loss, and with both legs left in the dust somewhere northwest of Kajaki, Tom is rushed into intensive care from the helicopter which lands yards from the doors of the Camp Bastion hospital. His heart stops again in Bastion, and twice more under surgery in the UK. Somehow he does survive.[3]

---

3 Tom Neathway lost both legs and his left arm. Eight months later he was skiing and sky diving.

About five wagons have turned up: some of the new Jackal mine-proof trucks, and the Vector ambulance to carry the two combat-shock victims back to Kajaki. The sun is sliding into the horizon. It's about an hour to sunset, but there's no easing of the heat. Corporal Jason Barnes is driving the Vector ambulance. A Royal Electrical and Mechanical Engineer armourer by trade, he's squeezed into the truck behind the steering wheel. He's got about an inch of head clearance. He feels like he's in an armoured kiln. The two combat-shock victims are being treated by the doctor in the back. Behind the Vector is the quad with a trailer. Fossey's group are following on foot. The adrenalin from the fighting and the bomb blast has subsided. Now everyone feels like fish left flapping on a beach. They have a long walk back to the Kajaki base – downhill and then by the northern banks of the river along what they call the coast road. They know they are being watched by the Taleban. Four of the 7-tonne Jackals take the lead; the lighter vehicles like the Vector are at the back.

Jason's Vector rears. It crashes down with its nose skewed left across the track. Fossey falls, curls up like a baby in the dirt, and wraps his arms across his face, huddling against the blizzard-blast of flying rock and metal.

'Check for casualties!' Lance Corporal Dougie Sneddon roars. Fossey is on his knees, moving into a run and getting up at the same time.

'Stay off the track,' he yells back.

He runs past the doctor and his two shock patients who are on their knees, covered in white dust. They're crawling around and lurching like old soaks on a pavement but not badly hurt. There is silence, as if the crack of the explosives has sucked all sound out of the air.

Fossey runs on to the front of the Vector and opens the passenger door. Metal girders from the chassis have been forced up through the floor and the passenger seat. The cushion looks like it has been bitten in half, but no one had been sitting on it. The cab is white with settling dust. Fossey can just see Jason in the driver's seat on the other side of the truck. He runs around with Dougie. He can see nothing through the thick armoured window glass of the door: it has been frosted by the blast. He pulls on its heavy handle. Jason is sitting at the wheel. Dougie tries to pull Jason out but can't – he's wedged in.

'I'll do it,' says Fossey, pulling Dougie roughly out of the way by the webbing across his back.

Fossey tears at Jason, using so much strength he fears he might break a bone. Jason is freed suddenly which sends Fossey staggering back. Then the major scoops him out of the Vector, like a parent carrying a sleeping child. Jason is floppy and lifeless. Fossey lays the dead driver down gently, so as not to wake him.

The platoon is ordered into a defensive circle while another helicopter is summoned. The light has gone. Fossey is staring into the desert. He hasn't got a pair of Night Vision Goggles – there aren't enough to go around. He's looking out into the gloom and wondering what he can now do with the wreck of the Vector. It will have to be stripped of all the secret radio equipment, and blown up.

He gets permission to destroy the Vector from the brigade head-quarters: his men snigger when Fossey, a demolition expert, is told to 'attack the wheels and axles' as if he were a trainee. He packs the Vector with 30kg of plastic explosive and it's turned into small chewed fragments in a gigantic explosion. Everyone knows the Taleban will have seen the blast and will know British troops have been hurt.

'Sir.' A young voice in the dark. 'If we had the right number of troops in Kajaki we could go and kick these fuckers – we could do them.'

'If the turbine move goes ahead and we bring it up here – there will be time for payback. There will be boots on the ground, lots of boots,' Fossey says.

That night Fossey hardly sleeps. He stays up talking through the details of the patrol that killed Jason, and maimed Tom, with their friends. Although only thirty-two, his mild manner and grey hair means that the soldiers look to him for wisdom. He doesn't feel wise. He doesn't feel as if he knows what to say. But he listens. He tells them that there will be a chance to punish the Taleban for what they have done. He isn't sure that driving a convoy of slow-moving unarmoured trucks right through the Taleban's strongholds will really give young paratroopers the chance to take the blood price that they crave. More likely, it will give the Taleban the chance to shed more British blood. But he knows the paratroopers and engineers need to hear that there is more to look forward to in Helmand than relentless patrols back and forth against an elastic front line.

The next morning he flies back to Bastion and pushes through the black plastic door to his squadron headquarters.

Squadron Sergeant Major Alan 'Paddy' Beattie is a heavyweight giant with a squared-off jaw. Intimidating piles of muscle have accumulated on the ridges of his shoulders. He slaps his hands together and stares at Fossey, his boss. A commando-trained paratrooper and rugby fanatic, he's the squadron commander's fixer and enforcer – and sometimes the major's gruff military nanny. Fossey appears to have aged and lost weight.

'Brew sir? NATO standard? Milk and two sugars? Coming up,' he says as Fossey pushes through his cramped operations room to the office he shares with Beattie at the back.

'Thanks sarn't major. I will.' He sits, and runs his hands through his hair.

'What the fuck is that in your arms, sir?'

'Uh – dunno. What do you mean?' he inspects the backs of his forearms. They are tattooed with bits of grey stone and metal which was blasted into his skin when he curled up to protect himself against the bomb that killed Jason Barnes.

'You're going to the hospital, sir, you're going right now,' says

Beattie. For an hour and a half nurses pick the pieces out of him with tweezers. The pain of their pincers and the sting of the iodine is worth it. Fossey has ninety minutes with nothing to think about but little holes and scratches.

Two days later he's in Lashkar Gah and has joined Major Y's planning team. The turbine move – Operation Oqab Tsuka, Eagle's Summit – is growing in momentum. No one has given the brigade the orders to move the equipment yet – and the main parts are stuck in Kabul anyway. Hugh Powell and Sir Sherard remain convinced that moving the turbine along the 611 is too risky. But Mark Carleton-Smith is demanding solutions.

The pendant – a thick black arrow on a sky blue and maroon striped background – flaps like a slapping hand as a desert wind rips through the Pathfinder camp. Men wearing T-shirts, sandals and baseball hats, many sporting long sideburns, and longer hair than military regulation would allow, even in the field, are bustling back and forth between metal shipping containers. Grenade launchers and heavy machine guns are being quickly fitted into the turrets of the Jackal vehicles. Rations and water are stacked in the back; radio equipment tested.

Just as these men look different to ordinary soldiers, they behave differently too. There's an air of the pirate about them: to swagger in flip-flops takes self-belief. It's impossible to tell the officers from the other ranks as everyone is on first-name terms. Recruited from across the whole army, Pathfinder volunteers go through intense physical trials on their selection course and serve a twelve-month probation period once they get into the Pathfinder Platoon. It is an anomaly in the British Army – the only free-standing platoon; it isn't part of a battalion or regiment. Other brigades have reconnaissance units but none so highly trained as 16 Air Assault Brigade's Pathfinders. Their role, as their name suggests, is to go deep into enemy territory ahead of other units to scout-out routes and spy on the opposition. They use 'Halo' – High Altitude Low Opening parachute techniques, which involve plunging from 30,000 feet and opening at 500 feet to avoid detection, and High Altitude High Opening (Haho) jumps which allow them to leap out at 30,000 feet, then sail for up to 40 kilometres beneath their canopies, to get to their targets. On the ground they usually work in four- or six-man teams with each member further trained in specialist skills.

They are different. They don't use the standard British rifle, they get the Diemaco C4 – a modernised version of the old American M16. They get fancy sights and handles to fit on it, and it has an extending stock. Pathfinders are also issued with the American type Gentex helmet, which is lighter than the British standard Mark 6A (which looks like a potty). They are allowed to wear non-standard body armour. The Pathfinders have many of the same weapons as the Special Air Service and Special Boat Service, but they are not, strictly speaking, 'Special Forces'. But they are an elite and within the tribal system of the British Army they have earned the right to show off their combat plumage. The Pathfinders are commanded by a major – Mat Taylor. He has two captains under him, and a sergeant major – all of the trappings of a full company even though there's only about forty Pathfinders. When they're off duty their tents are a frequent scene of adoring pilgrimage for female soldiers. They get to race across the desert in their Jackals; they star in their own twenty-first-century *Mad Max* adventures. Other units are jealous of them. Some senior officers are enraged by their laid-back attitude and idiosyncrasies.

'I've never understood what the whole point of the Pathfinders really is,' one senior officer in the brigade said to Taylor when he was appointed to command the unit. 'They're not special and they're expensive. I'd disband the whole fucking lot.'

Taylor has only just been promoted to major. As the Pathfinders roll out of their little camp, inside Bastion, everyone is quiet. The first rule is 'no roads or tracks', so they head off into the desert ocean. The sky gets bigger, the stars pulsate; there's a schoolboy skip in the stomach as the patrol feels the adventure begin. They've escaped the stifling tedium of Camp Bastion. The latest mission statement is: to scout in the area of Malmand and Wushtan, report on 'atmospherics' and get an idea of the Taleban's intent, strengths and locations – and report on any narcotics activity.

Malmand sits on a large tributary of the Helmand River, the Darreh-ye-Malmand, about 10 kilometres southeast of Sangin. Wushtan is on another, bigger, tributary – the Dey Ghurak Lowy Mandah, a few kilometres further north. It's very close to the narrow Gorak Pass between the Abu Hassan and Gavkhaneh mountain ranges. The area seldom gets visited by NATO troops and is believed to be a major drug-processing and marketing centre. The brigadier and his planners need to know what effect the Taleban could have if they come down the two river valleys and attack the turbine convoy as it grinds its way along the 611.

The Jackals with their huge wheels and air suspension sail across the bumps in the desert. In the moonlight they look like boats, trailing wakes of roiling dust behind. It is early in the morning of 21 July. Over the next three days the Pathfinders and a small detachment of Afghan Special Forces soldiers known as the Helmand Scouts visit villages and cross-question people at road blocks, slowly gathering intelligence. They are being watched by Taleban dickers who relay their movements to their commanders using walkie-talkie radios. On 22 July the Pathfinders finish a series of meetings in a village not far from Wushtan. They move into the desert and stop to get the next set of orders from Taylor.

The air screams, there's a crack, and the desert erupts about 300 metres away. A jet of grey smoke is driven into the sky and the air fills with bits of fizzing stone. The Taleban have fired a 107mm rocket.

'I've fired a rocket at them. I am now escaping,' a Taleban fighter is heard to say over his radio. The Pathfinders identify the firing point out in the desert and shoot at it with grenades and a Javelin rocket.

'Fire another rocket,' the commander says.

'I am going to. I am just working out the angles.'

'They have moved a little bit,' says a third voice – a dicker.

'Prepare the rocket.'

'I am moving to another location.'

'Be careful.'

'We are just about to fire another rocket.'

The Pathfinders are hit again. This time the rocket falls inside their perimeter defences – they return fire – then, silence.

The next day the Pathfinders continue their patrol. They manage to catch four men on two motorbikes who have been shadowing them. One of the men has wire flex, a piece of wood with metal contacts built into it, and some silver paper. The Afghan Army suspect him of being a bomb maker or a courier for a bomb maker. Another in the group has two sets of remote-control key fobs for Mercedes cars – but no car. The remotes are often used to detonate bombs. The four men are interrogated, and released. The Afghans know they would never get a successful prosecution with such circumstantial evidence. There are other details of Taleban movements that emerge from talking to local people, but the Pathfinders don't feel as though they've hit the jackpot.

Soon after dawn the next morning, Pathfinders with six Jackals set up a checkpoint on what appears to be a busy track running north to south close to the Gorak Pass. About fifteen vehicles head south and five north in two hours. Their passengers don't have much to say about the Taleban, aside from the predictable condemnation of them as foreign invaders. But chatting through an interpreter with them, Taylor makes an astonishing discovery: the Pathfinders are standing on a busy commuter route between Kajaki and Kandahar. The passengers and drivers say that it takes just four to five hours to drive it. The 611 is too dangerous and expensive because of Taleban tolls at checkpoints, fighting, and mines. This back route between Kandahar and Kajaki costs only 800 Pakistani rupees in a taxi – $12 per person.

The turbine might be moved along this new desert route – completely bypassing the 611. The Pathfinders seem to have found a solution – they have earned their plumage.

10

DECEPTION

Hissing. All he can hear is hissing. His back is sore and his back-side hurts. And there's this hissing which won't go away. Etienne le Roux can smell the diesel on top of the sharp and sulphurous taste of explosive. He can't see anything except the wheel of the Jackal on his right. His world has shrunk to a boiling fog of dust. He puts his hands to his crotch. He's alright there. He begins to slide his hands down his thighs, hesitates.

He'd seen what happened to Tom Neathway. He'd been in Major Joe Fossey's group which had looked after Tom when his legs and arm were torn off. He'd seen Jason Barnes die at the cab of his Vector. He's not sure he wants to know what's not below his knees. He feels the fraying cloth of his combat trousers – finds his boots, with feet in them. He bends his legs. He looks around him – still just dust and smoke. He can't see the top gunner or the vehicle commander. The hissing is coming from behind him. He turns his head and sees the open mouth of a broken black rubber air suspension pipe swaying at him, like a rinkhals cobra, so common in the veld in his home town near Johannesburg.

'Okay. That was an IED – we hit an IED. That wasn't a rocket attack from the side. The truck was thrown up in the air – that's why I'm alive. IED.'

A soldier is running towards him, mouthing words he cannot hear – his head is full of a high-pitched screech. The soldier helps him to his feet and, putting his shoulder in Etienne's armpit, begins walking him to the Jackal in front. 'How come we got hit and they didn't – we were at the back – three trucks went over that bomb before us? Weird,' Etienne thinks.

The soldier is saying something but it's just a collection of disjointed noises.

'Huh?'

'Contact! We're in contact!' the soldier shouts and drags Etienne more quickly towards cover from Taleban bullets. Etienne stoops to his left and picks up his helmet. It is lying in the road at least 20 metres from his truck. It was torn from his head by the blast. He's made to sit by the undamaged Jackal. He can hear hammering – it must be British troops shooting at the Taleban, but it sounds like someone bashing wood. A medic strips off his Osprey body armour and checks out his back for what he calls 'scrap metal'. There are no holes in Etienne. The two other members of his crew come staggering in – they too are uninjured – saved by the thick V-shaped hull of the Jackal, which has no roof, so they were catapulted free by the blast.

Etienne, a sapper with Fossey's 9 Parachute Squadron, has been blown up because of a short verbal exchange in Lashkar Gah.

Brigade headquarters are delighted with the Pathfinders' discovery of the desert route between Kandahar and Kajaki. The Pathfinders returned for a second reconnaissance, with a driver from the Royal Logistic Corps, to say whether a Heavy Equipment Transport (HET), a tank-transporter lorry which is designed to move vast loads along German motorways, could make it through the desert carrying the turbine and its parts. The articulated lorries have a ground clearance of little more than 6 inches. The HET driver says he is confident the transporter will get through. Now known as 'Route Harriet', the desert road means that the convoy will only have to travel about 6 kilometres of the 611 – the last stretch of track before Kajaki itself.

Mark Carleton-Smith is comfortable that the insurgents can be held off in the village of Kajaki Sofla while the convoy is driven through this last stretch. But it is not clear whether the HET can make it through the last few obstacles, including a reverse camber on the corniche along the edge of the Green Zone, and a checkpoint the British have built. A convoy stuck on this short road risks being cut to pieces.

'We think it will be fine,' someone says at the briefing on the route. 'It should fit through.'

'Think. Should. We need to know for sure. We need certainty,' Carleton-Smith replies.

Etienne is part of a group sent down to measure the route and clear the obstacles, after this brief exchange. His is one of dozens of operations which the army calls 'setting the conditions' for the main operation. By early August the plan for the biggest military convoy mounted by the British armed forces since the end of the Second World War is in place.

Central to Operation Oqab Tsuka is a lie which has been accidentally, but elaborately, set up during the planning to take the turbine up the dangerous 611. The discovery of Route Harriet is top secret. Any coverage of the operation to take the turbine to Kajaki is subjected to a news blackout. But the Taleban already know that the turbine move is being planned, because their local leaders, and drug barons, have been approached by British go-betweens who have tried to get it through their territory – in return for cash.

The Taleban do not know when it will come. And once it is decided that the convoy will take the desert route, agents working for the British continue to hint that they are looking for a deal on the 611. The Taleban are encouraged to believe that the British are going to be crazy enough to drive a hundred trucks up a valley which appears to have been purpose-built for ambushes.

A rehearsal and equipment test of the HETs, which involves sending a convoy part of the way up the 611, reinforces the widespread belief that the turbine will be going that way. A road convoy, led by the Royal Logistic Corps and protected by out-riding Wimiks, is driven from Camp Bastion north in early August. It passes, as all convoys do, through Gereshk, over the bridge across the Helmand River, and then hooks up through the desert. It then swings back into the 611. It makes painful progress. It comes constantly under attack from the Taleban and in the last 18 kilometres search teams uncover twenty-two IEDs. The HET tank transporters meanwhile, collapse. Their brakes and wheels seize and they have to be dragged like sledges to safety.

Lieutenant Colonel Rufus McNeil – a suave and intellectual officer whose last job was as private secretary to the British Secretary of State for Defence, Des Browne – is to lead the real turbine convoy, as commanding officer of 13 Air Assault Support Regiment of the Royal Logistic Corps (RLC). The corps is among the least glamorous units of the British Army: it's responsible for getting stuff from A to B. Its members are frequently derided as 'fat loggies'. In the tribal hierarchy of the British Army, the Logistics Corps rank very low: if some units are dismissed as 'fish and chip regiments', the loggies are seen as the military equivalent of Spam. The corps history has been lost and mired in name changes and amalgamations. Formed in 1993, the RLC combined the Royal Corps of Transport, Royal Army Ordnance Corps, the Pioneer Corps, the Catering Corps, and the postal department of the Royal Engineers. But McNeil, an officer tipped for the highest ranks, loves it.

'There's something wonderful, beautiful even, about a massive convoy and I just love the logistics, fitting all the pieces together. It's what makes me tick,' he says.

And for loggies, Afghanistan is different. While infantry move between forts and camps in helicopters, only the loggies travel exclusively on the ground – delivering food, fuel, building supplies and ammunition, all over Helmand. They are targeted constantly, which explains why, while other units seek out the Taleban enemy and try to provoke fighting, the aim of the logistics convoys is to circumnavigate where the enemy might be. The trucks never take the same route across the desert twice, and hide in darkness. The dust thrown up from a convoy in daylight can be seen for 40 kilometres. So every convoy that the loggies run gets shot at or blown up, or both.

When they arrive at places like Fob Gibraltar and Musa Qal'ah, paratroopers and battle-hardened Scottish infantrymen greet them with open admiration. And manly nods of respect towards the cabs of the unarmoured trucks, as they sweep into unloading bays, stop – midway through the gesture – when the drivers climb down, take off their body armour, and shake out their hair. Women!

Now, on the eve of departure for Operation Oqab Tsuka, Dani Hanwell and Nikki Tindle, both drivers of a container carrying 'DROPS' trucks, wear their combat trousers on their hips and hold court to a circle of other drivers from 63 Squadron. The men laugh with exaggeration at the girls' jokes. The girls slide into silence and look at the ground when the attention gets too much – a scene from every shopping mall atrium in the world. Their banter fades to a murmur as Colonel McNeil stands in front of them to address them.

'You are at the highest level of readiness and experience for what you do. You've been doing it for five months and that is why we have been chosen for this operation – because we are at our peak. But let's be confident – but not overconfident. I want to bring you all back in one piece and that means we can be cautious – we can take our time and move with deliberation.

'This operation will dramatically improve the lives of the Afghan people. That is what we are here for. If their lives improve it is less

likely that al Qaeda will be able to recruit and our families will be
safer back home. I wish you all the best of luck – and will see you on
the road.'

A padre follows up with a prayer. Dani and Nikki stop shifting
their weight impatiently from foot to foot, and stare intently at him
as he implores the Almighty to watch over the convoy. He tells his
audience that God will do all he can to 'bring you back to your loved
ones'.

'What if he's not watching? What if he's busy? That quite freaked
me out. I was alright up to then but the vicar made me think that
maybe if God's not concentrating something will go wrong,' says
Dani in the canteen at Bastion, which is serving tea and biscuits,
before the convoy sets off.

The Pathfinders in Jackals and the Queens Royal Lancers in
Viking armoured vehicles, dragging troop-carrying trailers, set off
thirty-six and twenty-four hours earlier. Their role is to screen ahead
of the convoy, discreetly driving up either side of Route Harriet
to snow-plough the Taleban away, and then stop infiltrators from
laying bombs on the road north. The main deception – a decoy
convoy made up of more than twenty trucks escorted by the Danish
battle group out of Gereshk – is ordered onto the road north. In
Fob Inkerman, the most northerly Fob before Sangin, 2 and 3 Para
launch an operation to set up a new base, Fob Emerald, 1.5 kilometres north of the main base on the 611. The idea is to ram home the
lie that the turbine is heading up the 611.

Fossey and his engineers, as well as a fleet of DROPS vehicles,
high-risk IED search teams, bomb-disposal experts and drivers for
two diggers (one of them a new armoured version with solid tyres),
the commanding officer's group, and a mine search team led by
Adam Ireland from Fob Gibraltar, do a late-night circuit of Camp
Bastion in convoy and turn right onto the 601.

Coming towards them from Kandahar is the rest of the convoy
under the command of Major Iain Bayliss with his 13 RLC Regiment's

15 Squadron plus Canadian and American troops. The two groups are scheduled to meet at Maiwand.

The British and Afghans have fought each another before at Maiwand. But if any British officers are aware of the significance of the fly-blown mud hamlet, they do not let on. A hundred and thirty years earlier, to the day, a British brigade of around 2,600 men and 3,000 camp followers collided here with 8,500 men led by the Afghan prince, Ayub Khan. The British and native Indian troops were better equipped. They had Martini-Henry and Snider rifles, capable of firing ten to twenty rounds a minute while the Afghans mostly had muzzle-loading muskets which fired, at most, three shots a minute. So, although outnumbered, the British should have had the edge. But, according to military historians Lester Grau and Ali Jalali (who also made definitive studies of the Soviet occupation of Afghanistan), the British were routed because they relied too heavily on the 'strength of their technology, and chose their battle site in open ground surrounded by flanking ravines'[4]. They were outwitted by the local Afghans who used the undulations of the ground to escape the wall of bullets, get close to the British and cut them to pieces.

The British were destroyed – losing '1,757 dead and 175 wounded, seven artillery pieces, 1,000 rifles, 2,425 transport animals, more than 200 horses, 278,200 rifle bullets and 448 artillery shells'.[5] The rout was compared to the retreat from Kabul during the First Afghan War, when an estimated 16,500 perished in 1842. It caused outrage and consternation in Victorian England and is often used to prove the argument that wars in Afghanistan are 'unwinnable'.

Sergeant Joe McMahon waves at the driver of the armoured digger, frantically chopping at his own throat. 'Turn it off. Turn it off.' The gunners on the 15 Close Support Land Rovers, who are out

---

4 'Expeditionary Forces: Superior Technology Defeated – The Battle of Maiwand', Lester Grau and Ali Jalali, *Military Review*, June 2001.

5 *Ibid.*

to the flanks of the convoy, swing their guns outwards – preparing for an ambush. Joe Fossey, who is on foot beyond the diggers, feels dangerously exposed. The British are back in Maiwand.

Lance Corporal Mat Dalton turns the key and the engine dies away with a shudder. The bucket at the front freezes about 30 centimetres off the ground. A copper pot emerges from the sliding dirt. The convoy is about 2 kilometres short of the rendezvous where the British will collect the turbine from its Canadian escort. Dozens of vehicles have already been up and down this track. Joe McMahon can see wires coming out of the pot – and a flat piece of wood wrapped in black rubber inner tube.

'Sir. You better have a look at this. It's given me a bit of a turn,' says McMahon.

'You're a very lucky team. I'm sure you will stay that way,' says Fossey after Major Wayne, the commander of the Explosive Ordnance Disposal Group in Afghanistan, has taken a look at the bomb. 'It was wired to explode but they hadn't connected the pressure pad to the battery.' Wayne took the bomb away, and thirty-seven minutes after it was found, he blows it up.

The turbine parts, which include a stator, the turbine itself, and several other massive pieces of equipment, have been hidden in fake metal shipping containers to camouflage and protect them. An Afghan government religious leader, an imam, has authorised the use of Koranic verses which have been painted on Perspex hoardings, and hung on the sides of the vast boxes. Officers and NCOs have been instructed to tell every soldier, male or female, that they are not allowed to touch the verses – and above all they should not 'wash, eat, piss or shit anywhere near them'. The idea is to convince the Taleban that attacking the turbine parts would be sacrilege – so no one wants non-Muslim troops desecrating holy texts. The containers are higher than normal ones, and bits of the turbine are sticking out the top; but the Taleban would struggle to figure out which one they would want to attack – there are about half a dozen.

A Taleban radio transmission reports that the road ahead has been sown with 'water melons' – Taleban code for bombs – and that two rockets are ready to be fired into the train of military vehicles and a 60-tonne civilian crane, which stretches over 3 kilometres. There's a steady drip of intelligence warnings. Dickers on motorbikes flit about in the middle distance. The sun begins to set behind the Garmabak Mountain to the west. Joe McMahon and Mat Dalton are working constantly in their diggers smoothing the road out by filling trucks with stones and dumping them in holes, shaving off the steep sides of wadis.

The convoy curls back along a grey stone wadi cut into a dun-coloured plain which erupts on either side into sharp-edged mountains. Small villages huddle against the valley walls and creep down to the edge of the wadi thirstily probing for water. We pass a graveyard; red, black, and green flags snap in the hot wind. Over the radio someone is getting excited about a lone white flag further on – it could be marking the site of a bomb beneath the earth, warning local people. It turns out to be just a flag.

Adam Ireland's team from Fob Gib are resting in their Vector. Four Mastiff trucks in front have churned up the gravel on the ground in front. His driver spots something dark in the road.

'Adam what's that?'

'Stop!'

They approach the small black shape about the size of the top of a tin can. As they go forward the metal detectors screech. Major Wayne, the bomb-disposal expert, is called back and gingerly brushes away the dirt. The black shape is an anti-personnel mine. Underneath it is a brown plastic anti-tank mine the size of the wheel of a Mini. Wayne defuses it. They're in a vulnerable spot: the mountains have closed in around them. Adam's team spreads out to protect the static vehicles. One of his team finds a slab of rock; on it someone has painted the scene of an ambush. It shows mujahideen fighters shooting at a helicopter with a heavy machine gun and others firing RPGs into a convoy of Russian armoured personnel carriers.

A spy plane shadowing the British convoy picks up a Taleban message: 'We are preparing the big one. We are ready and laid on target, we await further direction.'

The convoy quickly gets under way.

'Shoot. Why aren't you shooting at them?' a Taleban commander complains.

'There are too many of them. The helicopters are above us,' a plaintive fighter replies.

Fossey, who is commanding the engineers and the front half of the convoy, chuckles.

'So someone doesn't want to be a martyr today. I bet he'll get his arse kicked when we've gone,' he says. The valley opens up again, rises slowly, and the desert rolls away like sea swell on either side.

Thump. A grey geyser bursts about 100 metres east of the back end of the convoy.

'That looks like a contact. Let's wait for the report,' says Fossey. He gets a message that the Taleban are telling each other that they can see the convoy and are going to attack. American Kiowa helicopters sweep and dip along the ravines and cliffs on the edge of the valley. Iain Bayliss confirms that there has been an attack – a mortar or rocket. British Special Forces teams are known to be patrolling the mountains and 15 Close Support Squadron are in charge of protecting the convoy, so no one on the trucks is allowed to cock their weapons – but they swing their barrels ready to shoot anyway.

Silence.

The convoy moves on.

An American Special Forces unit, Task Force 71, has set itself up on two towering sugarloaf mountains, Black Rock and Brown Rock, which choke the Helmand River valley about 2 kilometres south of Kajaki Sofla on the 611 – the other side of the mountains from the British convoy. Their commander 'Major Mat', a short, bearded and intense officer, has attended the British brigadier's rehearsals and agreed that his unit's role will be to prevent Taleban reinforcements from heading north up the valley to support. The distant crump and thud of artillery and aerial bombardment from their area echoes across the ridgeline. No one knows what's going on there: the Americans are on a different radio network.

Between 22 and 26 August, 3 Para are flown in to Kajaki, along with a *kandak* of 380 Afghan troops and mentors from the Royal Irish Regiment – a massive airlift of over a thousand men and 300 tonnes of food and ammunition. The sudden increase in British troop numbers immediately provokes a reaction from the Taleban. They begin to reinforce their positions in Kajaki Sofla by linking their two main areas of concentration, known to the British as Big Top, on the east side of the valley, and Sentry Compound on the west. British drone spy planes film the Taleban digging trench lines and bunkers, while 3 Para and the Afghan troops move into compounds south of the main British base at the dam.

But the British don't want to fight. Secret agents have been continuing in their efforts to persuade the leaders further south in the valley that the turbine will benefit all Afghans and that they should allow it free passage. Since the Taleban control most of the territory, and are also charging people to use electrical power, it is also pointed out that they stand to make money out of boosted electricity production. In Kajaki Sofla the local government officials send feelers out to community leaders, who agree to attend a *shura* with 3 Para and the Afghan Army two days before Operation Oqab Tsuka is due to be launched.

About twenty village elders turn up for the meeting. They are friendly and readily agree to a proposal to take to the local Taleban leadership: to accept a fee of $25,000 to allow the convoy through. A small group of younger unsmiling men hang around at the back of the room. They are assumed to be insurgents. They scowl at the

British and sneer extravagantly when the offer of money is made.
The elders later contact the British and say that the Taleban will
only allow the convoy through if they can search it to make sure that
it only carries the turbine and its parts. The insurgents insist that
they have intelligence that the turbine is a ruse to smuggle a 'super
gun' to Kajaki which the British are going to use to attack Iran.

No deal. The British warn the elders to leave the area and say that
they now have no choice but to 'fight the turbine through' Kajaki
Sofla.

The British insist that they are not trying to change the security situation on the ground but that they want safe passage for the
turbine. They also warn local civilians to stay off the streets and out
of the way if they see troops or the convoy coming through. Leaflets,
radio broadcasts and loudhailers are used to drive the peaceful
message home. But the Taleban keep building their trenches.

On 26 August, 'X' Company of 2 Para, Kajaki's resident unit,
patrol south to try to work out the extent and location of the new
Taleban defences. As they approach the front line, two American
helicopters appear in the valley to their east. The 3 Para battle group,
of which Lieutenant Colonel Huw Williams is in overall command,
has no idea what the American Chinook pilots are doing in the
area – and they do not communicate with anyone on the ground.
The British assume they are 'sightseeing' at the dam. The Taleban,
however, assume that the aircraft are part of a British attack and open
fire with every weapon they've placed in their new hidden trenches
and bunkers. 'X' Company's commander, Major Simon Britton,
cannot get the helicopters out of the airspace and warn them they
are being shot at – he can see that they are being hit. Their loss is his
gain: they have accidentally provoked the Taleban into revealing all
of their new firing points, which Britton duly notes and passes on to
the mortars, artillery and jets.

Within seconds the air is filled with the onrushing-train sound of
the incoming rounds and the crunch as they hit the Taleban positions

with 280 mortar bombs. The flow of high-explosive mortars into the Taleban is so steady it looks as though a giant hosepipe is being used to blast ants along a dusty path. This is followed with a hundred 105mm rounds from Australian gunners attached to the Royal Horse Artillery at Kajaki – and three 500lb bombs dropped by jets.

The next day the Afghan *kandak*, and their British mentors, move in two groups to leapfrog past 'X' Company. The Taleban have managed to reinforce their troops overnight and meet the Afghan government probes with a wall of fire. Again the jets, artillery, and rockets fired from Fob Edinburgh pour down onto their positions. This second tidal wave of high-explosive bombardment begins to break the Taleban's will to fight.

'Attack the foreigners. In the name of Allah, fire!'

'We cannot. We are too weak and many of us are wounded and dead. They are too strong,' says one exchange picked up by the British.

On 28 August the ANA are ordered to begin their assault on Big Top and Sentry Compounds. Captain Steve Swann is mentoring a company of Afghan soldiers. He finds himself wading through fields flooded by the Taleban, and then crashing about in thick plantations of corn 3 metres high. He can hear shooting as ANA soldiers blast the locks off doors and clear through compounds. But he feels disorientated and nervous – the artillery and jets are hitting targets directly in front of his men but he cannot see where. The ground shakes. The tops of the maize bend in with the shockwaves of the explosions.

Monitoring the Taleban radio channels, the British hear: 'Push the children forward. Send the children to find out where the British are.'

Swann ignores it. He's been told that there are no civilians in the area and that the only Afghans he will see will be 'Fighting Age Males'.

Emerging from a field the British are confronted with the sight of two small boys on their knees scratching at the ground. They cannot

make out what the children are doing. Two Afghan soldiers take
off after them like hounds after rabbits, grab them by their collars,
drag them back to the narrow path where they'd first been seen. An
Afghan soldier kicks at the ground – two electrical wires appear.
The children have been laying a bomb. One of the boys is eight; the
other is six years old. The British are worried for the kids; they have
no jurisdiction over the Afghan troops who have a reputation for
shooting Taleban prisoners.

The boys are crying and are trying to wriggle free. They insist that
they had just been playing with the bomb which they had found
on the ground; they didn't know it was dangerous. 'We're only
children' the older one pleads through his heaving snivels. His eyes
are wide with terror. He looks to one Afghan soldier and then to
another searching their faces for mercy. His green *shalwar kameez* is
covered in a dusty layer of brown, it darkens around the crotch.

'Where are the people who sent you? Where are the people who
sent you? You are in great danger – you could have been killed. You
must tell us where they are.'

An Afghan officer sits down next to them and puts his hand on
the older boy's shoulder. 'What is your name?'

The boy shakes his head.

'Don't worry. We don't need your name, little man. We'll look
after you. You didn't know what you were doing. It is not your fault.
I am just happy that you are safe. Who sent you? We need to know
that.'

The boy shakes his head again; his eyes bubble with tears. The
kandak commanders are anxious to get moving quickly. The boys
are led to an abandoned compound, given a box of rations each, and
told to stay out of the way until the fighting is over. Later they are
handed to neighbours from the village who agree to look after them.

That night the government troops are told to hold their positions. The convoy is making slower progress than they are. There is
a danger that the infantry, who have moved south from Kajaki, will

have to hold Taleban positions they have just overrun for too long. This would give the insurgents the chance to organise a counter-attack – and risk the destruction of civilian homes which, until then, have been safely behind Taleban lines.

The morning of 29 August, Swann and his Afghans take Sentry Compound, unopposed. The Afghan soldier who leads the assault carries a rifle in one hand and a teapot in the other. Swann and his rangers are incredulous – but the Taleban have fled.

On the east, Colour Sergeant John 'Strawman' Brennan, the Irish-Mancunian pugilist giant who had fought in Musa Qal'ah, is in charge of assaulting Big Top – a cluster of compounds which straddle the 611 road and press up against the valley's sides. The morning sun catches the shark's-teeth peaks of Zamindavar in the west as Strawman moves forward through the tight maze of build-ings. Machine-gun rounds start hitting the ground a few metres away. Rockets are bursting in the air above. Strawman is now in open ground 200 metres short of the target. He has no choice but to charge the Taleban positions; to stay in the open would risk being cut down as the insurgents improve their aim. He finds himself standing on the rim of a crater about 10 metres deep – the result of a 1,000lb bomb dropped that morning. Facing him across it is a bunker which has been splashed with shrapnel but is still intact. His stomach lurches: gunmen in the bunker could hose him down. He needs to keep the momentum going or he'll die.

He spreads his long arms and waves the Afghan troops on into compounds on his right and left. The Taleban have run back a couple of hundred metres – their bullets continue to harass the Afghan government troops as they advance. Random shots splash on the walls by their faces and at their feet. The government troops begin to falter. They are spooked by the British artillery which is firing deeper into the Taleban lines.

'Make them stop. Make them stop the shelling. It is very dangerous for us, very dangerous,' an Afghan officer begs Strawman.

'They won't hit us, we're controlling them, so we are,' says Strawman.

The Taleban bunkers have been staggeringly well constructed; many are made out of concrete. When Strawman throws grenades into them smoke puffs out of the gun slits in their walls, but they remain intact. Both Strawman and Swann are having trouble motivating the government soldiers to assault the bunkers and clear compounds. They hang back from taking the risk of charging into closed spaces, and complain constantly that they fear being bombed by aircraft. Strawman has no option but to charge ahead of the government forces.

'I'll fucking shame you into doing your job,' he thinks.

He makes sure he keeps the senior Afghan officer close to him. The Afghan Army must be seen to be leading the fight – to prove to the rest of the population that the government is not just a fig leaf to legitimise the presence of foreign troops, as the Taleban claims. Strawman is surprised that the government troops begin to 'chicken out'. He'd become used to their reckless bravery. They seem stunned and sickened by the scale of the artillery and aerial bombardment. Still he sprints ahead and half a dozen more bunkers are cleared with grenades and bursts of automatic fire.

In the middle distance, Taleban fighters buzz around on motorbikes evacuating wounded and re-supplying the front. Strawman realises that he is now about 200 metres beyond the point at which he was supposed to have stopped. He orders a halt.

He is kneeling by a wall talking on his radio when a burst of bullets smashes into the dried mud above his head. His long arms almost drag on the ground as he crouches and runs into cover behind the wall. Then he pops back up to return fire. He can see muzzle flashes from three weapons in a bunker about 160 metres to his left on some high ground. His team fires two anti-tank rockets at the bunker, each time hitting it; each time the Taleban inside survive and continue to pin down his Afghan soldiers. British artillery rounds land all around it but fail to score a direct hit. An Apache approaches and pauses. There's a *shoosh* and a trail of vapour points down into the redoubt which explodes like a balloon. The helicopter gunner sees three men running away from its rear exit; they vanish in churning dust thrown up by his cannon shells.

Strawman is now under attack from a sniper. The rounds are missing the Afghan troops but frightening them into taking cover and not returning fire. He spots the smoke from the sniper's barrels and tries to explain where it is to his mortar fire controller who can't hear enough to figure out what he's talking about. Strawman grabs a Jimpy from another Ranger.

'Watch my tracer. That's the target,' he says, standing in a doorway firing a long burst into the compound used by the sniper.

'You got that?'

'Got it mate', says the mortar expert, who Strawman knows only as 'Smudge' (and that he is on loan from the Paras). The air between them zips as three rounds bisect the 30 centimetres between the two men.

'Fucking hell – that was close. I felt the wind on my face.'

'Me too,' said Smudge who's already given the coordinates of the compound to the mortars. They watch the bombs crash into the compound. The sniper stops shooting.

As evening falls the Taleban fighting fades like evening birdsong down to silence.

'Sir, there's no road,' says Paddy Beattie, the giant engineer sergeant major.

'Sarn't major, you must be mistaken. The route's been recce'd and the map says it takes us up to the Forward Rendezvous,' an already exhausted Fossey replies.

'Sir. There's No. Fucking. Road.'

'Fuck . . . sergeant major . . . find me another road.'

Route Harriet has vanished to a goat track in a deep wadi and then for 1.8 kilometres is hill. There's no way that any of the HETs can make it: they would tear their undercarriages off, and fall over. It's just got dark. The convoy is about 4 kilometres short of the last rendezvous before the final leg through Kajaki Sofla. 3 Para and Afghan troops are sitting poised to secure the final part of the village and are putting pressure on Rufus McNeil to get a move on.

Fossey walks up and down the route. There's no choice: he's going to have to build a road from scratch. Joe McMahon and Mat Dalton, the digger drivers, have had about five hours' sleep in the last thirty-six. They will have to work through the night carving a road out of the gravelly hillside.

'Sorry Paddy,' Fossey says to his giant sergeant major. 'We're committed to this; there's no turning back. We're going to have to take this on the chin and smash it through.'

'Bring it on, boss.'

The diggers scoop and dump their way up the hill. Watching is an Afghan translator travelling with the Lancers, who have taken up positions on a nearby hill to protect the convoy against ambush while it sits in the valley below.

Elections are scheduled for next summer – August 2009. Jaweed is an ethnic Pashtun – like the locals in the valley, although he comes from Kabul. He's sipping a cup of sweet black tea. Hamed Karzai, the Afghan President, is also a Pashtun. He needs as many votes as he can garner in the south of the country where his tribe dominate. The turbine is a way to boost his support and prove to sceptical Helmandis that a central government is worth backing.

Jaweed is not impressed. 'Here we vote for people we don't know. If we've heard of them then that is a bad thing because it means they have done bad things. It means they are criminals and war lords. I voted for Karzai in the last elections because even though he's Pashtun – I hadn't heard of him. Those politicians I do know, I do not trust. I'll vote for Karzai I guess in the next election – unless there is a candidate I've never heard of,' Jaweed says.

The road is built in eight hours. The convoy, a military circus train of snub-nosed pig-like Viking troop carriers, broad-shouldered DROPS trucks, the long, low dinosaur HETs, Mastiffs, Vectors and Land Rovers, draws up in its final rendezvous, looking down into the Helmand River valley. Mud-walled hamlets usher Route Harriet towards the 611. The sounds of occasional explosions echo up into the desert – 3 Para are blowing up Taleban bunkers.

Waiting at the crest of a hill Joe Fossey scans the outer edges of Kajaki Sofla for British troops. Little groups of brown figures are scuttling down alleys and vanishing. A platoon of about thirty men from 3 Para appear on the road. Fossey's column leads the convoy down to them. There are brief handshakes and a discussion about the route which, it is estimated, will take five hours to travel. Kajaki Sofla is silent. A digger is brought in to knock down the wall of a garden compound to make room for the HETs to turn.

Jerry-rigged electrical cables crisscross the road. They will snag on the convoy's loads. An exhausted but jubilant Fossey has the lines tested to check whether they are live or not and then pulls out his Letherman pliers. Standing on the roof of his Mastiff he drives the last kilometres to the dam – snipping off the cables to get the front of the convoy through.

'The irony of what I am doing is not lost on me. Here I am disconnecting a whole town to get an electrical generator through. Something's a bit wrong here.'

He then drives back down the route cutting any wires that could be caught on the higher loads with his pliers fixed to the tip of a bamboo pole, assisted by Sergeant Gaz Jones. The Taleban try to kill them, twice, with rockets which come close enough to make the two engineers giggle.

The first vehicles in the convoy arrive in little over an hour; they have had no problems getting through Kajaki. A handful of locals turn out to wave but most hide in their homes. The route is lined by 3 Para and government troops. Oqab Tsuka is a triumph. No British soldier has been killed and only one government private has been wounded. The only British casualty is a mechanic, who was injured repairing a HET. The Taleban have been spectacularly tricked into thinking that the convoy would fight all the way up the 611 road. A headline in *The Times* declares: 'Triumph for British forces in Boy's Own-Style Kajaki Mission'. More than a hundred vehicles, 2,000 men and women, have travelled over 180 kilometres in five days to deliver the hydroelectric plant turbine to Kajaki. It is supposed to provide power for 1.9 million Afghans. British commanders guess that they have killed 200 Taleban – although there's no way they can know.

The turbine isn't expected to generate any power for a year or two because it still has to be fitted into the generating hall at the dam. And while the Taleban holds most of the territory in Helmand it will be impossible to upgrade the distribution network to either carry the additional load, or to reach new customers. The turbine itself cost £3.4 million and many more millions have been spent getting it to Kajaki.

Still the British are proud. They were set a task – and they pulled it off.

Tired and filthy, most of them rush to swim in the shallows of the river that tumbles across flat rocks below the Turbine Hall. They splash and torment one another like toddlers. But Adam Ireland and the rest of the team from Fob Gib sit on a bank behind their Vector. Life in the beleaguered Fob has taught them to stay in cover – they can see no one guarding the far side of the river bank.

'They're daft going out there – there could be Taleban on those banks, there probably is. This is nuts,' says Adam.

A Kajaki-based paratrooper comes down to chat with them. 'It's all right mate – there's no one who can get eyes on you down there – just don't get washed away.'

Adam's group wanders down to the river, still warily watching the opposite banks.

'When you come from Fob Gib, it's a bit hard to believe that you can relax anywhere in Afghanistan,' says Adam as he sinks into the cold water.

First there are two local men who are delivered in a car to the gates of Fob Inkerman, 30 kilometres south of Kajaki. One is missing two legs and an arm. He's still alive. The other has a bad head wound. Lance Corporal Charlotte Davidson, twenty-three, from Aberystwyth, can see grey matter leaking from his skull. They are rushed into the medical centre and evacuated by helicopter.

Five children and a young woman appear. They all have shrapnel wounds. There are two more young men, suspected of being Taleban, who are treated for severe wounds to their arms and flown out to Bastion. Then more and more women and children.

They all come from the area where the American Task Force 71 has been operating. Their tactics have been anathema to the British for months because they prefer to stay in their Humvees and call air strikes in to deal with Taleban gunmen, rather than patrol on foot. They have also used the AC-130 Spectre gunship, which carries a 105mm artillery piece, heavy cannon and Gatling guns, to 'suppress' the Taleban around Black Rock.

In June, Mark Carleton-Smith had given a half-hour briefing on counterinsurgency from a TF71 captain at their base at Fob Robinson. The young captain explained that the only way he would deal with Afghans was 'from a position of strength'. Carleton-Smith discreetly tried to persuade the American Special Forces group, which was outside of his chain of command, to take a more subtle approach to counterinsurgency. He was getting nowhere. When he heard this he rolled his eyes:

'We drive up to the outskirts of a village and wait. If we are shot at then we bring some heavy firepower down on the heads of the shooters. Pretty soon the local elders come out to talk to us. We say to them "Look at us, we're the guys with beards. You have to

know that when you see the guys with beards you've got to stop the
Taleban from attacking – or there will be heavy penalties. It's up to
you." '

Carleton-Smith was surprised by their heavy-handed and unsubtle
approach. But in the ensuing weeks, during the planning of the
turbine move, he had extracted from 'Mat', the major in charge of
TF71, an understanding that his men would act only to block the
Taleban from reinforcing their fighters at Kajaki Sofla. The British
brigadier had also managed to get the Americans to take a British
liaison officer with them. But once the Americans got into the field
they returned to using the same tactics; standing off and dropping
bombs which risked high civilian casualties.

At Fob Inkerman one wounded child, who later dies, and more
than sixty injured – mostly women and children – come through the
medical centre. Supplies of bandages and medications fall dangerously low and are re-supplied by helicopter. Patrols are reduced so
that soldiers with medical training can be brought in to treat what
are assumed to be the victims of American air strikes.

In Sangin, another 8 kilometres south, Lieutenant Colonel Joe
O'Sullivan of 2 Para is called to the medical centre. Injured civilians
have been turning up there too. He sees a girl of about sixteen with a
pretty face distorted by pain. She's being helped to walk by an older
man, probably her father: she's bleeding from the leg and pelvis.

O'Sullivan looks inside the centre. A boy of about six is whim-
pering in pain; stuff is leaking out of his back and he's got an oxygen
mask on his face. In Sangin the medics treat about sixty patients.
Some of the wounded say that they were close to Taleban positions
which had been attacked; but this makes no difference to the Paras'
commanding officer. He believes that many civilian Afghans must
have been killed if there were this many emerging from the valley
with such severe wounds.

'Why were we killing all these civilians? The answer is we weren't
– the Americans were. There is a moral point – it ain't right to kill

the population in any significant number. We know as a battalion that that method of operating, using bombing, is neither practically nor morally necessary. On 24 June we fought a seventeen-hour battle [on Operation Talander] in that area and dropped just one 500lb bomb. There's also a practical issue. We want to move forward. Our guys are getting killed to move the campaign forward but if you're killing civilians you're not moving things on – so it doesn't make military sense.

'The American Special Forces were put in that position to do a blocking job. But [they interpret this as]: "If you see the enemy drop a bomb." How do you know they are the enemy? "Well, they are blokes with rifles and they are shooting at us." Okay, they are shooting at you – are they killing any of you? Can you manoeuvre? Can you do it a different way? The population are the vital ground so it's just stupid to risk killing them.'

He adds: 'There was some very unattractive chest-beating about that operation – I felt that quite strongly because a lot of civilians have been killed.'

II

Hospital Pass

They've spent the last two days pecking at the outskirts of Marjah like a mongoose baiting a snake, running fake raids in to distract the enemy from the resident Afghan National Police and their mentors. It has been dirty and tiring. This morning they get orders to push deeper in.

No one seems to know much about Marjah. There are plenty of drug lords, that is obvious: thousands of hectares of heavily irrigated rich land have been given over to growing poppy. Marjah is just 15 kilometres southwest of Lashkar Gah – but there is no permanent ISAF base in it. An area of about 50 square kilometres right next to the provincial capital has been ignored.

'Man Down! Man Down!' someone is shouting over the platoon's radio net. The vehicles in front and behind have stopped moving. There are RPGs flying by with a *shoosh* noise, 'like fireworks', she thinks.

Chantelle drops down into the body of the lightly armoured Snatch Land Rover. Bullets are hitting the sides making a pinging sound. She bounces back up through the roof hatch exposing her head and shoulders.

'What the fuck?'

A Taleban fighter is standing in a field about 40 metres away. He's got a gun and he's shooting at her. Chantelle swings her rifle onto him. He's so close he almost fills the sights of her stubby SA80 rifle. Snap. Snap. She shoots twice; each time her gun leaps.

'Contact left! Contact Left!' she shouts.

'I can't fucking believe it. He's just standing there, in the field, and he's shooting at me,' Chantelle thinks. The noise is terrible. The chainsaw racket of Minimi machine guns firing from the Land Rover in front, and another on her own wagon, makes it hard to think. She pulls off another five shots, individually aimed. The man flops to the ground, out of sight, behind an irrigation channel. Chantelle doesn't know if she's killed him or not. Doesn't care – so long as he's not shooting at her any more.

In the vehicle at the back of the convoy an Argyll has been shot through the abdomen. The commander of the company, Major Harry Clark, is sitting in the front of Chantelle's Snatch Land Rover. The vehicle offers some protection against bullets and none against bombs. A lightly armoured box on wheels, with thin bullet-proof glass windows, it cuts anyone inside off from the outside world and Clark can't hear what's going on properly. Craning his neck around, Clark asks: 'What are you lot shooting at? Where is the firing coming from?'

'There's a dead guy in that field and we're under fire – sir.'

'Ah. Carry on Chantelle.'

He then leaps out of the vehicle to run towards his wounded soldier at the back of the convoy and Chantelle joins him. She is a medic, a sergeant in 16 Medical Regiment, a permanent part of the Air Assault Brigade. As she charges along the line of vehicles to the wounded man, bullets still crackle around her. She's stopped half way and told that she's not needed – another medic is dealing with him.

Soaked in her own sweat, and still under fire, Chantelle laughs, turns around and runs back to the Snatch.

She hadn't liked the atmosphere when the company had started to drive into Marjah. There were none of the obvious signs of an impending attack: women and children were not seen running away from their homes and the farmers were still in their fields. But it had felt wrong.

'Maybe,' she'd thought, 'if we were on foot we'd feel better.' Driving down roads that are no more than the banks of irrigation channels, with no way of escaping left or right, is against everything she'd been trained to do. Now thirty-two, she'd been in the army for ten years. When she joined she'd been working at Top Shop. She is blonde and has a no-nonsense walk. Her voice is soft, slightly inter-rogative. Charismatic and motherly, she is also feared. The young men under her command want to please and impress her. She's a fully qualified Urban Operations Instructor, which means that she teaches soldiers how to fight in towns.

'Something is wrong, very wrong,' she thinks.

Marjah is a mixture of town and country. Huge compounds surrounded by high thick brown mud walls create shoulder-wide alleyways. These open onto fields chopped into quadrangles by irri-gation channels. The roads are like tramlines with ditches running either side.

'The Taleban know every inch of it – we know fuck all,' Chantelle thinks. She's standing in the back of the Snatch with her rifle held loosely against her right shoulder. Part of a tiny force of about thirty people, she is certain that they are going to get ambushed.

She is excited. She's done tours in Iraq. She is a highly trained infantry instructor, even though women are not, technically, supposed to serve as combat troops. Like every other soldier in her vehicle, she is anxious to test her skills.

'I'm not going to come over all politically correct and pretend that I'm not first a soldier. When the shit hits the fan I'm just another weapon on the ground. If you're a medic and you're going to be out

on patrol then you had better be as good a soldier as you can be –
other people could die if you fuck it up,' she says.

The casualty is rushed to a hastily organised helicopter landing
site – one of the snipers in a Snatch has claimed two kills – and an
Apache attack helicopter has chewed up eight other fighters with its
30mm cannon.

'Job done – hectic and scary but exciting as well. It's what we
signed up for and it's what we're getting,' Chantelle says.

Based in Lashkar Gah, Harry Clark's 'B' Company of 5 SCOTS
has about 140 men to control a vast area which includes the whole
of the city and a radius of 40 kilometres around it. With one platoon
dedicated to protecting the Provincial Reconstruction Team and the
British headquarters at 'Lashkatraz', another set aside as the Quick
Reaction Force, Clark is left with thirty men 'to patrol an area the
size of Yorkshire'.

If there is little pressure in Lashkar Gah he could scrabble together
a couple of platoons by adding his own headquarters staff. And every
time he patrols out of the city, in any direction, he finds himself in
a fight.

In mid-June he is east of Lashkar Gah, with his two platoons.
They have had a short battle with a large force of Taleban and
are following them up. He is leading the company to a group of
compounds in a village about 10 kilometres east of Lashkar Gah,
close to the road to Kandahar. He is with Second Lieutenant Chris
Hesketh, and an Afghan translator. They approach a building hoping
to speak with its occupants. There is no one inside and so they walk
further forward up to an embankment to have a look ahead. The
landscape rolls away in front of them throwing up eddies of dust.
Throbbing with heat, the Red Desert of southern Helmand shim-
mers in a barren wilderness of orange dunes. Clark and Hesketh are
silent but relaxed. They are further away from the rest of the platoon
than is sensible, they know that, but the slight rise ahead of them
gives them the height they need to survey the ground.

They push through a few scrubby green prickly plants and instinctively crouch as they get closer to the top of a gentle bank. They find themselves on the edge of a wadi and 20 metres to their right a group of Taleban are coming the other way.

'Jesus!'

'W'Allah!'

The two groups immediately fire at each other. Hesketh and Clark fall onto their faces. They are pinned down; their translator runs away. Hesketh pulls out two grenades and tosses them into the ditch. There are quick cracks like the sound of a massive paddle hitting a carpet. The ground shakes and the air fills with gravel. Hesketh scrambles onto his knees with his rifle ready. He knows that he has a fraction of a second before survivors of his grenades get hold of their weapons to kill him. The grenades have no effect. The Taleban are hurrying closer. But they haven't seen him. He is above them on the embankment and signals to Clark's 'snap ambush' by miming the snapping of a twig. He stands up as they get close and fires a long burst into the men below him. One is killed instantly; two or three look like they are badly hit. The two officers run back to the rest of Hesketh's 5 Platoon.

They return to the site of the ambush with the rest of his men, and find the Taleban fighter he has killed. Hesketh is still excited. But he is surprised to find how completely indifferent he feels at having taken life from another human being. He's not been sure what to expect: delight, dismay – but not indifference. 'I'm glad it was him – could have been me – bet he wouldn't have shed a tear for me.'

The body is carried back closer to the road. A small team of four SAS reservists and an intelligence corps corporal, Sarah Bryant, are sent to collect it. They turn right off a main route onto a dirt track, crossing a culvert close to Clark's men, and vanish in a bulge of black smoke and fire. The Land Rover bucks into the air and comes down with a crash. Silence.

The Jocks stare as the smoking mess of metal, which is supposed to protect people from bombs and bullets but really just chews them up. Sarah, Corporal Sean Reeve, Lance Corporal Richard Larkin, and trooper Paul Stout, are killed instantly. One SAS soldier has survived, trapped behind the steering wheel.

Sarah Bryant had been working mainly on psychological operations. She is the first female soldier to die in Afghanistan. Pretty, blonde, recently married, and with a movie-star smile, she'd been hard to miss in the claustrophobic camp at Lashkar Gah. The thought of her being torn to pieces by a bomb was somehow indecent, dirty. She was no more, or less, loved than the others who died that day – but she was blonde, and pretty. Now she was no more than a body being zipped into a bag, loaded into a coffin and onto a Hercules aircraft amid bugles and flapping flags.

Her death, in the middle of June, caused a media sensation in Britain. But given that women are driving convoy trucks, which are attacked and blown up every day; that they are running intelligence and psychological operations, flying aircraft, dismantling bombs and patrolling with infantry every day, most soldiers in Helmand are surprised that more women have not been killed. The sight of a woman on the front line is now routine. But she died in a Snatch – the unpopular 'Magimix' vehicle which offers no protection against the mines which are the most common weapon in use against the British in Helmand. That they were the only vehicles available to them – who had to borrow them from other units anyway – two years into the war in Helmand showed to many officers and soldiers that the government had little idea about, and still less interest in, the realities of fighting on the ground.

The commander of the squadron in Lashkar Gah, Major Sebastian Morley, resigned in disgust when he returned to Britain. He said that the continued use of Snatch was 'cavalier at best, criminal at worst'. In response the Minister for Defence Equipment and Support, Quentin Davies, told the BBC that Morley's allegations were 'surprising and very sad', adding 'the idea that we have been cavalier with soldiers' lives is horrific'.

'I recently visited Afghanistan,' he insisted, after 16 Air Assault Brigade's tour had ended, 'and 100 per cent of those I asked said they were now satisfied with their equipment.' This, of course, was nonsense. SAS officers complained to me of a shortage of vehicles and that they were having to borrow weapons from other units. No one in the whole of Helmand who got into either a Snatch or a Vector – the jerry-rigged armoured ambulance and troop trans- porter – ever did so without trepidation. It is inconceivable that soldiers would say that they were happy with Snatch, or that they had enough helicopters.

He then went on to make matters even worse. He said: 'Given the nature of war, there may be occasions when in retrospect a commander chooses the wrong piece of equipment, the wrong vehicle, for the particular threat that the patrol or whatever it was encountered and we had some casualties as a result,' as the BBC reported. His attempt to blame commanders for using the 'wrong piece of equipment' resulted in immediate calls for his resignation. Commanders in Helmand have always faced a shortage of equipment and men – there has never been a choice about what vehicles could be taken.

In April 2008, the company commander from whom he took over in Lashkar Gah told Harry Clark: 'If you don't go to places like Marjah, the enemy won't bother you.' This didn't make much mili- tary sense to him – although he understood what was being said: 'There's a rock that's not worth turning over down there.'

But he felt that while Lashkar Gah might feel secure, he should remember that the Taleban were opportunists. And even if he had just thirty men and women, he would have to foray out of the city to keep the Taleban at bay. Very quickly, as he discovered in the patrol with Chantelle Taylor, 'We got the "fuck off" – as in ambushes – every time we went out.'

If this was true of the start of the tour in April and May, it was put down to the heavy presence of drug-production laboratories in the area. But by the end of June and early July, Afghan intelligence and police were claiming that the Taleban was moving on the western banks of the Helmand and threatening Lashkar Gah from Nawa, due south, Marjah, southwest, and Nad-e-Ali in the west.

The chief of police in the area repeatedly claimed that his men were under attack. Governor Mangal had begun to feel vulnerable. British military intelligence analysis was that there was no real concentration of Taleban in Marjah and that the threat was being exaggerated by Afghans for obscure, political reasons.

The military intelligence analysis was that the police chief was close to Sher Mohammed Akunzada (SMA) – the governor the British had had removed in 2006 after he was found with 9 tonnes of opium resin at his home. SMA was now in the Afghan parliament and was thought to be plotting to undermine Mangal to secure his own return to Helmand. He was close to President Karzai and was, according to intelligence sources in Kabul, constantly whispering malevolent disinformation into the Afghan President's ear. He was said to be telling the President that Mangal had lost control of Helmand and that the government risked losing Lashkar Gah itself. This would be a disaster for Karzai in the 2009 elections – he had to show he could hold some parts of southern Afghanistan where his own Pashto tribe dominated.

This was, perhaps, only part of the story.

From May through to July there had been constant reports of a growing Taleban presence in Marjah and Nad-e-Ali – most were coming from the former police chief Abdul Rahman Jan. Police checkpoints would collapse; the men would withdraw 'under fire' and then return.

From late July and into early August, while the British brigade focussed its efforts on moving the turbine into Kajaki, the Taleban infiltrated the towns around Lashkar Gah. But the turbine move absorbed a *kandak* of Afghan soldiers, the whole of 3 Para Battle Group, extra troops from 2 Para and several hundred on the convoy itself. There simply weren't any spare troops for other operations.

Governor Mangal backed the turbine move – but he didn't see it as a priority. The threat to his leadership and his personal survival was what worried him: he said that the Taleban were in his back garden. In early August a small unit of 21 SAS, who were in charge of mentoring the police in the area, was asked to bring an urgent re-supply to Afghan police who had been attacked over the previous day in Marjah. The SAS drove in with a small escort of Afghan army troops and discovered that the police had packed and were ready to withdraw. Captain Darren Pridmore, a Welsh Guards officer attached to the Afghan army, watched stunned as the number of Afghan police vehicles climbed steadily from a dozen to twenty-seven.

'They dumped one of their dead and a wounded policeman on us and drove off back to Lashkar Gah.' The British were ambushed on their way out.

On 15 August, while the brigade was waiting anxiously for all of the turbine parts to be assembled in Kandahar, intelligence filtered back to the British headquarters that the Afghan police in Marjah, who were mostly drawn from the local community, had opened negotiations with the Taleban. The Taleban claimed that it was in control of Marjah.

Mark Carleton-Smith's self-examination told him that while he was under pressure to pull off the turbine move – which was looking 'neat and doable' – there was a danger that the operation could obscure more important issues. He called his staff together.

'The propaganda threat out of Marjah is much more dangerous than anything that is happening in Musa Qal'ah, Sangin or anywhere else. We're very confident we can deal with a hard threat – but we're a bloody sight less well configured to deal with a soft information operation [run by the Taleban]. Clearly we're going to have to lean into the problem, physically.

'We need to get inside the information loop – when Governor Mangal has got a phone in each ear giving him a running commentary of [police] checkpoints falling in Nawa, and Marjah – we need to get our version of events across as well.

'Mangal has got the police saying that it's not their problem, the Afghan Army saying it's not their problem, he's got us saying it's not a problem – and he's saying it is a problem. We have to reassure him that we're behind him and that we take his problems seriously. We're much more likely to become unstitched by what happens in Marjah and Nawa than by an airburst from an RPG over Inkerman – that we can deal with. We don't know enough about what is happening in Marjah.'

He later met with his intelligence officer who stuck to his view that reports of Taleban successes west of Lashkar Gah were being exaggerated by Sher Mohammed Akunzada's supporters – who, in any case, were all in the opium business in Marjah and Nad-e-Ali. They had a stake in maintaining chaos and destroying Governor Mangal's efforts to persuade farmers to switch from poppy to wheat.

On 19 August the intelligence briefing on Nad-e-Ali and Marjah for Mark Carleton-Smith was that 'there are spurious reports of gathering enemy forces in these areas to attack Lashkar Gah – the reality is that the atmospherics in these areas are positive'.

The following morning I meet with Mangal. In the 1970s he had been an administrator in the Communist government but he joined the mujahideen after the Soviet invasion. Under President Karzai he had been a hugely successful governor of Laghman and Paktia provinces, where he managed to re-establish the central government's hold. He had taken on Helmand on the orders of President Karzai.

Mangal wears a turban and a short-sleeved collarless waistcoat

over a collarless shirt. His beard is shaved to a bristly shadow and his
rimless glasses are almost invisible. We sit in the 'purple room' – a
sitting area used by civilian staff to watch TV at the British headquarters in Lashkar Gah. He is despondent.

He explains that he has a vision for breaking the hold of the drug
lords and gangsters in Helmand which will, in turn, undermine
the Taleban. He wants to launch a public information package to
explain the benefits of government. He wants to distribute seeds free
of charge to farmers (who have to buy their poppy seeds from drug
dealers) and he wants to impose the rule of law.

'This campaign has provoked a group of individuals in Kabul
[Sher Mohammed Akunzada's clique] and they have reacted down
here. Their concern is that if the rule of law comes here then the
drug dealing will be over; and it's not the Taleban who make most
of the money from the drugs – it's people close to the President.
Therefore if chaos remains in Helmand – they make money. If they
get rid of me – then they can have their chaos. If the government
does not support me here then we will fail – and I already fear for
my own safety.'

Later that day he is sacked – although President Karzai does
not make the decision public. Britain's diplomats go into a frenzy
of activity. They feel personally, and they know that the British
public would agree with them, that it would be totally immoral
to ask British troops to fight and die in Helmand if the province
was ruled by Sher Mohammed Akunzada, a man caught storing
opium and who the British blame for undermining their reputation in Kabul. Mangal's sacking could result in strategic failure,
they say.

Carleton-Smith seizes the initiative. Mangal is fired the day
before the arrival of the British Prime Minister, Gordon Brown, for
a brief visit to Camp Bastion before heading off to Kabul. Carleton-
Smith escorts the Prime Minister to the Bastion hospital where a
soldier from 3 Para is being treated for a bullet wound which has

gone through his chest. The paratrooper's thorax is cracked open and surgeons are struggling to save his life.

'It's going to be pretty hard to justify why British troops would risk that for a man like Akunzada,' the brigadier quietly says to a visibly shaken Brown while they watch the surgeons save the paratrooper's life.

In Kabul, Brown's next stop, the British Prime Minister tells the Afghan President that sacking Mangal risks undermining British support for his government. Karzai reluctantly agrees to shelve the dismissal 'for the time being'. The already tense relations between Karzai and the British, who are keeping him in power with their troops, reaches a new low.

But the high-level politics throw little light on whether the Taleban do indeed pose a serious threat to Lashkar Gah from the western side of Helmand. Major Harry Clark is ordered to take a patrol into Nad-e-Ali to reassure the police and get a notion of ground truth.

On 23 August, four days before Operation Oqab Tsuka, the move to get the turbine to Kajaki is launched, Harry Clark takes his company headquarters – a total of about forty people, including Chantelle Taylor's medical team – on a twelve-hour 'look-see' patrol to Nad-e-Ali. The Afghan security forces claim the town is under constant attack and has been for days. He arrives, with the protection of an attack helicopter, at the Nad-e-Ali District Centre, in the pitch dark without any problems.

Within minutes of his arrival the police station, in the southeastern edge of the District Centre – a rectangular area about 500 by 240 metres – comes under attack. Four RPGs crash into the outer walls and burst overhead. On the roof of their station the Afghan police are firing constantly. Clark and his sergeant major have to run up a staircase on the side facing the Taleban to get the police under control before they spend all their ammunition shooting at shadows. Four Afghan policemen have been wounded, two of them badly. They are evacuated by helicopter just after midnight.

The next morning Clark has a meeting with the Afghan army commander, Major Nazim. He refuses to patrol to the west of the DC at all and says that he faces a force of at least 300 Taleban. Clark, who has heard the exaggerated estimates of the Afghans before, thinks this is an extravagant figure. But he's told by Acting Lieutenant Colonel Sandy Fitzpatrick, who's taken over Battle Group South from Nick Borton, to stay another twenty-four hours to reassure the Afghans further, and get a clearer understanding of the Taleban threat in the area.

The British set themselves up in a group of three buildings in the north-eastern part of the DC, which they call Patrol Base Argyll. South of them is a helicopter landing site on an old football pitch. The Afghan Army have a base in an abandoned prison on the eastern edge. The police mentoring team have brought enough food and water for twelve to fourteen hours, no extra clothing or ammunition, fuel, medical supplies or bedding. They will remain here for seven weeks.

At 1745 hours the DC is attacked again. This time the target is the British patrol base, PB Argyll. It is a pattern that will establish itself for most of the following weeks: the Taleban pouring machine-gun and rocket fire into the roof-top positions of the British, usually from locations less than 200 metres away. This time, though, the Afghan Army in the prison, behind the British, cannot resist the temptation to fire back at the Taleban, probably because the Taleban bullets are dropping into their lines. Clark watches a rocket streak across the sky towards a Taleban-held building known as Compound Blue. It drops short; there's a crash and a ball of white smoke. Clark runs across the open ground to see what damage it has done; it's smashed into the wall where his Jocks have been taking cover.

Corporal Tony McPortland is lying on the ground underneath

the splash mark of the rocket in the wall above him. His hand is pouring blood from where one of his fingers used to be – and he's badly injured down the left side of his body.

'Man Down! Man Down!'

Chantelle breaks cover from their improvised operating theatre, an old classroom, and scoops Tony onto a stretcher. That evening four more Afghan soldiers are also wounded in the attack on the DC – and all five are evacuated by 1900 hours that evening. Over the next six days, thirty British and Afghan soldiers are evacuated and one Afghan sergeant is killed.

Harry Clark's father was an Argyll; his older brother is also in the regiment. A Philosophy and Theology graduate of Bristol University and a father of two boys, he now finds himself fighting the same sort of battle which was the hallmark, and curse, of the British deployment in 2006. Back then, small numbers of lightly armed troops were sent into platoon houses up the Helmand River in Sangin and Musa Qal'ah and out in the desert at Now Zad. They'd been surrounded and forced to fight a Rorke's Drift type of defence against much larger Taleban forces, for months.

Clark is confident that the DC cannot be overrun. He knows that it is now a magnet for the Taleban – but he still does not have a clear idea of how many he is up against. On 25 August he sends Second Lieutenant Alexander 'Beatie' Barclay down to give security to a convoy in Nawa on a short patrol. In the meantime he sends his Jocks to reinforce Patrol Base Argyll – especially the sangar on its roof from which you can see all around the area, but which is also under constant attack.

Corporal Scottie Pew and two other riflemen are manning the newly rebuilt sangar, which has enough space for four men to squat under a camouflaged tarpaulin. Its walls are made of 1-metre high Hesco bags. As evening falls the air is ripped with the sounds of Jimpies engaging targets out to the west of the base. Scottie spots ten to fifteen Taleban trying to move north and west to attack the patrol base. He fires a long burst into them and watches in amazement as five or six men spin and collapse onto the ground.

'Get some!' he laughs.

Then he sees another group trying to get their own machine gun onto the roof of Compound Green – a spot frequently used by the Taleban as a fire base 150 metres east. Their aim is obvious – they want to get rid of Scottie. He guns them down. Then he shoots the men who chase up onto the roof to rescue their dead and wounded comrades. All he can see on the roof are men lying like dolls thrown down on top of one another. He kills another group which is trying to carry out a flanking attack on patrol base. By the end of the day he thinks he's killed nineteen people.

'That, sir, was a good day at work,' says Scottie when he reluctantly hands over to the next shift. 'You've got to give them credit – they are brave fuckers. They were never going to leave any of their wounded behind.'

'Nice work Pew. Glad you enjoyed yourself,' replies Clark.

'That was close. Sixteen men on base and several groups of twenty attacking us. That was as close to getting overrun as I ever want to get,' Clark thinks.

He settles down to write orders for a company operation to take a look at Shin Kalay, a village built on a dense grid of irrigation channels about 2 kilometres west. The Afghan Army have said the Taleban are based there. Overnight, Captain Colin Wood, the company second in command, is going to bring the rest of 6 Platoon and more supplies in from Lashkar Gah by road.

A Snatch Land Rover driver in Wood's convoy feels his left wheel suddenly give way and, like a horse tripped at a gallop, the Snatch tumbles forward onto its shoulder. The back end follows it into the steep-sided ditch.

'Fuuuuck. Water – we're in water, we're sinking, we've got to get out, get out, get out,' someone is yelling in the back. The two soldiers in the front seats heave against the right-hand passenger door. They're soaked; the door handle is slippery; there's water half way up the cab. Their backs and necks hurt and the door weighs a quarter of a tonne.

They're out – fresh air. They can hear banging inside the armoured box at the back. Someone leans back into the open door.

'Oi, you two. Are you injured? No? Then stop flapping and get out. The fucking wagon's not sinking, it's on the bottom, ya fuckin' gobshites.'

Wood has the convoy strung out along the roads but there's plenty of cover in the ditches. The minor injuries from the crash, whiplash and sore backs and a couple of cases of concussion, are being dealt with. A tow rope is fixed to the side of the Snatch and a Land Rover lurches forward to drag it out of the ditch; the Land Rover wheels spin loudly. Barclay is looking around him and can't seem to stand still.

'What's up, Beatie?' says Wilson.

'Well – er, I know this area; there are a few Taleban firing positions they use to attack the patrol base and it's getting light.'

'Ah – well – we'd better get a move on then and get the fuck out of Dodge. We'll have to leave the Snatch here and we'll deny it some other way.'

The Lashkar Gah convoy quickly scoots into Patrol Base Argyll. Barclay is immediately sent back out with his platoon sergeant, Scotty McFadden, an experienced senior sergeant, to destroy the Snatch, which is lying like a wounded animal on its side. They chuck plastic explosive and six bar mines (each one designed to destroy a tank) into the vehicle and take cover.

'That's great that is, boss. Thermonuclear. That's mega that is,' says Private Michael Duffy, eighteen, watching the dust and smoke mushroom into the sky. An irrepressibly naughty schoolboy of a soldier, 'Duffy' always manages to make Barclay smile, and feel a little older. At twenty-two Barclay only arrived with the battalion in May, after passing out of Sandhurst and completing his platoon commander's course. Broad shouldered, blond and as handsome as a ski instructor, he'd taken a gap year between school and university which turned into several more before he settled on joining the army. Though raised in a small village on the Suffolk coast, he applied to join a Scottish regiment as his maternal grandfather had served with the Black Watch. He chose the Argylls because they 'didn't seem too posh'.

Scotty McFadden has let him grow into his job and is relieved to find that the young officer has checked his plans and decisions with him before giving orders. That way it isn't necessary to correct the young officer in front of his platoon. The two men are becoming friends.

Major Clark's own plan, of a company patrol to Shin Kalay, has been wrecked by the Land Rover crash. It has taken away any chance of sneaking into the area and surprising the Taleban before dawn. So he orders Barclay to take his platoon out to Compounds 'Blue' and 'Green', a couple of hundred yards from the gates of Patrol Base Argyll. Under normal circumstances this would be a two-minute walk. But within about four minutes of leaving the base and patrolling gingerly down the narrow alleyways and ditches, 4 Platoon come under fire. They duck into cover and start trying to win the firefight against the insurgents. They also call for an Apache helicopter to spot and destroy the Taleban firing positions. The helicopter replies that it cannot open fire – it would risk hitting civilians who are close to the Taleban. So Barclay orders an assault on Compound Blue where he finds blood trails and the brass cartridges of spent bullets, but no Taleban. His 'platoon' is, in fact, just two sections of six men, plus his sergeant, two medics, and himself – sixteen soldiers. A few days later he would shake his head with amazement and guilt that he had so underestimated the Taleban that he thought it would be possible to go out with such a small force and come back alive.

He assaults through Compound Green about 100 metres further

west – deeper into Taleban territory, where he finds some more blood and brass and there's a brief exchange of fire.

At three in the afternoon, Barclay is back out again, on his fourth patrol in eighteen hours. This time he's got to take his platoon in six Land Rovers – half open-topped Wimiks, the others, Snatch – to investigate routes into Shin Kalay. The Afghans insist that they should go in the middle of the convoy in their three Ford Rangers with three British vehicles each side.

'I reckon we should cut north because there haven't been any reports of Taleban in that area, then hook a left going west and come in to Shin Kalay from the top and see how far we get – no?'

'Looks like a plan,' says Scotty McFadden.

Barclay takes the lead. His driver is a stoic Afrikaner called Wynand 'Vin' le Roux. Duffy is manning the .50 calibre in the gun turret behind, and Barclay has a Jimpy fixed to the bonnet in front of him. It's a relief to be back in vehicles. The platoon is already tired – but still pumped up on adrenalin from the fighting earlier on in the day and the pace of their patrolling seems to carry them along on its own wave. Barclay is leading. He heads north, turning right out of the DC, then on for about 1.5 kilometres, then takes a left. There are open fields immediately on his left and some compounds about 150 metres south. On his right the fields are dense with okra and maize. He's approaching a 'choke point' between tall mulberry trees with some buildings on his right. Rockets crash into the ground about 10 metres to his left – Taleban gunners have got their range wrong. The air fills with the football rattle of bullets and the dissonant irregular *ping* when they make contact with metal.

'Contact, wait out,' Barclay signals back to Clark.

'Lads, we're going to fight straight through this and turn right at the next junction, where we will rendezvous. Get those rounds down and keep the enemy's fucking heads down,' he tells his men over the platoon network. He need not have bothered. Duffy is grinning and blasting to the south with his heavy machine gun.

The Afghan soldiers are standing in their pickup trucks firing volleys of rockets and shooting their rifles from the hip with one hand and hanging on to the trucks with the other. Their cars are kangarooing forward.

Barclay can see the right-hand turn which will give him a safe area clear of the ambush. His heart is pounding and as the Land Rover swings off the main drag he thinks, 'Oh fuck – what if they've got a cut-off group here?' It would be obvious to have a second ambush team ready to kill anyone escaping up this track. He stops as soon as he's out of sight of the Taleban attackers. The Afghan troops pull in behind, and McFadden roars up alongside and hits a bump in the road. All four wheels are hanging uselessly in the air – the sergeant's Land Rover rocks on a fulcrum of baked mud.

'Boss – the rear vehicle is missing – we're one vehicle down.'

Barclay's chest leaps. He calls the bad news through to Harry Clark who asks for drones and an Apache helicopter to try to spot the missing Land Rover – and the three men inside. 'I've got to get them back before they get their heads chopped off,' Barclay thinks. This is a commander's worst nightmare. Not very far away three British soldiers could be facing a slow and terrifying death.

Out loud Barclay says: 'The sergeant's group will remain here to extract their vehicle and provide support. We've got three British soldiers missing somewhere back there and we've got to make all haste to get them out before the Taleban capture them. The ANA can wait here and I'll take my three wagons. We're going back in the way we came out.'

In Patrol Base Argyll, Clark is watching a video downlink of the scene. He can see Barclay's group – but there is no sign of the Land Rover – it has vanished. 'Jesus. The best we can hope for now is that they're killed in action not missing in action. Please God we don't end up with British soldiers being dragged around by their ankles behind a Taleban pickup truck,' he thinks, recalling the television images broadcast from Mogadishu in October 1993 when American

Black Hawk helicopter pilots were killed, stripped, and towed through the streets by screaming mobs.

Corporal Garrie Wallace, a Territorial Army soldier, Air Troopers Craig Woods and Matty Readshaw, were in the rear Land Rover. When the ambush started, Matty, the driver, had lost his bearings in the smoke and noise. He crashed into a ditch – rolling the vehicle onto its side.

With the Land Rover three quarters over and held up only by its .50 calibre turret, Wallace is trapped in the passenger seat. The two Air Corps soldiers who, like him, have been drafted into the Argylls to make up the numbers while in Helmand, have crawled free. Bullets are smashing into the armoured underside of the open-topped Land Rover. Matty shoves his arms into the water and drags his commander free.

'They can't see us. So don't return fire or you'll give away our location. Let's get the fuck out of here,' says Garrie. He tosses a phosphorous grenade into the Land Rover to try to burn out any radio equipment on board, and the three men tuck themselves behind a low bank of earth with trees running along it, and sneak away. Their feet slip in the clay. The shallow water holds them back like a childhood nightmare when you're running from a monster but your legs won't work. They slide and stagger. They half grunt and sort of sob with frustration. They keep low. With bullets tearing the air above them they scuttle along. Garrie is thinking with more clarity than he can ever remember. A cold calmness has come over him which he knows he needs if he's going to stay alive.

A slaughterman by profession from Ayr he knows what a prize captured British troops would be to the Taleban. 'They're not going to fucking get me and cut my throat like a fuckin' animal,' he thinks. He looks around at Matty. His eyes have gone very wide.

They come to the metal door of a compound about 50 metres away from their vehicle – although it feels like they've moved much further. It seems the Taleban don't realise they've crashed yet and are still firing blindly into their stricken Land Rover. Garrie knows he's got to get off the road and out of sight and asks Craig to slip the latch on the door. He pushes into the compound and the other two follow – there's no one in it. At the back are two small rooms with windows looking towards the main entrance.

Matty has gone green. Having rescued Garrie he's close to exhaustion and collapse, so Garrie tells him to lie down while he takes his grenades which are then piled up in front of the two windows.

'Don't worry lads. I'll get you out of this and the platoon will come back to get us. We're going to be fine,' says Garrie. He catches Craig's eyes. 'He knows we're fucked,' Garrie thinks, but no one wants to say so.

Barclay stops his truck about a hundred metres from the killing zone at the centre of the ambush he's just escaped and ducks into a drainage ditch. He runs along as far as is safe and inches onto his stomach onto the road. He cranes his neck. But there's no sign of the Land Rover. He runs back to his three trucks to find that the government troops have joined him. The Taleban see them and open fire.

'They might have done one of two things. Maybe they were able to stay out of the ambush and head north and then west and are heading for the rallying point. You head east and look for them there. I'll look west – they might have missed the turning,' he says to McFadden.

'Roger.'

Garrie can hear the shooting and now he can hear Barclay driving away.

Barclay can see a vehicle moving about a kilometre away close to the edge of the desert. It might be them. He heads off to look for them and in less than 300 metres he sees a mosque to his left. Bullets stream from its forecourt and from behind its walls. His team sprays bullets back at the holy site as they race past and get to the end of the road – no sign of the missing truck. They turn around and head back, past the mosque and through another ambush.

McFadden has been blocked from heading east. He's been ambushed and is now on the radio saying that he's fighting his way back to the original rallying point. This time the weight of fire from the mosque is even heavier. Barclay feels the wind of a bullet pass his face.

Inside the compound the sound of shooting has died down. Garrie can hear Taleban voices outside the door. He prepares to fight to the last bullet and gets the air troopers into positions. They don't want to be captured alive.

'We're going to die here. But we're not going to get captured – no fucking way – no one's going to see me getting my head cut off on youtube,' Garrie thinks.

He turns to Craig. 'If anyone comes through that door we let them have the good news and keep shooting as long as the bullets last. Then switch to the grenades. You know what to do with the last one . . . ' Craig nods.

Barclay has only one choice. He decides he's going to relive the ambush by driving straight back into the killing zone. He's convinced his missing men are somewhere in there.

'You know we've got three men stuck in that killing zone and the only way we're going to get them out is to go back in and fight for them. There will be no spectators. You see anyone in that area to your south you fucking shoot them,' he tells his men before they set off, then clambers into the front seat of his Land Rover.

'You sure you want to do this, boss?' says Vin le Roux.

'Yes – I'm sure.'

'Let's go then,' says the Afrikaner, and guns his engine.

The platoon tears off – every ditch and alleyway, every compound wall and tree that flashes by is a potential hiding place for more ambushes. Vin throws his wheel to the right and drives straight into the ambush, hitting the accelerator. There are more Taleban and they're closer to the road now. Bullets are smacking off the sides of the vehicles and tearing through the bodywork.

Vin jams on the brakes. He's spotted the Land Rover on its side under some trees in the ditch.

'There's the fucking wagon boss, there it is!'

Inside the compound Garrie hears the telltale screech of Land Rover brakes. He bursts through the door, sprints and dives into Barclay's car. The others jump into the back of the Land Rovers behind. Barclay sees a group of seven Taleban about 20 metres away and fires a burst from his Jimpy into them. He's moving and can't see if he's hit anyone.

A Taleban fighter erupts from a hiding place in a ditch on the edge of the road about 5 metres from him. Barclay swings his Jimpy and fires – the Taleban does the same getting off an eight-round burst before he's thrown backwards in pieces. Barclay feels a sharp smack in the bag of his leg – 'like I'd been hit with a hockey stick'. They race out of the ambush for the second time and meet again at the rallying point which Scotty McFadden has also managed to fight his way back to. Barclay is in pain but his leg still works and he's not losing a lot of blood, so he ignores his wound and has a quick conference with his sergeant. Scotty explains that they are going to have to go north and then cut east to get around the Taleban he's just been fighting in order to get back to Patrol Base Argyll.

In a few minutes they find themselves in a Taleban shooting gallery running a gauntlet of fire a thousand metres long. Apache helicopters are unable to give covering fire because they can't make out who is a fighter and who is a civilian. They see a man working in a field who picks up a weapon, shoots at them, then puts it back down on the ground and sits down. He knows that the British won't shoot him when he's unarmed.

The road in front of Vin erupts with whirring metal and dirt. An RPG explodes so close that when Vin has stopped shaking his head, Barclay can see blood dribbling out of his ears. Duffy's .50 calibre has jumped off its bracket but he's got two 66mm rockets and his personal rifle. Garrie is shooting at Taleban fighters from the back of the Land Rover with his SA80.

Duffy spots the RPG gunner in a bunker about 200 metres away and fires a hopeful shot from his bouncing and racing Land Rover. It's a direct hit.

'Hey – did everybody see that! That was me. Whahay! I hope you all fucking saw that. That was genius. I got him everybody, I got him!' The teenage soldier is jumping up and down and waving his arms oblivious of the hundreds of bullets that are whipping around him. Barclay's seat is slick with his own blood. He smiles.

Pulling into the patrol base he gingerly hobbles to the medical centre where a female medic cuts off his trousers.

'Sorry – that's a nasty sight, haven't had a wash and I've been "going commando" for a few days.'

Scotty walks in with his right hand four times its normal size: somewhere along the way his Jimpy had caught on a wall and smashed his fist. Vin is grinning – and deaf: his eardrums have burst. The men who'd been stuck in a compound waiting to die for over an hour sit in a small, silent group, and are given cups of sweet tea.[6]

Barclay and the other wounded are evacuated that evening

Clark estimated that his company killed at least 150 Taleban in Nad-e-Ali during the fighting, which lasted until October.

But it wasn't enough.

When Brigadier Mark Carleton-Smith arrived back at RAF Brize Norton at the end of his six-month tour, on 10 October, he got a text message saying that Governor Mangal's offices in Lashkar Gah had been rocketed by the Taleban.

---

6 Second Lieutenant Alexander 'Beatie' Barclay won a Military Cross for gallantry as a result of his actions that day.

EPILOGUE

. . . If in some smothering dreams you too could pace
Behind the wagon that we flung him in,
And watch the white eyes writhing in his face,
His hanging face, like a devil's sick of sin;
If you could hear, at every jolt, the blood
Come gargling from the froth-corrupted lungs,
Obscene as cancer, bitter as the cud
Of vile, incurable sores on innocent tongues,
My friend, you would not tell with such high zest
To children ardent for some desperate glory,
The old Lie. Dulce et Decorum est
Pro patria mori.

Dulce et Decorum est, Wilfred Owen, 1917

I was ten when I first heard this poem. It was read to us by my English teacher in our classroom, with its blue plastic floor tiles and walls that echoed, at the end of the New Block. In those days we had teachers who kept their ranks from their service in the Second World War. One, Colonel Hulton, was a kind, grandfatherly figure with a grey nailbrush moustache, who had won the Military Cross in France. Sometimes the colonel would pause mid-syllable, turn his head very slowly to the left and stare out of the window. Several minutes would go by, tears would roll down his cheeks. He never told us what he saw in those long reveries framed by the plate glass window. We sat and waited in silence. He would turn back to the classroom, clear his throat, rub his face and eyes with the white hankie that he kept in his jacket pocket and say: 'Sorry chaps – got a bit lost.'

These gentlemen-warriors in their thick tweed, and shoes that crunched on gravel, were a living connection with the *Commando* and *Victor* comic characters who tore through Jerry and the Japs. They were our heroes. We knew they had been damaged by the war. But we didn't understand quite where Colonel Hulton went when he 'got lost'.

Owen's verses made me feel guilty. Through them we perhaps saw some of the movie that ran through the colonel's head. I felt guilty because I knew, because I had seen it in Colonel Hulton's eyes, that the poet was right. But I didn't believe him. I could not help myself.

How many men can honestly claim they've never fantasised about charging a machine-gun post, lobbing in grenades, butchering the enemy, and returning home a hero? We do it as kids and we do it as adults. This is a basic male instinct, though not one to be proud of. It is juvenile.

The army takes this instinct and nurtures and refines it. It teaches soldiers to remain dignified amid the mind-battering mayhem of combat. It teaches them to think of the needs of others. Soldiers nurture an incomparable love for one another. And when they're not fighting – they play like puppies in the sand, ragging and pulling each other's ears because soldiers are men, and men are boys. Their eternal youth and optimism is beautiful. They will not grow old now as the years condemn because, as Major Iain Bayliss said on the way back from the Kajaki turbine operation, 'When you join the army . . . you never have to grow up.'

Not at first that is. Almost every front-line soldier I met in Helmand was loving the war – they were getting to play the most dangerous and exhilarating game man has ever invented – the original sport. They were proud of the intensity of fighting that bore comparison with the Korean War, there was even a guilty pride in the casualty rates – more than six times higher than the war in Iraq. These facts drove home that what they were doing was the real thing. 'Real war fighting' they call it.

But they also know that they do not have enough troops to hold the ground they are taking. Each time they patrol out of their Fobs to fight they know that they are building sandcastles on the beach that will be washed away overnight. They know that they will be back, day after day, to fight the same battles in the same places.

Those who survived 16 Air Assault Brigade's tour, Operation Herrick Eight, are at home now. Other units continue to fight – it has just been reported (in the summer of 2009) that there has been a 62 per cent increase in the numbers of NATO casualties since 2008. I can only marvel at the absurdity of fighting a war for a government that does not resource these men and women for victory. The war in Helmand is not unwinnable. But it cannot be won with the tiny number of troops the British government is prepared to send. Every soldier who has set foot in Helmand knows this.

But still they go. They have to satisfy the strange yearning so many men have to prove themselves in war. The British Army makes a virtue out of coping with poor equipment and meagre supplies; this has been its greatest pride and its greatest curse. The determination of soldiers to shoulder whatever burdens are thrown at them has meant that they have managed to survive the poor political decisions that have taken them to Helmand underequipped, and undermanned. This has been their desperate glory.

As the years go by there will be many hundreds of men and women who fought in Helmand who will break off mid-sentence as they recall what they saw, what they did, and those who did not return – and in silence tears will roll down their cheeks.

GLOSSARY OF TERMS

.50 calibre: British forces L1A1 heavy machine gun – 12.7mm (.50 inch) tripod-mounted or vehicle-mounted.

105mm field gun: artillery piece firing shells up to 15km.

107mm Katyusha rocket: a simple high-explosive rocket with a range of up to 9km.

AC-130 Spectre Gunship: a C-130 Hercules carrying a 105mm artillery gun, as well as 40mm Bofors and 20mm Vulcan cannon and an array of 7.62 Gatling guns. A ground attack aircraft usually deployed in support of American Special Forces; the British do not own any.

AK47: 7.62mm short cartridge rifle; effective range 300–500m.

Apache: attack helicopter flown by British, Dutch and American pilots in Helmand.

Chinook: CH47 double rotor helicopter capable of carrying up to fifty-four people.

CAS: (Close Air Support) – fast jets attacking ground targets in support of infantry.

Contact: military language for being attacked.

Bowman: the unpopular and unreliable but secure British military radio and data communications system; often derided as 'Better Off With Map and Nokia', the Ministry of Defence announced an upgrade of the system in May 2009.

Dragunov: 7.62mm Soviet-designed long-barrelled sniper rifle.

'Dushka': 12.7mm Soviet-designed heavy machine gun – the equivalent of the .50 calibre.

Diemarco C4: 5.56mm rifle favoured by Pathfinders and Special Forces.

ECM: (Electronic Counter Measures) – top-secret equipment used to disable radio-controlled bombs.

Fast air: Harrier GR7/&A, F16/F17/F18, fighter/bombers flown out of Kandahar airfield.

Green Zone: the fertile strip of irrigated land either side of the Helmand and its tributaries.

Grenade Machine Gun: (GMG) – fires 40mm grenades at 340 rounds a minute up to 2,200m.

Hesco: dirt-filled sacks held in a wire-mesh frame used to build blast-proof walls.

Humvee: US four-wheel-drive (short for High Mobility Multipurpose Wheeled Vehicle – HMMWV).

Improvised Explosive Device: (IED) – a hidden bomb made from components such as old ammunition, pressure cookers filled with homemade explosives, or purposed-built mines. These are the biggest killer of foreign troops in Afghanistan.

ISAF: (International Security Assistance Force) – the NATO force in Afghanistan with around thirty-four contributing nations with dozens of limitations placed on the parent governments as to how those troops can be used.

kandak: an Afghan National Army battalion.

HLS: Helicopter Landing Site.

Jackal: Mobility Weapons Installation Kit – the 7-tonne patrol vehicle with a V-shaped hull armed with a .50 calibre machine gun or a Grenade Machine Gun. Originally developed for the SAS it is now being brought into service in various forms as a replacement for the Land Rover series of vehicles in many combat and support roles.

Jimpy: British slang for a belt-fed 7.62 General Purpose Machine Gun.

Mastiff: heavily armoured six-wheel-drive truck based on a South African design. Its V-shaped hull offers a high level of protection against IEDs and its bar-armour (in the British version) makes it almost impregnable to RPGs.

Minimi: Soldiers' name for the 5.56 Light Machine Gun firing up to 1,150 rounds a minute with an effective range of up to 600m.

Pinzgauer: un-armoured four- or six-wheeled light off-road vehicle.

PKM: the Soviet equivalent of a British General Purpose Machine Gun; belt-fed it fires 600–800 rounds per minute up to 1,600m. It is light and rests on a bipod.

Snatch: a lightly armoured Land Rover much despised by the troops who have to travel in it.

RPG: Rocket Propelled Grenade. Ubiquitous, cheap, easy to use and devastating man-portable reusable rocket launcher armed with a variety of missiles including air burst, armour-piercing and high explosive.

shura: a meeting/convention.

Vector: the armoured version of the Pinzgauer.

Viking: armoured and articulated tracked vehicle developed for the Royal Marines for Arctic warfare, now used as a troop carrier in Helmand.

wadi: river bed, usually dry and subjected to seasonal flooding.

Warrior: tracked British armoured personnel carrier with a 30mm cannon capable of carrying eight passengers.

WMIK: open-topped Land Rover which carries a Weapons Mounted Installation Kit, usually a .50 calibre.

ACKNOWLEDGEMENTS

Dozens of people have helped me to write this book. I am indebted to them all. It could never have been contemplated had Mark Carleton-Smith not agreed to take the extraordinary risk of backing the idea that a writer should accompany his brigade, for a full tour of Afghanistan, and have unrestricted access throughout Helmand. His staff at 16 Air Assault Brigade Headquarters, Colonel Neil Hutton, Major Simon Gilderson, Major Chips Broughton, Major Andy Rhodes, Captain Andy Rogers, Captain Jim Crompton, Lieutenant Colonels David Reynolds and Robin Matthews, and many others, were unstinting in their courtesy and support to me.

Commanding officers Lieutenant Colonels David Williams, Rufus McNeil, James Learmont, Nick Borton, David Richmond, Huw Williams, Sandy Fitzpatrick, and Joe O'Sullivan allowed me to roam around their respective military tribes and gave generously of their time, and hospitality, in very trying circumstances.

Infectiously enthusiastic Majors Harry Clark, Neil Den-McKay, Dave Kelly, Adam Dawson, Dave Lee, Joe Fossey, Nick Calder, Jason Calder, Russell Lewis, and Wayne Davidson offered guidance and friendship to a lone traveller hitching rides across the province on scarce helicopters or their personal vehicles. They somehow spread the notion that relentless fighting, terrible food, malnutrition, sleep deprivation, and outright exhaustion were a privilege for the men and women under their command. These men and women, some of whom appear in this book, are too numerous to thank here in person but if they felt uncomfortable with a stranger in their midst, they had the good manners to hide it. Thank you.

In London, at the Ministry of Defence, Colonel Ben Bathurst, and later Colonel Andrew Jackson, supported the genesis of this project and Paula Edwards kindly saw it through to its conclusion, frequently smoothing away bureaucratic sand traps.

The families of Jay Bateman and Jeff Doherty were kind enough to share their memories with me. I would like to thank Joyce Wakefield, Jeff Doherty senior, and Victoria Bateman in particular.

Natasha Fairweather, my friend of many years who, against her better judgement, is also my agent, has been a source of great encouragement and rigorous editing. I have always wanted, and failed, to be half as stylish as Richard Beeston; a true gentleman and a great journalist, he remains an inspiration to many of us lesser hacks.

My editor at Bloomsbury, Michael Fishwick, has been an invaluable guide to a novice author and Katie Johnson's meticulous efforts to turn my prose into English were close to miraculous. Anna Simpson somehow got this book through the production process. Lavina Penrys-Evans did sterling work turning many hundreds of hours of interviews into text. Henry Edwardes-Evans offered perspicacious comments on an early draft. Olivia Tollemache caught several solecisms in the text. Theresa Tollemache has provided our families with a happy *manyatta*. This book was put to bed at Charlotte Scott's incomparable *Trasierra*. I have been proud to follow in the footsteps of my father, the journalist and author Dennis Kiley.

Above all my thanks and love must go to my children, Ella and Fynn, and my Editor-in-Chief, Melissa Kiley. Not only did Melissa comb through this book and help sew it together, she is the very fabric of my life. Those of us who choose to go to war leave behind husbands, wives and children who do not choose to be left. They are the heroes.

INDEX

A NOTE ON THE TYPE

The text of this book is set Adobe Garamond. It is one of several versions of Garamond based on the designs of Claude Garamond. It is thought that Garamond based his font on Bembo, cut in 1495 by Francesco Griffo in collaboration with the Italian printer Aldus Manutius. Garamond types were first used in books printed in Paris around 1532. Many of the present-day versions of this type are based on the *Typi Academiae* of Jean Jannon cut in Sedan in 1615.

Claude Garamond was born in Paris in 1480. He learned how to cut type from his father and by the age of fifteen he was able to fashion steel punches the size of a pica with great precision. At the age of sixty he was commissioned by King Francis I to design a Greek alphabet; for this he was given the honourable title of royal type founder. He died in 1561.